Narrative Research

MW01716358

Rachael Dwyer • Ian Davis • elke emerald
Editors

Narrative Research in Practice

Stories from the Field

Springer

Editors
Rachael Dwyer
Queensland Conservatorium
Research Centre
Griffith University
Brisbane, Australia

Ian Davis
Griffith Institute for Educational Research
Griffith University
Brisbane, Australia

elke emerald
Griffith University
Brisbane, Australia

ISBN 978-981-10-9391-3 ISBN 978-981-10-1579-3 (eBook)
DOI 10.1007/978-981-10-1579-3

© Springer Science+Business Media Singapore 2017
Softcover reprint of the hardcover 1st edition 2016
This work is subject to copyright. All rights are reserved by the Publisher, whether the whole or part of the material is concerned, specifically the rights of translation, reprinting, reuse of illustrations, recitation, broadcasting, reproduction on microfilms or in any other physical way, and transmission or information storage and retrieval, electronic adaptation, computer software, or by similar or dissimilar methodology now known or hereafter developed.
The use of general descriptive names, registered names, trademarks, service marks, etc. in this publication does not imply, even in the absence of a specific statement, that such names are exempt from the relevant protective laws and regulations and therefore free for general use.
The publisher, the authors and the editors are safe to assume that the advice and information in this book are believed to be true and accurate at the date of publication. Neither the publisher nor the authors or the editors give a warranty, express or implied, with respect to the material contained herein or for any errors or omissions that may have been made.

This Springer imprint is published by Springer Nature
The registered company is Springer Science+Business Media Singapore Pte Ltd.

Preface

The impetus for undertaking this book comes from two sources. Firstly, there was a strong desire to produce something from our collaborations as a narrative research group, something that would provide a resource for other narrative researchers. Secondly, there was a common experience of those within our narrative group of encountering difficulty in navigating the diversity of literature surrounding narrative research. At times, there appear to be contradictions between research that uses similar labels and clearly delineated 'camps' or factions of researchers. For many of us, this caused difficulties knowing how to encompass theoretical positions that were in alignment with our desires for our research and the needs of our project. The purpose of this volume is to attempt to look across the entire landscape of narrative methods drawing out significant perspectives and identify the variety of theoretical positions. Some of this work has been started by others (Squire, Andrews and Tamboukou 2008; Pinnegar and Daynes 2007; Clandinin and Murphy 2007; Bamberg 2007), and we draw heavily on their work as we attempt to synthesise their ideas and present a possible framework for understanding the diverse possibilities for research that uses narrative methods.

Chapter 1 begins this volume with Dwyer and emerald's endeavour to create a map of the landscape of narrative inquiry, discussing the similarities and differences between the work of various narrative researchers and highlighting the alignments, synergies and contrasts between them. Chapter 2 sees emerald and Carpenter offering a brief outline on some of the tenets of autoethnography, exploring how an autoethnographic writer can achieve that connection between the story and the wider cultural point that shifts a story from just interesting to research. In Chap. 3, Davis and Johnson explore a new innovation in narrative research by the influence of fictional narratives on the construction and performance of masculinities within educational environments. In Chap. 4 Kennelly, Ledger and Flynn present three narratives that undertake to explore narrative research with music therapy clients or colleagues. The authors go on to highlight five critical junctures in narrative research and identify common strategies for negotiating challenges in the research process.

Chapter 5 by lisahunter draws on their own research and the work of scholars who have contributed to research associated with visual narrative to illustrate how the visual may be harnessed in conjunction with narrative. As a frame to guide this exploration, lisahunter uses Clandinin and Connelly's three research moment texts: field texts, interim texts and research texts (2000). In Chap. 6, O'Bryan discusses the use of video in the study and considers some of the benefits and hazards of storying video data in narrative inquiry methods. In Chap. 7, lisahunter and elke emerald discuss how sensual and sensory methods and methodologies can help us to capture our storied worlds in ways that reveal complex embodied, emplaced, multisensorial social phenomena. They discuss how narrative inquirers face two particular challenges when considering questions of the sense-body and that body in place. Firstly, how to capture, analyse and represent storied worlds in embodied ways and also how to capture sensed and embodied experiences in narrative. Chapter 8 sees Rojas-Lizana demonstrating how the nature of co-constructed interviews is discursively present in the perceived discrimination discourse of two stigmatised groups in Australia through key linguistic devices and strategies. In Chap. 9, Ronksley-Pavia and Grootenboer describe the fluid methodologies used in a narrative research study involving interviewing children identified as gifted and also having a disability. Chapter 10 details Yucel and Iwashita's discussion regarding how a narrative approach can be used to investigate the key constructs of language, culture, identity and learner beliefs about English language testing.

Finally, Chap. 11 uses data collected from three interviews with leaders in the field of narrative methods to identify the tensions that arise when considering definition and delineation of the terms and approaches concerning the use of narrative methods as a research tool. The chapter considers the differences, both ethical and practical, in how narrative data is collected and used, as well as the differences in the historical trajectory of how narrative methods have been utilised in research.

This project has been the work of 3 years and has brought together the thought and discoveries of a group of authors, some of whom work closely as part of a local narrative network in Australia and others who are part of a more informal global network of scholars working as researchers employing narrative methods. It is the hope of the editors that this volume will address the diversity that exists in the landscape of narrative methods, illuminating specific significant theoretical and methodological perspectives.

Brisbane, Australia
March 2016

Rachael Dwyer
Ian Davis
elke emerald

Acknowledgements

The success of a project like this is based on the ability of a team of people working together towards one common aim. To this end, there are many within that team to thank. Firstly, we thank all the authors represented here for their dedication, patience and talent. Your work and your words have inspired us to forge on and have reinforced how vital it is to get your ideas out into the field. Next, thank you everyone who has supported the project either financially or by offering resources such as office space and meeting rooms. Particularly we would like to thank Greer Johnson and the team at Griffith Institute for Educational Research and Queensland Conservatorium Research Centre for their ongoing practical support. Finally, we would like to thank our colleagues who developed and grew the narrative research network, namely, Paula Myatt, Wendy Green and Ann Webster Wright.

March 2016

Rachael Dwyer
Ian Davis
elke emerald

Contents

Contributors

Lorelei Carpenter is adjunct senior lecturer in the School of Education and Professional Studies at Griffith University in Australia. She has used narrative inquiry methodology in her main research areas of mothering, attention-deficit/hyperactivity disorder (ADHD) and autism spectrum disorder (ASD). She currently uses autoethnography in her work as a form of self-reflection that assists her to connect to and explore a range of sociopolitical issues.

Ian Davis is an educator of 15 years with a primary interest in narrative masculinity and education. Ian has worked at both Sydney University and now Griffith University with the Institute for Educational Research where he has recently completed his doctoral thesis. Before moving to Australia, he worked in London at Croydon College of Higher Education where he was the head of the Critical and Theoretical Studies Department and before that as a lecturer in the Education Studies Department. Previous to that, he worked as a social worker and was seconded as a practice teacher to the University of the West of England and University College Northampton developing a degree pathway in social work specialising in youth mental health. Ian has a new book *Stories of Men and Teaching* published by Springer.

Rachael Dwyer is a lecturer in the School of Education at the University of the Sunshine Coast, and has previously lectured in music education at Griffith University and the University of Queensland. She spent a number of years as a music specialist teacher in primary and secondary schools prior to completing her doctoral research which sought to investigate how music teachers' values and beliefs shape their practice. Rachael's research interests include teacher education, research pedagogy, critical pedagogy and narrative inquiry.

elke emerald is in the School of Education and Professional Studies at Griffith University, Australia. Her publications currently explore methodological advances in qualitative research and the work of academics in neoliberal times. She uses narrative, autoethnographic and arts-based methodologies.

Libby Flynn is a Brisbane-based music therapist, researcher and musician who completed both her master's training and her PhD through the University of Queensland. Libby's primary field of therapy work has been based within adult mental health, and she has published her research covering substance abuse, dissociative identity disorder and cognitive behavioural music therapy in highly ranked national and international journals. In 2012, Libby became the national chair of ethics for the Australian Music Therapy Association, a role in which she has been looking closely at the ethical implications of social media within the health profession. Libby is currently a research assistant at UQ and is working on Professor Margaret Barrett's ARC study which is looking at the provision of music in early childhood education and care in Queensland and Australia.

Peter Grootenboer was a school teacher and leader for 12 years before moving into the tertiary sector. In 1997, he received a Jim Campbell Award – a national award for teaching excellence in mathematics in New Zealand. Peter completed his MEd and EdD through the University of Waikato focussing on mathematics education and educational leadership (staff development and appraisal). He is now an associate professor in education at Griffith University and a member of the Griffith Institute for Educational Research. His research interests include practice theory, educational leading, mathematics education and action research. He has recently published 2 books with colleagues through Springer: *Changing Practices, Changing Education* (2014) and *Mathematics, Affect and Learning: Middle School Students' beliefs and Attitudes About Mathematics Education* (2016).

Noriko Iwashita is a senior lecturer in applied linguistics at the University of Queensland. Her research interests include the interfaces of language assessment and SLA, task-based assessment and crosslinguistic investigation of four major language traits. Her work has appeared in *Language Testing, Applied Linguistics, Language Learning,* and *Studies in Second Language Acquisition*.

Greer Johnson is a professor in education at Griffith University. She is director of the Griffith Institute for Educational Research and convenor for the Area of Strategic Investment (education). Her research is focused primarily on leadership for learning. She is involved in Australian federal, state and territory governments working with principals in primary and secondary schools to improve children's literacy outcomes, especially in disadvantaged circumstances. Recently she led and completed the Principals as Literacy Leaders with Indigenous Communities research and development project, in association with the Australian Primary Principals Association (APPA). Additionally, she has completed ARC Discovery projects on examining the issues associated with school-to-work/further study transitions for at-risk students and another international project on the learning needs of older workers.

Jeanette Kennelly is an experienced music therapist, academic lecturer and professional supervisor who has worked across a range of paediatric clinical areas since

1995. Specialising in the fields of paediatric neuro-rehabilitation and professional supervision, Jeanette has presented widely on these topics and is published in a variety of music therapy and non-music therapy-specific refereed journals and books. Following the completion of her PhD, Jeanette received the Dean's Award for Research Higher Degree Excellence and is now an honorary research fellow with the School of Music, University of Queensland. Jeanette currently delivers clinical music therapy services to two sites in Brisbane, the Mater Cancer Care Centre and The Possums Clinic, and runs a private practice, *Inspiravision*, which specialises in music-centred supervision practice.

Alison Ledger trained as a music therapist at the University of Queensland. She is best known for her work and publications in the areas of music therapy and dementia care, music therapy and paediatrics and music therapy service development. This narrative research chapter is based on her Irish Health Research Board-funded doctoral research undertaken at the University of Limerick, Ireland. Alison has developed expertise in arts-based, narrative and ethnographic research methods, which she now draws on in her current lecturing post at the Leeds Institute of Medical Education, University of Leeds, UK.

lisahunter works with personal and cultural narrative as a field text, as research analysis, and in the production of research texts to capture experiences and stories of those in schooling, teacher education, sex/gender/sexualities, surfing and relationships with the sea. Fascinated by methodologies of sensory and visual narrative as part of participatory research, lisahunter is a freelance academic/independent scholar and has recently published: "HPE: Pedagogy, sexualities and queer theory', in *The Handbook of Feminisms in Sport, Leisure and Physical Education*; 'Pulling the monstrosity of (hetero)normativity out of the closet: Teacher education as a problem and an answer' in *Sexual Cultures in Aotearoa/New Zealand Education*; 'Seaspaces: Surfing the sea as pedagogy of self' in *Seascapes: Shaped by the Sea*; 'Visual narratives of 'female' as a political position': Pedagogies of surfing events and their media' in *Women in Action Sport Cultures: Identity, Politics, Experience and Pedagogy*.

Sol Rojas-Lizana is a lecturer at the School of Languages and Cultures, the University of Queensland. Sol's main areas of publications are discourse analysis and pragmatics. She has research interests in everyday discourses of discrimination, stigma and exclusion in connection with theories of decoloniality and border thinking. Her work has been published in the *Journal of Pragmatics*, *Languages in Contrast*, *Babel*, *JILAR* and *PORTAL*, among others. She is currently working on her second academic book called *Perceived Discrimination Among Minorities in Australia: A Discourse Analytic Perspective*. Sol is also a professional translator and co-author of a historical autobiographic graphic novel that is currently being made into an animated documentary.

Michelle Ronksley-Pavia since migrating to Australia from Belgium, has continued her visual arts practice following her success as a student at the Ecole Des Beaux Arts in Brussels. Since completing her undergraduate and postgraduate degrees, Michelle taught in ACE and TAFE colleges, and at a number of schools both in New South Wales and Queensland over the last 20 years. Michelle has worked with gifted and talented students and in special education across P-12 schooling sectors. Michelle's qualifications include a master's degree in gifted and talented education. Michelle was recently awarded a PhD by Griffith University, Queensland, Australia, and has research interests in creativity, disability studies, gifted education, twice exceptional research and narrative inquiry. Michelle lectures in undergraduate and postgraduate primary and secondary education courses. Her specialist areas are visual arts, disability studies and gifted and special education. Michelle has published numerous journal articles and conference papers on gifted and talented children, twice exceptional children, creativity and differentiation. Michelle is past president of the Queensland Association for Gifted & Talented Children (GC Branch) and is a member of the World Council for Gifted & Talented Children and a member of the European Narratology Network.

Megan Yucel teaches at the Institute of Continuing and TESOL Education of the University of Queensland (ICTE-UQ). She has worked as an English language teacher, examiner, textbook author and test writer in Turkey, the UK and Australia. She is currently a PhD candidate at the University of Queensland.

List of Figures

List of Images

Chapter 1
Narrative Research in Practice: Navigating the Terrain

Rachael Dwyer and elke emerald

Abstract This chapter endeavors to map the terrain of the narrative landscape. In so doing we use two broad categories, firstly *methodological questions*, which includes the ontological and epistemological basis of the research, the nature of the relationship between the researcher and researched, and whether the research focuses on the individual or on societal contexts and concerns. Secondly *method questions*, which includes the nature of the evidence, the analytical processes used, and the representation of the research product. We seek to draw attention to the way the same terms are used by different authors in different ways. We hope this assists narrative researchers in the field further develop ideas in a continued commitment to the scholarship of narrative research.

Keywords Narrative • Methodology • Method • Epistemology • Ontology • Research design

Introduction

Telling stories as a way of making sense of the world is, as far as we can tell, a uniquely human trait. The stories people live and tell are a rich source of knowing and meaning making. Qualitative approaches to research that draw upon "stories" are numerous, encompassing ethnography, autoethnography, narrative inquiry, life history research, phenomenology, and others. Stories and narratives may themselves be the "data" for the research, the mode of analysis, or they may be the form in which the data is (re)presented (Polkinghorne 1995).

There is a wide range of divergent approaches that are described as making use of narrative methods. Stories may be fully formed by the participant then analysed by the researcher, or take the form of snippets of data that are "storied" by the

R. Dwyer (✉)
Queensland Conservatorium Research Centre, Griffith University, Brisbane, Australia
e-mail: rachael@rachaeldwyer.com

e. emerald
School of Education and Professional Studies, Griffith University, Brisbane, Australia

© Springer Science+Business Media Singapore 2017

R. Dwyer et al. (eds.), *Narrative Research in Practice*,
DOI 10.1007/978-981-10-1579-3_1

researcher. The inquiry may focus on the experiences of the individual, or seek to illuminate larger scale social narratives. The wide variety of approaches are flexible and highly contextualised, meaning the researcher must make decisions about which approach is most suited to the specific study undertaken. This makes the journey of becoming a narrative researcher perilous and uncertain, with an absence of clearly defined rules or processes that can be learned and simply applied. Some of those writing about narrative research acknowledge the diversity of narrative approaches to research, while others overlook the differences in attempting to present a consistent field or a definitive approach. As others have said before us, policing the use of the terms is not appropriate (see Clandinin and Murphy 2007) and not what we want to do here; yet an absence of policing has lead to a state of immense confusion and contradiction, felt most profoundly for those new to the field. So, while policing boundaries is not our aim, we seek to draw up some form of map of the terrain of narrative methods that can be used as a navigation aid.

The question that underpinned the development of this chapter was ultimately selfish in nature: "what would I have wanted to read at the start of my journey with narrative research?" This is itself a daunting question: as Corrine Squire, Molly Andrews and Maria Tamboukou comment in the introduction to *Doing Narrative Research* (2013):

> … narrative research offers no automatic starting and finishing points…the definition of narrative is itself in dispute … as indeed is the need for having one in the first place … there are no self evident categories on which to focus … Clear accounts of how to analyse the data … are rare. There are few well defined debates on conflicting approaches … and how to balance them … narrative research offers no overall rules about suitable materials or modes of investigation … (p. 1)

This is hardly reassuring to the novice researcher, but in chaos there is opportunity: we propose that these open questions for narrative inquiry are also its strength.

Narrative research can be broadly divided into two waves: an initial canon of work that sought to establish a place for narrative knowing in the academy of human and social sciences (Bruner 1986; Labov 1972, 1997; Mishler 1999; Polkinghorne 1988, 1995; see Pinnegar and Daynes 2007 for a thorough review); and the body of work that followed, which outlines the principles, methods, approaches and processes of conducting narrative research. This chapter draws heavily on the methodological work of leading narrative scholars from this "second wave", some of whose names very rarely appear in close proximity: Molly Andrews, Michael Bamberg, Jean Clandinin, Michael Connelly, Alexandra Georgakopoulou, Corrine Squire, Catherine Kohler Riessman and Maria Tamboukou. The outputs of these scholars cover a diverse range of disciplines, and diverge in fundamental epistemological premises and in methods.

The task we have set for ourselves in this chapter is ambitious, probably too ambitious for a chapter of this size. As Clandinin and Rosiek (2007) caution:

> any attempt to organize these divergent views into a summary representation inevitably risks shortchanging one view in favor of the priorities of another. There are, however, real differences of opinion on the epistemological, ideological, and ontological commitments of narrative inquirers as well as real differences with those who do not identify as narrative inquirers. (p. 37)

However, as we find ourselves reading and re-reading the work of others who have attempted to synthesize the key ideas from sections of this sprawling, unbounded field (particularly Squire et al. 2013; Clandinin and Rosiek 2007) we are mindful of not repeating their excellent work here. Our intention is to piece those syntheses together in a way that provides a useful starting point, and assists in gaining an understanding of how the work of these various scholars fits together.

To organise the key ideas, we use two broad categories: *methodological questions*, which includes the ontological and epistemological basis of the research, the nature of the relationship between the researcher and researched, and whether the research focuses on the individual or on societal contexts and concerns; and *method questions*, including the nature of the evidence, the analytical processes used, and the representation of the research product.

We use this organisational structure as a way of creating something of a map of the landscape of narrative inquiry, discussing the similarities and differences between the work of various narrative researchers and highlighting the alignments, synergies and contrasts between them. Most importantly, we seek to draw attention to the way the same terms are used by different authors in different ways. In turn, we hope that others will take what we offer in this chapter and build upon it, further developing the ideas in a continued commitment to the scholarship of narrative research.

Methodological Questions

These methodological questions or concerns, including their underpinning theoretical drivers, in an ideal world, are the ones that would be considered first – at the very outset of the research. The position you adopt in response to these questions will underpin all the decisions you make about the research, including methodology, methods and representation.

Story and Narrative – An Ontological Concern

One of the most frequently posed questions in the burgeoning field of narrative research in the social sciences is the simple ontological one: "What is narrative?" (Tamboukou 2008, p. 283) Narrative is a word that is used across a broad range of contexts, and its meaning varies accordingly. As Riessman and Speedy (2007) note:

> beginning in the late 1960s and continuing at a hectic pace, the idea of narrative has penetrated almost every discipline and school. No longer the sole province of literary scholarship, narrative study is now cross-disciplinary, not fitting within the boundaries of any single scholarly field. (pp. 426–427)

The terms "story" and "narrative" are words that come freighted with commonsense meanings and further, with several definitions in different research contexts. Some research uses the terms "story" and "narrative" interchangeably; others make a clear distinction. For example, because it is a focal point of their analysis, Carpenter and emerald (2009) make a clear distinction between "stories" and "narratives" in their *Stories from the Margin*. They utilise the understanding of a story offered by Poirier and Ayers (1997) and Sarbin (1986) to inform their definition of story as a structure used by an individual for the communication of an experience and as a re-presentation of action. For them, stories, in the main, provide meanings for past events, that is, they are a context for knowledge production. Whereas they use the term narratives as "a scheme used by people to give meaning to their experience" (McAllister 2001, p. 391). This distinction is important in Carpenter and emerald's work as they trace the relationships between individuals stories of their mothering and cultural narratives of "good motherhood".

Together with a definition of story and/or narrative, as researcher, the question of what a story is an ontological one. For example, Squire et al. (2013) note that one division in thinking is whether stories are social, dialogically constructed artefacts, or individual expressions of internal states (p. 5). It is almost customary now to open a narrative inquiry with a quote from Jerome Bruner about the centrality of story to human existence; often suggesting that narrative knowing is a primary act of mind (1986). Claninin and Rosiek (2007) position stories as central to human meaning making, they see narrative inquiry is the study of experience as evident in story:

> The only thing that keeps us from floating off with the wind is our stories. They give us a name and put us in a place, allow us to keep on touching … lived and told stories and the talk about the stories are one of the ways that we fill our world with meaning and enlist one another's assistance in building lives and communities. (p. 35)

Huber et al. (2013) position story as central to identity making:

> Throughout the ages and across cultures story continues to express the fundamental nature of humanity. … Our very identities as human beings are inextricably linked to the stories we tell of ourselves, both to ourselves and with one another. (p. 214)

Each of these positions on the nature of story and narrative speaks to the ontological foundation of research and has implications for research design.

What Counts as Knowing? Epistemological Concerns

Just as there is a need to understand the ontological question of what story and narrative are, there is also a need to consider how you understand the "nature of knowledge" (epistemology): what counts as knowledge, where/who does it come from, and the criteria that it needs to meet to be considered knowledge. Epistemology has a direct correlation with the types of methods and techniques used in the research; it will determine the ways in which evidence is gathered, interpreted and presented. Lincoln et al. (2011) describe epistemological standpoints using terms such as objectivist (singular "truth"[1]), transactional/subjectivist (knowledge is created in social contexts), value-mediated findings (researcher uses theories to reach findings, particularly critical/feminist/post-structural theories), and co-created findings (findings are a result of the contribution of both researcher and participant, including the researcher's personal history). Qualitative research in the social sciences typically necessitates the researcher adopting a reflexive stance, whereby they acknowledge, question and reflect upon the ways in which their presence has shaped what is occurring. This reflexivity cuts across all research and is not limited to narrative work. As Bourdieu (1999) explains:

> The positivist dream of an epistemological state of perfect innocence papers over the fact that the crucial difference is not between a science that effects a construction and one that does not, but between a science that does this without knowing it and one that, being aware of the work of construction, strives to discover and master as completely as possible the nature of its inevitable acts of construction and the equally inevitable effects those acts produce. (p. 608)

In simpler terms, knowledge generated through social research can never be entirely objective, but acknowledging and attending to the ways in which the researcher's presence contributes to and affects the construction of the knowledge means that the level of transparency is increased.

Narrative work is typically within a transactional frame – focused on the way knowledge is created in social settings, whether that is in the interactions between the researcher and participants and/or between participants and others. However, the way findings are developed, along with the relationship between researcher and participants, influence the epistemological stance.

In recognizing the variety of epistemological approaches to narrative research, Bamberg (2009) describes three approaches: Psychoanalytic, Phenomenological and Discursive. Consideration of these is a useful broad sweep entry in to the field; they are by no means exhaustive, but provide a means of illustrating how epistemology shapes research design and processes. In brief, psychoanalytic approaches seek access to a truth behind the story, or a deeper truth, perhaps not even known the teller of the story. Psychoanalytic approaches search stories for the internal motivations of the storyteller and seek the conflict at the core of the story. Squire, Andrews and Tamboukou see this take on narrative inquiry as interpreting research materials almost as if they were materials from an analytic session (2013, pp. 10–11).

Phenomenological approaches adopt a constructivist/interpretivist epistemology, to glimpse in to the lived experience of individuals, which brings with it a respect for the participants' perception of reality; a belief that reality is multiple and situational. The research takes the form of an in-depth understanding in pursuit of the essence of experience, and so is interested in fine-grained descriptions. In some ways Clandinin and colleagues' approach can be understood in these terms. For example, in the research reported in the book *Composing Diverse Identities* (Clandinin et al. 2006), the seven-member research team lived alongside teachers, students, administrators and families for 18 months in order to "understand diverse

[1] Not commonly associated with qualitative research.

individual's experience as they lived out in dynamic relation to people, places and things, in and outside of school" (p. 2). Their investigation entails a rich, detailed and extended account of the research site.

Bamberg (2011) works within the discursive approach, which recognizes that the story and the telling of the story are in relationship. Storying is a pervasive strategy in social interaction and this approach notices how story is remade in the telling, and as such, the telling itself requires as much attention as the story. For example, in *Narrative Practice and Identity Navigation*, Bamberg (2011) examines the storying process: that is, "what speakers tend to accomplish when breaking into narrative and making use of narrative performance features" (2011, p. 100) in the discursive construction of the self in the context of identity research. He opens this paper with an example from a movie in which the character has misunderstood the routine structures and purposes of storying practices in an anger management therapy session. He then uses extracts from three different interviews in which the question of "who are you" was pertinent, to examine routine storying practices, how they are used and resisted or subverted, and what they achieve. The analytic unit for Bamberg in this case, is not the story, rather the story in context, as co-constructed. His focus is the practice of storying (p. 107) and he uses close-grained conversation analytic techniques.

Some of the work in the field of Discursive Psychology presents something of an overlap – as it uses the discourse analytic techniques of, for example, conversation analysis or critical discourse analysis, to look at how people deploy commonsense psychological ideas. "Rather than taking those ideas out of context and finding that they amount to a messy, contradictory and inaccurate theory of mind, we explore how people actually put them to use in their everyday lives, when accounting for actions and events" (Spears et al. 2005, p. 546). The field of Discursive Psychology might take stories that people produce to understand the ways that routine storylines or story structures might be used construct the world in certain ways.

Clearly then, the epistemological position of the research shapes the way data is collected, analysed, interrogated and presented, all of which are research design questions to be unpacked later in this chapter.

Relationships Between Researcher and Researched

Questions of epistemology are deeply connected to the question of the relationship between the researcher and the researched. The adopted epistemological position shapes the types of questions that the research can seek to answer, and what you can take "inquiry" to be – and these both influence, and are influenced by, the nature of the interactions between researcher and participants. Pinnegar and Daynes (2007) describe the change of relationship between the researcher and "the researched" as the most significant shift in the "turn" towards narrative inquiry. Human "subjects" in social sciences research are no longer treated as fixed in place, that is, as static, atemporal, and decontextualized. When drawing on the methodology of narrative inquiry, which explores stories, narratives of experience, as the phenomenon of interest, narrative inquirers "embrace a relational understanding of the roles and interactions of the researcher and the researched" (Pinnegar and Daynes 2007, p. 15). This section focuses on the complexities that arise in negotiating relationships between researchers and participants when moving beyond a distanced, objective stance.

Many narrative researchers take on a highly "relational" perspective on how they interact with their participants. For Clandinin and Connelly (2000), "relationship is key to what it is that narrative inquirers do" (p. 189). In a phenomenologically informed narrative inquiry, the desire for deep understanding of the people and context, the researchers' presence in the field will likely take on roles other than a non-participant, "fly-on-the-wall" observer. Their presence may influence what takes place, but a richer and more nuanced understanding of the phenomenon is made possible where research relationships are trusting and lasting.

The relationships between researcher and researched influence the types of data that are generated, and level of depth to which the data can be interrogated. In Rachael's (Dwyer 2016) work with four teachers, each of the participants differed in the level of openness during the research process; with some there was a level of defensiveness about interpretations of the data, with others those interpretations sparked reflective cycles that may not have otherwise occurred, and this reflectiveness enriched the narrative. The differing relationships resulted in widely varying degrees of depth and criticality in the four narratives.

Another aspect that can complicate research relationships is when the researcher needs to balance multiple roles and/or there is a need for the relationship to last longer than the research itself. Flynn (2014), in her work with bereaved parents, balanced a dual role of music therapist and researcher with these highly vulnerable participants. For Kennelly (2013) and Ledger (2010), their professional colleagues formed the participant pool, requiring research relationships to be negotiated in a way that would maintain positive relationships beyond the course of the research. Jackie Smith (2015) was a therapist for the organization in which she conducted her research. While not therapist to the research participants themselves, she has maintained an ongoing "support group" type of relationship with those who asked for an ongoing connection with the support group that developed around the research.

In addition, it is necessary at times to attend to the specific needs of a particular group of participants. In her chapter, Sol (Rojas-Lizana, Chap. 8 this volume) explored the co-constructed nature of interview data when conducted by an "in-group" interviewer. Michelle (Ronksly-Pavia and Grootenboer, Chap. 9 this volume) attended to and problematized the interview process of working with children with exceptional needs, to ensure that the research was both ethical and inclusive.

Research relationships, as well as being underpinned by epistemological concerns, are closely connected with ethical considerations. University ethical clearance processes are generally designed to deal with research conducted under a positivist framework, but work that falls outside that paradigm may be significantly more complex. Research informed by post-colonial and feminist research ethics seeks to avoid the colonial/imperialist model of plundering a research site for "data" and leaving. The feminist concern to create genuine relationships, respect participants social and cultural context and "give back" to the participants in some way has informed many research designs, although a desire to respect cultural practices can sometimes bring ethical questions. For example, Cassim et al. (2016) felt they could not conduct their research without abiding by the cultural necessity to both accept food when they visited people in their homes (despite the intense discomfort of accepting food from impoverished and traumatised people) and to bring a small gift to their participants, even though the research ethics committee might consider such a gift an "inducement".

Another important ethical decision that is tied to the relationships with research participants is the decision of whether to engage in a process of member checking. Member checking is the process of going back to the participants and asking them to check the accuracy of the texts. This can include only interview transcripts (which is usually considered desirable by ethical review boards), but can be extended to asking participants to read, comment on and clarify your interpretations and analysis so they can "check" it is the "truth": that it is the whole story, or the story they wanted to tell. This process might elicit more detail and elaboration on the themes, and through this process the researcher might access a deeper, more reflective response.

Some researchers take member checking to be an ideological/philosophical stance that aligns with their concern to treat participants respectfully as co-researcher. Yucel and Iwashita (Chap. 10, this volume) developed narrative accounts that were treated as interim texts (Clandinin and Connelly 2000). These were shared with the participants for the purpose of "verification" as an accurate account. Dwyer (2016) also shared narrative accounts with participants, and the conversations about the interpretations they contained were written into the final versions of the narratives.

In some cases, member checking may actually pose a significant ethical risk to participants. For example, in her work with bereaved parents, Flynn (2014) asked participants to read the interview transcripts shortly after the interview, but by the time the narrative accounts were developed several years later, revisiting their grief through reading the narratives posed a potential risk of retraumatisation, which may have a negative impact on their psychological state.

Another perspective on member checking is that it is a pointless exercise. If you understand that a story is not the truth or not itself an experience, but rather, what someone said about the experience, then a member check is simply another step back from experience again – that is, what someone said about what they said about the experience. Therefore, your stance on member checking will have its foundations in your epistemological commitments to what counts as knowledge and knowledge production, and your ontological commitments about the nature of story, as well as being concerned with the nature of the phenomenon under research and the vulnerability of the participants.

While relationships with participants can be carefully cultivated, unexpected occurrences can present challenges for the researcher. Vera Caine and Andrew

Estafan (2011) are researchers who are sincerely concerned with honouring and respecting participants as co-researchers. Each of them had the disquieting experience of a participant leaving the research. In Vera Caine's research, the participant, quite literally, disappeared, with the ensuing police investigation finding no trace. Andrew Estafan had a participant simply fall out of contact, no longer answering emails, but then, when he did reappear years later, he said he was simply done with the research, he felt he had had his say and did not feel he needed to participate any more. Caine and Estafan rather wryly remind us that participants are not always as excited as we are about our work. Caine and Estafan faced an ethical dilemma as they wondered over the ethical way to treat these people's stories, given that their routine, ethically driven, member checking was not possible.

Whatever decisions are made, it is essential that there is a congruency between the epistemology, desired and possible relationships with participants, and the questions that the research seeks to answer.

So What? Who Cares? What Next? The Question and Purpose of the Research

It is possible for narrative research to fulfill a wide range of purposes. As Squire et al. (2013) identify, the divisions between these positions are often treated as more rigid than is truly necessary, and complementary and dialogical movement between them is appropriate at times. However, each brings with it a set of ontological, epistemological and ethical assumptions, and it is therefore useful to have a clear conception of the purpose of the research (or the work that it produces) from the outset.

It is possible for a narrative approach to yield richly detailed accounts of a single person or case study, with a focus on the particular, the unique and the individual. Don Polkinghorne (in Clandinin and Murphy 2007) suggests that narrative focuses on individual lives, as a means of understanding human existence (p. 633). This aligns with the approach to narrative research that has its roots in phenomenology, and also connects strongly to a life history biographical tradition.

While this focus on the individual may be the primary purpose of the research, all narrative research acknowledges the way individuals are situated in social contexts. As described more fully in later sections of this chapter, a focus on the micro-linguistic features of talk in social settings has the potential to illuminate social identities (Bamberg 2007; Georgakopoulou 2007), drawing attention to the ways in which linguistic interactions between agents shape and are shaped by identities.

It is also possible to take a more encompassing look at the social interactions, by examining the ways in which individual experiences align with or resist broader social attitudes. Clandinin and Connelly (1998) use the expression "stories to live by" to describe the way roles, tropes or "master narratives" shape identities and are used to make sense of the social world. Clandinin and Rosiek (2007) draw comparisons between social theorists and narrative researchers. They posit "narrative inquirers and Marxist-influenced scholars working in the applied social sciences often share an interest in analyzing the way large institutions dehumanise, anesthetise, and alienate the people living and working within them" (p. 47). As well as this shared ontological starting point, they suggest that both have a shared goal of "generating scholarship that transforms the ontological conditions of living" (p. 49). The difference between them comes with how these ontological commitments are approached, with critical theorists being primarily concerned with the macrosocial impact on individuals, while narrative inquirers are concerned with the experiences of individuals and how this influences the macrosocial. Social theorists use different terms to describe these macrosocial narratives or forces: Bourdieu adopts the classical notion of *doxa* to describe the unquestioned and unquestionable values of the dominant members of a field and how these shape the experiences of individuals; Foucault writes of a *regime of truth*, an invisible web of power; Lyotard uses the concept of *master narrative* to describe a story that is beyond interrogation, one that is intended to represent the experiences of society rather than individuals (cited in Barone).

Many have identified the potential for narrative research to give voice to the marginalised (Andrews, 2004; Barone 2000, 2001, 2009; Clandinin and Murphy 2009), and to draw attention to power relationships and issues of justice and injustice within social contexts (Barone 2000, 2001). Molly Andrews (2004) draws attention to the potential for narrative research to give voice to "counter-narratives", personal stories that "go against the social grain" (p. 11). For example, Austin and Carpenter (2008) and Carpenter and emerald (2009) heard women's stories of mothering and the ways these aligned with or contradicted the cultural narratives of "good mothering". They heard women's counter narratives of their good mothering in the ways they sometimes stated mothering practices that might be understood in the metanarratives as "bad mothering", as evidence of their "good mothering". In one example, in the context of their work the question of medication for ADHD was a lively and often fraught debate—and some women declared medicating their children as evidence of their good mothering in the face of accusations that is was evidence of their poor mothering.

Taking this a step further, Barone (2000) suggests that narrative (fictional and non-fictional) texts may provide opportunities for readers to engage in "acts of conspiracy" (2000) and critical analysis (2001). Barone (2009) draws on the work of Rorty (1989) and Sartre (1949), both of whom identify the power of storytelling to be emancipatory, mind-changing, and political, or what Sartre labelled *littérature engagée* (Barone 2009, p. 593). While not always identified as narrative research, rather, research presented as narratives, arts-based research is underpinned by the idea that artistic works have the potential to produce texts that inspire transformative experiences for readers (see Leavy 2015; Sleeter 2014).

Whatever you desire the purpose of your research to be, it needs to be informed by your ontological and epistemological position, and align with the selected methods of gathering evidence, drawing meaning from evidence and (re)presentation.

Method Questions

Once the decisions regarding methodology have been made—especially those regarding the question/s you are going to address and your preferences for interacting with participants—the design questions of the research methods should be easier to answer. In reality, designing research is seldom a linear process, often itself iterative. You may find yourself questioning your decisions or assumptions and cycling back to redesign your method until you have coherence across the design stages.

Much has been written about the need to distinguish qualitative research from quantitative through the use of distinctive terms, rejecting the use of terms such as "data", "analysis" and "writing up". Clandinin and Connelly (2000) use the terms field, interim and research texts to describe three moments in the research process. They use the word "moment" to capture something of the ongoing flow of research and the permeability of research phases. In a narrative inquiry it may not be easy, or even sensible to delineate "phases" of data collection, analysis and presentation, especially when the research design is deliberately iterative or cyclic.

In this chapter, we will think about methods in terms of evidence, analysis and (re)presentation. While you are coming to understand the ontological and epistemological foundations of your research, you will be facing a pivotal question in understanding your narrative inquiry design: "where in the research is the narrative?". Story or narrative could be an integral element of any or all of these moments of research (see Fig. 1.1) and as such, there are a myriad of research designs.

What Counts as Evidence? From Whence Does It Come?

All researchers make decisions about the evidence they gather. There is more or less room for flexibility in these choices depending on the traditions associated with particular disciplines. The possibilities for forms of evidence in narrative research

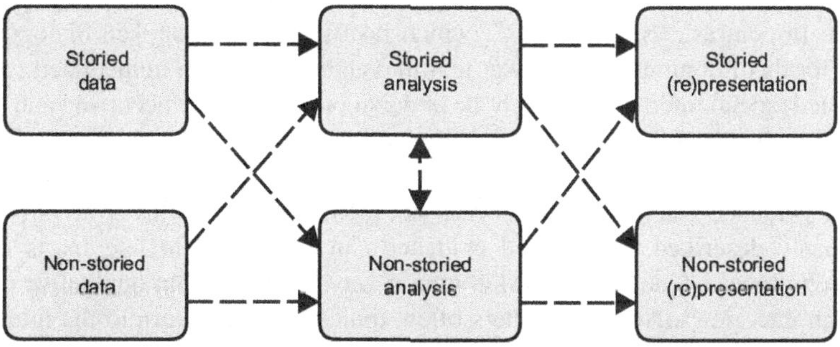

Fig. 1.1 Position of narrative research design (Copyright 2016 R. Dwyer & e. emerald)

are many: field notes, observations, stories, scripts, interviews, films, photographs, conversations, walk-a-longs, collages, photo elicitation interviews and so forth, and likewise, the medium can be written, spoken, film, audio, and more. In this section, rather than focusing on what can be done and how, we explore the issues associated with determining what evidence will be the best suited for your research questions, and problematize the often-tacit decisions about "data collection".

The question of what evidence to gather, create, collect, select or generate, and why, is driven by the underlying tenets of the research itself, founded in your epistemological and ontological commitments. For example, Clandinin and Connelly (2000) suggest that use of the term field text helps us shift the concept of "objective reality" embedded in the notion of "data" and acknowledge, "how imbued field texts are with interpretation" (p. 93). For Clandinin and Connelly, field texts constitute the evidence upon which claims are made, what others might call "data".

Another question to be considered is whether the evidence would have existed without your intervention as a researcher. David Silverman (2007) refers to this as a distinction between naturally occurring or "manufactured" data (data that only occurs because the researcher is there). Coming from the theoretical foundation of ethnomethodology, Silverman (2007) makes a strong argument for the use of naturally occurring data, and demonstrates some of the pitfalls of manufactured data. He alerts us to procedural consequentiality—that is, how the way we gather data influences its "reliability" (p. 58). He makes the important point that researchers must "attend to and demonstrate that they have thought through the extent to which their findings may simply be an artefact of their chosen method." (p. 58).

This distinction between naturally occurring and manufactured evidence resonates with the conversation about using "big stories" or "small stories" as evidence (see Bamberg 2007). Small stories are small conversational exchanges and big stories are life stories and autobiographical accounts (Georgakopoulou and Bamberg 2005). Bamberg (2007) notes that the differences between "big" and "small" stories denote very different approaches to narrative inquiry, claiming that re-positioning big story approaches as grounded in dialogical/discursive approaches such as small story research will theoretically and methodologically enrich narrative inquiry in a radical way. As Freeman (2007) identifies, "big stories" (evidence generated in settings such as interviews, clinical sessions, written reflections) are a step removed from the action itself and are reflective by nature rather than a "true" account of the action. In contrast, "small stories", which take the form of spoken dialogue and other forms of communication (e.g. text messages, emails) in unmediated (or less mediated) social interactions, might be understood as naturally occurring and hence a more authentic reflection of social life as the evidence was generated with less intrusion from researchers (Bamberg 2007).

The evidence you gather may or may not themselves be stories or narratives. As previously described, non-storied evidence can be storied in later parts of the research process. One of the most common ways of generating qualitative data is through interviews. New researchers often, quite innocently, turn to the interview, approaching it as if it is somehow a neutral means of extracting information, without recognizing the contested and debated territory on which interview as a research method sits (Holstein and Gubrium 2004; Honan 2014). Alerted to David Silverman's caution of procedural consequentiality mentioned above (Silverman 2007), many narrative researchers strike something of a middle ground in narrative interviews. For example, Wendy Holloway, uses the "free association narrative interview method" (Spears et al. 2005, p. 545), hoping to avoid constraining respondents by the assumptions embedded in interview questions, as a way of reaching beyond the constraints of the structured interview:

> to elicit deeply felt and difficult emotions, possibly conflictual, as well as taken-for-granted issues like identity and identifications… The resulting narratives are developed by follow-up questions following the ordering and wording of the interviewee, based on the principle that the researcher should elicit participants' experiences meanings and free associations, imposing as little as is possible of their own. Analysis of data involves, among many other things, noticing signs of the affect and potential conflict interviewees show in their narratives. (Spears et al. 2005, p. 545)

Narrative researchers might open an interview with a broad question such as "tell me about your experience of …" This may allow the respondent to set the agenda, and as an interviewer you may or may not then have some probes on hand to examine a point of particular interest to the research. In her work with music teachers, Rachael (Dwyer 2016) used themes from the literature to prompt the teacher participants to speak to particular themes. Carpenter and emerald (2009) took a slightly different approach. They started with open interviews, and as their work progressed over time and number of interviews, they identified several developing themes that powerfully spoke to their research topic. These themes came up in most interviews unprompted, but if they didn't, Lorelei or elke would introduce them towards the end of the interview, with a statement something like "Many other mothers have spoken about … Do you have any thoughts on that?". As such a reflective and reflexive cycle developed. Aware of procedural consequentiality, in their analysis, Carpenter and emerald noted where this topic was prompted and when it arose unbidden.

Every introductory research text will have a taxonomy of interview types and a "how to" section including such terms as structured, semi structured, conversational, and focus groups. Qualitative researchers have fruitfully employed a range of other story gathering techniques: walk-a-long interviews (that create a conversational space that may well be responsive to the space you are walking through) photo elicitation (either historical photos—say for life history research or asking participants to respond to photos they have taken) and digital storytelling. Both big story and small story research use stories as the evidence, focusing on the way the storytellers (participants) structure their stories and make use of linguistic devices. However, evidence need not always be collected in storied form. Clandinin and Connelly (2000; Connelly and Clandinin 2006) describe generating evidence through "telling", where more often than not, the "tellings" are storied in at least some sense, but also through "living alongside". Living alongside participants includes observing interactions in the field as well as informal conversations that naturally occur when the researcher is a presence in the field setting. These pieces of evidence are not coherent, structured stories in themselves, but are "storied" by the researcher, or by the participant and researcher together (this will be discussed in more depth in the next section).

The question of "standards of evidence" is alive in all research, and perhaps moreso in a space like narrative inquiry, which encourages a range, richness and variety and, depending on the approach you take, is unlikely to adhere to fixed procedures. The question of how we determine whether evidence is rigorous and reliable and valid has been approached in different ways. Freeman et al. (2007), the five authors themselves not agreeing, review some of the ways that issues a research 'validity' and 'reliability' have been addressed in qualitative methods and give particular attention to how we determine 'good' evidence; For example, they summarise Wilson (1994) and Lincoln (2002) as two possible criteria for evaluating the nature of evidence. Wilson offers:

> evidence should be consistent with a researcher's chosen epistemology or perspective;
> evidence should be observable;
> evidence should be gathered through systematic procedures;
> evidence should be shared and made public, and,
> evidence should be compelling (Wilson 1994, pp. 26–30)

Whereas Lincoln (2002) offers:

> researchers should have been deeply involved and closely connected to the scene;
> researchers should achieve enough distance from the phenomenon to permit recording action and interpretations relatively free of the researcher's own stake;
> claims should be based on an adequate selection of the total corpus of data;
> data should come, at least partly, from publicly accessible observation records, and,
> data and analysis should include consideration of inferences and interpretations, as well as concrete phenomena (Lincoln 2002, p. 9).

Criteria such as these draw our attention as researchers to how we operationalise our epistemological, ontological and ethical commitments. As a researcher you will be called upon to justify your evidence as part of the work of validating your research outcomes. It is wise to consider this question deeply and carefully before you start gathering/collecting/creating data/evidence.

While the approaches described thus far in this section present a range of methods, they are commonly used in combination, as a bricolage. What follows is a series of examples of how evidence has been generated in a range of narrative inquiries. It is essential to note that the methods selected for generating evidence are guided by both the research questions and the field context: planning and reflexivity replace hard-and-fast rules.

Examples of Evidence

elke emerald and Fiona Ewing (2015) capture something of the notion of lived stories as data sources. elke and Fe have been friends for nigh on 30 years. They have spent many days and nights storytelling their lives to each other around Fe's kitchen table. For the purposes of research though, they spent three deliberate days, around that same table, but this time with a recorder, and in walk-along "interviews", recounting Fe's stories of life at sea. The depth of a 30-year relationship sat behind the storytelling, which deliberately set out to examine the one phenomenon under study—life at sea for a "woman in a man's world".

Cassim et al. (2016), examining the use of Western and Indigenous psychology, gathered the life narratives of five Sri Lankans affected by the 2004 Indian Ocean tsunami using semi-structured and walk-along interviews. The walk-along technique enabled richly layered stories as participants interacted with community and responded to the environment—eliciting stories and memories that might otherwise not have been available. The memories and artefacts, and interactions with community members enriched the stories. Further, as community members related their stories in talking "incidentally" with the passing researcher and participant, a richly layered story of the tsunami and its consequences and the subsequent healing journeys emerged.

Vera Caine (2010) gave 6th grade students cameras to take home with only one brief instruction—to photograph "community". These photos were used to elicit discussion with students about what community meant to them. This method elicited a variety and depth of perception that may not have otherwise emerged. Students explored the concept in their own spaces, rather than being influenced by some predetermined definition of community, with one student even contributing photographs of his home's resident ghost.

A stark question/answer interview technique would elicit little or no response in some cultural settings. Susan Faoagali, Eileen Honan and Timote M. Vaioleti use talanoa, a Pacifica storytelling dialogue as the conversational platform for gathering narratives (Faoagali and Honan 2015; Vaioleti 2006). The talanoa is a storytelling dialogue itself and the ritual sharing of stories and cultural passing of permission to speak from one member to another facilitates iterative and layered storying.

In his exploration of the lives of boys with ADHD, Brenton Prosser (2006) uses the boys' poetry and stories to present their lives. He also presents a story that several boys wrote together about the experiences at school of a fictional composite character. This collaborative writing arguably allowed the boys to express a richer story than any one boy could tell.

Pithouse-Morgan et al. (2012), in their exploration of student life for one international student in a South African University, used interviews and collage making. The collages expressed an element of experience and also facilitated a relaxed and open talking space. Their aim was not ascertain the number of participants who had similar or different experiences, but rather to "re-present and make meaning from the texture, depth, and complexity of one participant's stories of lived experience" (p. 77).

Georgakopoulou (2007) argues that conversational small stories are "crucial sites of subjectivity" (p. 89), that have the potential to illuminate social identities. Small stories data may be from research-driven events (group interviews) or naturally occurring data such as verbal exchanges or text messages, and allow the researcher to attend to the social interactions between participants in ways that individual interviews do not. In her work with school students, Georgakopoulou (2014) used ethnographic observations, radio microphone recordings of students' in-class and playground talk, formal interviews, "playback sessions", in which the researcher and student participant listened to and discussed selected excerpts of the recorded data, as well as demographic information about students and the school. This rich dataset allows for a focus on the micro-linguistic features of social interactions, as well as providing opportunities for those interactions to be contextualized.

What Does It Mean? How do I Know?

Approaches to analyzing or interpreting research evidence are perhaps the most contested aspect of narrative research. There is an inherited view from the "hard sciences"/positivist/quantitative disciplines that analysis must be rigid in order to be rigorous; that evidence must be "proven true" in order to be considered knowledge. It is important to recognise that there are several ways to understand the value of research, and all research should be evaluated in terms of its own parameters. Many of the concepts and words we are used to using come from the positivist paradigm, and make a lot of sense in quantitative research—but perhaps are not so applicable to qualitative research. Guba and Lincoln (2005) suggested that the concept of research 'rigour'—with the associated criteria of validity, generalizability, reliability and objectivity, which harken to the assumption that inquiry is objective and value free—be rethought for the qualitative context. For example, they suggest the use of the concept of trustworthiness in place of rigour, with criteria of credibility, transferability, dependability, and confirmability. They developed this as something of a mirror of positivist criteria, but recognising that inquiry is contextual and value laden. In their publications in the late 1980s Lincoln and Guba (see a more recent version in Lincoln, Lynham and Guba, 2011) asked qualitative researchers to take on the challenge of considering how we evaluate qualitative research and move the field forward. Lively debate has moved qualitative research well beyond justifying itself, with frameworks for evaluating research directly responsive to the nature and goals of the research itself.

For example Laurel Richardson (2000) suggested consideration of whether the research:

makes a substantive contribution,
shows aesthetic merit,
demonstrates reflexivity,
has impact, and,
expresses a reality.

Tracy (2010) suggested we consider evaluative criteria in terms of:

whether is it is a worthy topic,
demonstrates rich rigor,
shows sincerity,
demonstrates credibility,
has resonance,
makes a significant contribution,
is ethical,
and shows meaningful coherence.

Freeman et al. 2007 suggested research reports be read with attention to thorough description of design and methods in reports, adequate demonstration of the relationship of claims to data, and thoughtful consideration by the researcher of the strengths and limitations of the study.

Clandinin and Caine (2012) turned their attention very specifically to their rendering of narrative inquiry to develop their touchstone criteria for evaluating the rigor of a narrative inquiry:

Attending to relational responsibilities.
Recognition of being in the midst.
Negotiation of relationships.
Narrative beginnings.
Negotiating entry into the field.
Moving from field to field texts.
Moving from field texts to interim texts and final research texts.
Representing narratives of experiences in ways that show temporality, sociality, and place.
Relational response communities.
Justifications.
Attentive to multiple audiences.
Commitment to understanding lives in motion.

As they appear here, these may just look like empty lists. Each of the authors of course articulates these criteria in some depth. We do not have space here to unpack all the frameworks, but take it as our task in this chapter to alert you to this consideration in your research. A clear sense of your commitments to research quality can drive your project in productive ways.

Again, the epistemological foundation of the research will drive the choice of approach to analysis, along with the research questions and purpose.

Polkinghorne (1995) puts approaches to analysis into two broad categories: "analysis of narratives", which he considers to be a form of qualitative research more generally, and "narrative analysis", where the analysis is a "storying" of the evidence by the researcher (Clandinin and Murphy 2007, p. 635). For Polkinghorne, the point of narrative is not to find the commonalities, but rather the particularities of experience; the temporal development and unique histories, looking for things that are common across people. This focus understands that the knowledge we get from narrative is knowledge of the particular rather than general.

However, there are many researchers who call their work "narrative" who fall outside of Polkinghorne's definition. Approaches are varied, ranging from highly structured linguistics-informed approaches (Bamberg 2007; Georgakopoulou 2007; Labov 1997), more thematically-informed approaches, research guided by dimensions of temporality, sociality and place (Clandinin and Connelly 2000; Connelly and Clandinin 2006), narrative as a synthesis of evidence (Polkinghorne 1995) or a myriad of others. Again, and as always, approaches are informed by the research questions and underlying theoretical and methodological tenets of the research.

It is beyond the scope of this chapter to articulate the processes of analytic methods, so here we'll describe a number of studies by way of example. First though, it may be pertinent to consider thematic analysis, as it is often the "go to" analytic for first-time narrative inquirers. The question of how themes (sometimes called narrative threads) are analytically derived from the research evidence will be, again, driven by your research methodology and underpinning philosophical tenets: systematic "highlighter and sticky note" coding as described by Brene Brown (2007); a "reading and re-reading" approach (Clandinin and Connelly 2000); software driven analysis (NVivo for example); careful coding, cross-coding with independent coders and cateorising described by Boyatzis (1998) and Braun and Clarke (2006).

By way of example, Megan Yucel and Noriko Iwashita (Chap. 10, this volume) gathered student stories through several interviews and then created narrative accounts which they reflected on in terms of the major themes arising from students' experience of engagement in the IELTS examination system. They use Barkhuizen's (2008) model of three interconnected stories to frame their analysis:

story—a particular individual's story.
Story—the wider context, beyond the personal level such as the school or workplace
STORY—the broader socio-political context in which teaching and learning takes place.

This distinction is important for Yucel and Iwashita as it enables an understanding of the layers of context in the stories of international students studying for IELTS (International English Language Testing System) tests: how the educational experience of English language proficiency is inherently connected with the students' sense of past, present and future selves, and the ways in which the learning is part of larger social and political structures.

Molly Andrews (2004) listened for the counter narratives—the moments when participants countered or resisted their culture's driving narratives. She spoke with people in their eighties, recounting their experience of being mothered around 70 years prior to the interview. She found that rather than deferring to simple plotlines and explanations that cultural narratives might provide as explanations for, for example, "negligent mothering", they would at times challenge these cultural narratives, recognising circumstances and contexts as complicating factors. Andrews found that "speakers in my study dip in and out of dominant cultural scripts of motherhood, manipulating and reformulating them in ways that are not always immediately apparent. The end result is a very subtle subversion of the well-worn tale, with the mythology of motherhood at its centre (Andrews 2004, p. 9).

Carpenter and emerald (2009) used a systematic and rigorous method developed from Boyatsis (1998) to find the themes arising from their interviews with women and then scanned media, movies and blogs to find the abiding cultural narratives of motherhood. They then examined the way that women confirmed or resisted these narratives in their stories of mothering.

Taking the understanding that narratives can give meaning to and structure life events, and further, that the structure and form of a life story is as important as the content, Cassim, Hodgetts and Stolte (2016) analysed features of narrative in their endeavor to understand healing after tragedy. They explored the form and structure of the stories of Sri Lankan tsunami survivors and considered the "plotlines" that connected and organised experiences into episodes. They recognized that narrative structures differ across cultures, therefore adapted and combined Western narrative methods in a way that successfully translated and applied to the Sri Lankan cultural setting. In addition to listening to and analysing verbal accounts of participant life narratives, they also focused on, and interpreted, the everyday practices of members of the community. Informed by practice theory, they understood that one of the ways that individuals and communities come to understand the world around them is through the routine doing of everyday social practices. This analytic enabled Cassim et al. to understand the individuals and the community as skilled agents in managing their healing after tragedy.

In their studies of curriculum, Anne Murray Orr and Margaret Olsen (2007) found that Clandinin and Connelly's (2000) three dimensional narrative inquiry space—the temporal, the personal/social (a continuum between the two), and place—provided a scaffold for analysis and interpretation that allowed them new to see their curriculum moments from varied perspectives, leading to "possibilities for seeing differently" (Murray Orr and Olsen 2007, p. 821).

In contrast to these relatively open and flexible frameworks, analytical approaches that have developed out of linguistic traditions can provide much more systematized processes for analysis. Labov's (1972) approach to analyzing narratives focuses on the description of particular events. Labov's six-part model categorises each clause of the text according to its function: abstract, orientation, complicating action, result, evaluation or coda, allowing a detailed understanding of the structure and function of clauses within the narrative. The purpose of this approach is to gain a sense of how people use narrative devices to make meaning and construct their identities. As Patterson (2013) identifies, this approach is most meaningful when used to analyse stories that are produced naturally rather than in research-driven situations.

Bamberg (2004) proposes a narrative inquiry method by suggesting that each of the narrative elements—form, content and function—can be put to work in terms of three levels of positioning analysis: Level 1: the characters in a story world. Level 2: Interactive positioning, and Level 3: the story's intersection with dominant discourses. Bamberg and colleagues are concerned to notice the ways that all these elements of analysis are a function of interactional engagement—important insights are available when we consider the interactive context that enables and constrains a story. So, for example, Bamberg and Georgakopoulou (2008) explore of the detail of four 10 year old boys' storytelling in a conversation by layering their inquiry in steps:

Step one: Who are the characters and how are they relationally positioned? (Positioning Level 1)
Step two: the interactive accomplishment of "narrating"? (Positioning Level 2)
Step three: How is the speaker positioned within the interactive flow of turns that constitute the situation as "research"? (Positioning Level 2)
Step four: How is the relation between the four boys managed? (Positioning Level 2)
Step five: Who am I in all this? (Positioning Level 3)

While it is beyond the scope of this chapter to provide a thorough review of analytical processes, the examples above illustrate the diversity of approaches, and the possibilities for developing methods that suit the individual project.

(Re)presenting the Research

The question of how, when and in what form to present the research will be informed by questions of audience, context, theory, methodology and epistemology. And again, the research text may or may not be in the form of a narrative or have narrative elements. Options abound for (re)presentation, both within and beyond print genres. Narratives researchers have presented research as narrative within traditional, text-based academic outputs (journal articles, books or chapters), as well as in other mediums, such as performance, art works, music, drama, creative writing (fiction and non-fiction), poetry, and film. The chapter in this volume on sensory narrative describes examples of performance, installations using sound, vision and movement, and arts-based (re)presentation.

A fairly common and effective format in a journal article or chapter, is to intersperse elements of story with commentary and analysis. As Pithouse-Morgan et al. (2012) remind us:

> Researchers who use alternative methods of data re-presentation acknowledge the value of facts and interview quotes, but see these as raw material for constructing evocative re-presentations that "deploy literary devices to recreate lived experience and evoke emotional responses (Richardson 2000, p. 11)" (Pithouse-Morgan et al. 2012, p. 77).

The question of (re)presentation can require the consideration of ethical and methodological concerns. Alison Ledger (2010) found in her study of music therapists' experiences of clinical supervision, that the stories participants wrote of their own experience would have been too ethically dangerous to print as they were; as they may have implicated others or revealed participants to readers, being part of a small professional community. Alison asked participants to prepare a written or oral narrative, which were treated as interim texts, and then wrote her own poetry inspired by each of the narratives (see Kennelly, Ledger and Flynn, Chap. 4, this volume for an example).

It is in the question of (re)presentation that many narrative inquirers may feel frustrated by the limitations of the printed word, although many print publications allow limited photographs and visuals, and electronic formats are loosening the boundaries and creating new opportunities for (re)presentation of research.

Examples of (Re)presentation

In an ideal world with unlimited space, we would reproduce full, "real" examples of innovative approaches to presenting narrative research. However, we hope that the wonders of technology will put these examples within easy reach.

Pithouse-Morgan et al. (2012) peppered their journal article about "Jack's" experiences of racism at University with narrative vignettes—these were brief evocative scenes or accounts that re-presented the field texts of unstructured interviews and collage-making in storied form. These vignettes invite the reader to see and hear through the sensibilities and emotions of this one focus character "Jack". They interspersed the vignettes and interpretive discussion, which drew on literature to consider what we can learn about a university campus as a pedagogic setting from Jack's experience and then caste a forward looking glance to the possibilities for fostering different sorts of pedagogic settings, where stories such as Jack's were not possible.

emerald and Ewing (2015) use a similar threading of story, interpretation and theory to tell Fe's stories. The chapter is framed in the story of 3 days of storytelling, during which many stories are told, so the focus moves back and forward in time, and is interleaved with interpretation and theorizing, often framed in the story world as elke's ruminating on Fe's stories.

Concluding Thoughts

As we attempt to somehow sum up this chapter, we feel that we have perhaps attempted to cover too much ground. Our intention was to shine a light across the landscape of narrative research, to provide an introduction to what is there, and some useful signposts to mark areas that may be worthy of closer examination. While this chapter might be seen as something of a map, it is important to note that a map is not the terrain itself. Detailed study of those who have come before is an essential part of the process of researching, and allows for more informed, and more likely successful, innovation. As we have stated repeatedly throughout this chapter, the decisions about what, why and how to undertake a research project are both personal and contextual. Thorough consideration of each of the seven key issues that we describe in this chapter, we believe, will set a course for coherent and rigorous research.

Discussion Questions

1. Map your own research (or a project you have read about in a journal article, book or dissertation) on the 'position of narrative' diagram (Fig. 1.1). Consider what this means in terms of what the data/evidence, analysis and (re)presentation of the research.
2. Choose the author/s cited who you think aligns best with your own ideas about narrative and research. Write a paragraph explaining your choice.

References

Andrews, M. (2004). Counter narratives and the power to oppose. In M. Bamberg & M. Andrews (Eds.), *Considering counter-narratives: Narrating, resisting, making sense* (pp. 1–6). Amsterdam: John Benjamins Publishing.

Austin, H., & Carpenter, L. (2008). Troubled, troublesome, troubling mothers: The dilemma of difference in women's personal motherhood narratives. *Narrative Inquiry, 18*(2), 378–392.

Bamberg, M. (2004). Considering counter narratives. In M. Bamberg & M. Andrews (Eds.), *Considering counter-narratives: Narrating, resisting, making sense* (pp. 1–6). Amsterdam: John Benjamins Publishing.

Bamberg, M. (2007). Stories: Big or small: Why do we care? In M. Bamberg (Ed.), *Narrative: State of the art* (pp. 165–174). Amsterdam: John Benjamins Publishing.

Bamberg, M. (2009, July 20–24). *Doing narrative analysis: frameworks, methods, and exercises*. Workshop and Seminar Griffith University, Brisbane.

Bamberg, M. (2011). Narrative practice and identity navigation. In J. A. Holstein & J. F. Gubrium (Eds.), *Varieties of narrative analysis* (pp. 99–124). London: Sage Publications.

Bamberg, M., & Georgakopoulou, A. (2008). Small stories as a new perspective in narrative and identity analysis. Text & talk-an interdisciplinary. *Journal of Language, Discourse Communication Studies, 28*(3), 377–396.

Barkhuizen, G. (2008). A narrative approach to exploring context in language teaching. *ELT Journal, 62*(3), 231–239.

Barone, T. (2000). *Aesthetics, politics and educational inquiry: Essays and examples*. New York: Peter Lang.

Barone, T. (2001). *Touching eternity: The enduring outcomes of teaching*. New York: Teachers College Press.

Barone, T. (2009). Narrative researchers as witnesses of injustice and agents of social change? *Educational Researcher, 38*(8), 591–597.

Bourdieu, P. (1999). Understanding. In P. Bourdieu (Ed.), *The weight of the world: Social suffering in contemporary society*. Stanford: Stanford University Press.

Boyatzis, R. E. (1998). *Transforming qualitative information: Themeatic analysis and code development*. Thousand Oaks: Sage.

Braun, V., & Clarke, V. (2006). Using thematic analysis in psychology qualitative research. *Psychology, 3*, 77–101.

Brown, B. (2007). *I thought it was just me (but it isn't): Telling the truth about perfectionism, inadequacy, and power*. New York: Penguin/Gotham.

Bruner, J. (1986). *Actual minds, possible worlds*. Cambridge, MA: Harvard University Press.

Caine, V. (2010). Visualizing community: Understanding narrative inquiry as action research. *Educational Action Research* New York: Taylor & Francis

Caine, V., & Estafan, A. (2011). Living alongside the experience of waiting: Inquiry into the long-term relational responsibilities in narrative inquiry. *Qualitative Inquiry, 17*(10), 965–971. doi:10.1177/1077800411425152.

Carpenter, L., & Emerald, E. (2009). *Stories from the margin: Mothering a child with ADHD or ASD*. Teneriffe: Post Pressed.

Cassim, S., Hodgetts, D., & Stolte, O. (2016). Cultural consideration and mixed methods for psychological research: A Sri Lankan perspective. In R. Rinehart & E. Emerald (Eds.), *Ethnographies in Pan Pacific research: Tensions and positionings* (pp. 111–121). New York: Routledge.

Clandinin, D. J., & Caine, V. (2012). Narrative inquiry. In A. Trainor & E. Graue (Eds.), *Reviewing qualitative research in the social sciences*. New York: Taylor and Francis/Routledge.

Clandinin, D. J., & Connelly, F. M. (1998). Stories to live by: Narrative understandings of school reform. *Curriculum Inquiry, 28*(2), 149–164.

Clandinin, D. J., & Connelly, F. M. (2000). *Narrative inquiry: Experience and story in qualitative research*. San Francisco: Jossey-Bass.

Clandinin, D. J., & Murphy, M. S. (2007). Looking ahead: Conversations with Elliot Mishler, Don Polkinghorne, and Amia Lieblich. In D. J. Clandinin (Ed.), *Handbook of narrative inquiry: Mapping a methodology* (pp. 632–651). Thousand Oaks: Sage.

Clandinin, D. J., & Murphy, M. S. (2009). Relational ontological commitments in narrative inquiry. *Educational Researcher, 38*(8), 598–602.

Clandinin, D. J., & Rosiek, J. (2007). Mapping a landscape of narrative inquiry: Borderland spaces and tensions. In D. J. Clandinin (Ed.), *Handbook of narrative inquiry: Mapping a methodology* (pp. 35–72). Thousand Oaks: Sage.

Clandinin, D. J., Huber, J., Huber, M., Murphy, M. S., Orr, A. M., Pearce, M., & Steeves, P. (2006). *Composing diverse identities: Narrative inquiries into the interwoven lives of children and teachers*. Abingdon: Routledge.

Connelly, F. M., & Clandinin, D. J. (2006). Narrative inquiry. In J. L. Green, G. Camilli, & P. B. Elmore (Eds.), *Handbook of complementary methods in educational research* (pp. 477–488). Washington, DC: American Educational Research Association.

Dwyer, R. (2016). *Music teachers' values and beliefs: Stories from music education*. Abingdon, UK: Routledge.

Emerald, E., & Ewing, F. (2015). Shall we keel haul the little %$#@, or chuck him in the chain locker?: How life at sea becomes 'stories to live by' for a woman on a fishing vessel. In M. Brown & B. Humberstone (Eds.), *Seascapes: Shaped by the sea* (pp. 173–186). Farnham: Ashgate Press.

Faoagali, S., & Honan, E. (2015). A journey in-between: Using Talanoa in research reporting. In K. Trimmer, A. L. Black, & S. Riddle (Eds.), *Mainstreams, margins and the spaces in-between: New possibilities for education research* (pp. 239–252). Abingdon: Routledge. doi:10.4324/9781315777818.

Flynn, L. (2014). *The stories we haven't told: The lived experience of music used in therapy for bereaved parents*. Unpublished doctoral thesis, University of Queensland, Australia.

Freeman, M. (2007). Life "on holiday"? In defense of big stories. In M. Bamberg (Ed.), *Narrative: State of the art* (pp. 155–164). Amsterdam: John Benjamins Publishing.

Freeman, M., de Marrais, K., Preissle, J., Roulston, K., & St. Pierre, E. A. (2007). Standards of evidence in qualitative research: An incitement to discourse. *Educational Researcher, 36*(1), 25–32.

Georgakopoulou, A. (2007). Small stories, interaction and identities. In M. Bamberg (Ed.), *Narrative: State of the art* (pp. 145–154). Amsterdam: John Benjamins Publishing.

Georgakopoulou, A. (2014). Girlpower or girl (in) trouble?: Identities and discourses in the (new) media engagements of adolescents' school-based in interaction. In J. Androutsopoulos (Ed.), *Mediatization and sociolinguistic change* (pp. 217–244). Berlin: Walter de Gruyter.

Georgakopoulou, A., & Bamberg, M. (2005, July). Small is beautiful: Small stories as a new perspective in narrative analysis. In *9th International Pragmatics Association Conference, Riva del Garda* (pp. 10–15).

Guba, E. G., & Lincoln, Y. S. (2005). Paradigmatic controversies, contradictions, and emerging confluences. In N. K. Denzin & Y. S. Lincoln (Eds.), *The Sage handbook of qualitative research* (3rd ed., pp. 191–296). Thousand Oaks: Sage.

Holstein, J., & Gubrium, J. (2004). The active interview. In David Silverman (Ed.), *Qualitative research: Theory, method and practice* (2nd ed., pp. 140–161). London: SAGE.

Honan, E. (2014). Disrupting the habit of interviewing. *Reconceptualizing Educational Research Methodology, 5*(1) https://journals.hioa.no/index.php/rerm/article/view/929

Huber, J., Caine, V., Huber, M., & Steeves, P. (2013). Narrative inquiry as pedagogy in education the extraordinary potential of living, telling, retelling, and reliving stories of experience. *Review of Research in Education, 37*, 212–242. doi:10.3102/0091732X12458885.

Kennelly, J. (2013). *Sight, sounds and feelings: The views, experiences and practices regarding professional supervision for Australian-based music therapists*. Unpublished doctoral thesis, University of Queensland, Australia, available at https://espace.library.uq.edu.au/view/UQ:319389

Labov, W. (1972). *Language in the inner city: Studies in the Black English vernacular*. Oxford: Basil Blackwell.
Labov, W. (1997). Some further steps in narrative analysis. *Journal of Narrative and Life History, 7*(1–4), 395–415.
Leavy, P. (2015). *Low fat love*. Rotterdam: Sense.
Ledger, A. J. (2010). *Am I a founder or am I a fraud? Music therapists' experiences of developing services in healthcare organizations*. Doctoral thesis, University of Limerick, Ireland.
Lincoln, Y. S. (2002, November). *On the nature of qualitative evidence*. Paper presented at the annual meeting of the Association for the Study of Higher Education, Sacramento, CA.
Lincoln, Y. S., Lynham, S. A., & Guba, E. G. (2011). Paradigmatic controversies, contradictions, and emerging confluences, revisited. In N. K. Denzin & Y. S. Lincoln (Eds.), *The Sage handbook of qualitative research*. Thousand Oaks: Sage.
McAllister, M. M. (2001). In harm's way: A postmodern narrative inquiry. *Journal of Psychiatric and Mental Health Nursing, 8*, 391–397.
Mishler, E. (1999). *Storylines: Craftartists' narratives of identity*. Cambridge, MA: Harvard University Press.
Murray Orr, A., & Olsen, M. (2007). Transforming narrative encounters. *Canadian Journal of Education, 30*(3), 819–838.
Patterson, W. (2013). Narratives of events: Labovian narrative analysis and its limitations. In M. Andrews, C. Squire, & M. Tamboukou (Eds.), *Doing narrative research* (pp. 27–36). London: Sage.
Pinnegar, S., & Daynes, G. (2007). Locating narrative inquiry historically: Thematics in the turn to narrative. In D. J. Clandinin (Ed.), *Handbook of narrative inquiry: Mapping a methodology* (pp. 3–34). Thousand Oaks: Sage.
Pithouse-Morgan, K., Morojele, P., Pillay, D., Naicker, I., Chikoko, V., Ramkelawan, R., et al. (2012). "The air is hostile…" learning from an African international postgraduate student's stories of fear and isolation within a South African university campus. *Alternation, 19*(2), 73–93.
Poirier, S., & Ayers, L. (1997). Focus of qualitative methods: Endings, secrets and silences: Overreading in narrative inquiry. *Research in Nursing and Health, 20*, 551–557.
Polkinghorne, D. E. (1988). *Narrative knowing and the human sciences*. Albany: SUNY Press.
Polkinghorne, D. E. (1995). Narrative configuration in qualitative analysis. *International Journal of Qualitative Studies in Education, 8*(1), 5–23.
Prosser, B. (2006). *Seeing Red: Critical narrative in ADHD research*. Teneriffe: Post Pressed.
Richardson, L. (2000). Evaluating ethnography. *Qualitative Inquiry, 6*(2), 253–255.
Riessman, C., & Speedy, J. (2007). Narrative inquiry in the psychotherapy professions a critical review. In D. J. Clandinin (Ed.), *Handbook of narrative inquiry: Mapping a methodology* (pp. 426–457). Thousand Oaks: Sage.
Rorty, R. (1989). *Contingency, irony, and solidarity*. Cambridge: Cambridge University Press.
Sarbin, T. R. (1986). The narrative as a root metaphor for psychology. In T. R. Sarbin (Ed.), *Narrative psychology: The storied nature of human conduct* (pp. 3–21). New York: Praeger.
Sartre, J. P. (1949). *What is literature? And other essays* (B. Frechtman, Trans.). Cambridge: Cambridge University Press.
Silverman, D. (2007). *A very short, fairly interesting, and reasonably cheap book about qualitative research*. Thousand Oaks: Sage.
Sleeter, C. (2014). *White bread: Weaving cultural past into the present*. Rotterdam: Sense.
Smith, J. M. (2015). *Recovering from silence. Composing self in time, spaces, and friendships: A narrative inquiry with four mothers supporting adolescent children through long-term addictions treatment*. Unpublished doctoral thesis, University of Calgary, Canada.
Spears, R., Holloway, W., & Edwards, D. (2005). Three views on hate. *The Psychologist, 18*(9), 544–547.

Squire, C., Andrews, M., & Tamboukou, M. (2013). Introduction: What is narrative research. In M. Andrews, C. Squire, & M. Tamboukou (Eds.), *Doing narrative research* (pp. 1–26). London: Sage.

Tamboukou, M. (2008). Re-imagining the narratable subject. *Qualitative Research, 8*(3), 283–292.

Tracy, S. J. (2010). Qualitative quality: Eight "Big-Tent" criteria for excellent qualitative research. *Qualitative Inquiry, 16*, 837–851. doi:10.1177/1077800410383121.

Vaioleti, T. M. (2006). Talanoa research methodology: a developing position on pacific research Waikato. *Journal of Education, 12*(2), 21–34.

Wilson, B. J. (1994). A challenge to communication empiricists: Let's be more forthcoming about what we do. *Western Journal of Communication, 58*(1), 25–31.

Chapter 2
Autoethnography: Is My Own Story Narrative Research?

elke emerald and Lorelei Carpenter

Abstract Narrative researchers have long understood the power of a story to capture a reader's attention, link them emotionally to a topic and then use that attention and connection to communicate a theoretical or practical point. And further, the story can *itself* communicate the social/cultural/political. Autoethnography asserts that when we publically story our experiences, they transcend the private and the personal and assume political import. It is a particular research method that connects the personal to the political, social and cultural in captivating, stirring and most importantly, insightful ways that move us to action. Autoethnography is a comfortable companion for many forms of narrative research.

This chapter briefly outlines some of the tenets of autoethnography: exploring how an autoethnographic writer can achieve that connection between the story and the wider cultural point that shifts a story from just interesting, to research. We use some examples of autoethnographies to explore the extent to which authors can or should make the social/political/cultural points explicit for the reader, and present Lorelei's autoethnography of her 'near-miss' to elaborate and exemplify *one* way of facing the methodological and theoretical challenges of autoethnography.

Keywords Autoethnography • Narrative autoethnography • Field texts • Interim texts • Research texts

Introduction

> Qualitative writers are, thankfully, off the "science hook," so to speak. They don't have to try to play deity, writing as disembodied omniscient narrator, claiming, universal atemporal general knowledge; they can eschew the questionable metanarrative of scientific objectivity and still have plenty to say as situated speakers, subjectivities engaged in knowing/telling about the world as they perceive it. (Richardson, 1997, p. 88)

---

e. emerald (✉)
School of Education and Professional Studies, Griffith University, Brisbane, Australia
e-mail: e.emerald@griffith.edu.au

L. Carpenter
Griffith University, Brisbane, QLD, Australia

© Springer Science+Business Media Singapore 2017

R. Dwyer et al. (eds.), *Narrative Research in Practice*,
DOI 10.1007/978-981-10-1579-3_2

Narrative researchers have long understood the power of a story to capture a reader's attention, link them emotionally to a topic and then use that attention and connection to communicate a theoretical or practical point. And further, the story can *itself* communicate the social/cultural/political. Autoethnography asserts that when we publically story our experiences, they transcend the private and the personal and assume political agency. It is a particular research method that connects the personal to the political, social and cultural in captivating, stirring and most importantly, insightful ways that move us to action. Autoethnography has its roots in ethnography rather than narrative studies or narrative research (see Douglas and Carless 2013, in the Handbook of Autoethnography for a history) but, as a method that is intimately concerned with 'story', we feel that autoethnography is a comfortable companion for many forms of narrative research.

In this chapter we will briefly outline some of the tenets of autoethnography: We explore how an autoethnographic writer can achieve that connection between the story and the wider cultural point that shifts a story from just interesting, to research. We also explore the extent to which we as authors can or should make the social/political/cultural points explicit for the reader, or give over our trust to the reader and their reading and let them do the work of making those connections. We will show you some examples of different approaches. We then present Lorelei's autoethnography of her 'near-miss' to elaborate and exemplify *one* way of doing autoethnography so that the methodological and theoretical ideas described in the first part of the chapter are 'demonstrated in action'.

Autoethnography has attracted the criticism of being indulgent 'navel-gazing' and we understand how this misunderstanding can arise. (And conversely, Laurel Richardson (1997) argues it can be as equally narcissistic for a researcher to spend lengthy periods of time engaged in research that attracts a small reading audience and makes negligible impact. That is, she argues that so called 'objective' research can be narcissistic.) In any personal experience that is the focus of deep inquiry, the key and central question for us is always: What are the social/cultural/political conditions that are the circumstances of this experience happening, in *this* way, at *this* time, to *this* person? This is the question that distinguishes autoethnography from autobiography (of course, autobiography is itself a worthy pursuit—one with a different purpose to autoethnography). The foundational concern in the social/cultural/political is the question that brings the *research* in to the process. In answering this question, we can gain insight into how the social world works. In short—the key to autoethnography is in its name:

auto = self;
ethno = culture;
graphy = research.

Autoethnography then is exploring the cultural/social/political through deep reflection on the personal. Deeply introspective navel-gazing can most certainly be a starting point for many autoethnographies. The pivotal next step, though, is looking out, from the personal to the cultural, gaining research insight and stimulating some form of transformative action.

Many Narrative Inquirers will be familiar with Clandinin's use of the terms field text, interim text and research texts (Clandinin and Connelly, 2000) as a way to discuss the various 'moments' of the research process. She suggests these terms as a way to step beyond the positivist flavour of the terms data and analysis. (See the introductory chapter in this volume for a further exploration of these terms and lisahunter's chapters to see them operationalized (this volume).) All social research is a Gordian knot—here we'll attempt to untangle the knot of autoethnographic research by discussing these moments.

Field Texts

In autoethnography, our own story is often our primary field text. The form it takes may be, as Barbara Tedlock says "… the orchestration of various writing strategies—personal narrative, poetic inquiry, lyric essay, ethnodrama and analysis. Such techniques may be woven together with arts-based practices, including photography, music, drawing and the construction of multimedia collages." (Tedlock 2013, p. 385).

Qualitative researchers have sometimes shied away from our own stories. Sometimes for good reason and we'll discuss what some of those reasons might be below; but sometimes too, in the belief that we cannot attain appropriate researcher 'objectivity'; that we are 'contaminants' to our own writing, to borrow Richardson's (2001) forceful language. However objectivity comes at a price. Richardson argues that the author's voice is silenced when we attempt to write within the confines of science and attempt an objective stance: "Homogenization occurs through the suppression of individual voices and the acceptance of the omniscient voice of science or scholarship or the social-script as if it were our own." (p. 35). She claims that 'objective' writing suppresses the authenticity and authority of researchers' lived experiences. As scholars in pursuit of understanding of the social world, our own place in that world and experience of that world can be one of our first objects of inquiry.

Autoethnographic writing asks a lot of the writer. Firstly, Richardson (1994) and many others implore us to 'write well'.

> For 30 years I have yawned my way through numerous supposedly exemplary qualitative studies. Countless numbers of texts I have abandoned half-read, half-scanned. I'll order a new book with great anticipation, only to find the text boring. (p. 517)

In fact, it was engaging and evocative writing that drew us both to autoethnography. We discovered Carolyn Ellis (2004); Laurel Richardson (2001, 2013); Kathleen Stewart (1996, 2007) and Ruth Behar (1993, 1996)—and in comparing notes found ourselves recommending them to each other and discovered we were both reading into the night, unwilling to put aside a book or article half read. We had each had those times when we had a passion for a topic, but had to toil over dull or turgid text. But we both found these authors captivating.

Just as in Narrative Inquiry more generally, evocative writing aims to 'show, not tell'. Readers want to *feel* the pain, the loneliness, the excitement or the joy—or at least care that you feel them. Showing and telling is the difference between 'it was hot' and 'the dust settled on my feet, the hot air drying the inside of my nose, grass crunched underfoot, I felt my lips cracking'. Julia Colyar (2013) uses Britton's (1971) framework to distinguishing the expressive, transactional and poetic functions of writing to note that autoethnography asks for all three functions together. Expressive writing, explores, reflects on ideas, "foregrounds the personal and supports the building blocks of our arguments" (Colyar 2013 p. 366). It is active, energetic and emotional writing in which authors "locate their voices and their writerly selves", and it leads to purposeful action. Transactional writing communicates particular information. It may summarise, analyse or theorize. Poetic writing inspires and demands contemplation. In Pelias' (2011) terms, poetic writing is seductive in that it draws the reader in artfully and even stealthily, leading the reader to thoughtfulness, taking us to places we might not even have wanted to go. Autoethnography brings these forms together, no easy task, as, for example, the transactional and poetic modes can easily jar if not seamlessly interwoven. A reader knows when their author has lapsed into didacticism, and will resist. Much of this, the poetics and artistry, of course, is something of a judgement call. And for many of us, it can be something of a stretch, as we have been well schooled in clinical, objective transactional writing. More than one autoethnographer has taken a creative writing class.

Autoethnography is also a means of discovery, a reflection of community and social structures, a tool of empowerment and an instrument of clarity. Autoethnographers must be willing to record the complexity and richness of their lived human experience; and not just the extraordinary—but plumb the richness of the ordinary. In Kathleen Stewart's (2007) words, "Ordinary scenes can tempt the passerby with the promise of a story let out of the bag. Matters can shimmer with undetermined potential and the weight of received meaning" (p. 23). Sometimes the most ordinary things can be what Tripp (1990) describes as the 'critical incidents' that lead us to deeper understandings of the social world. As many writers attest, writing can be a surprising process, itself a method of inquiry:

> I write because I want to find something out. I write in order to learn something that I did not know before I wrote it. I was taught, though, as perhaps you were, too, not to write until I knew what I wanted to say, until my points were organized and outlined (Richardson, 2001, p. 34).

In our own experience, some of our most successful pieces of writing were not written to an agenda, rather they were explorations. The autoethnographic vignettes published in *Vulnerability and Emotions in Research: Risks, Dilemmas, and Doubts* (emerald and Carpenter 2015a), are a case in point. These grew from our debrief discussions as we pondered our research experiences, talked about the resilience of the mothers in our study and then turned to consider our own resilience, or not, as researchers. We each wrote about the experiences and then our stories bumped up (Clandinin et al.. 2006) against each other to create an added depth of insight.

> Lorelei's's Story
> I am sitting opposite my friend and colleague elke, who
> I have researched and written with for many years now.
> Over that time we have slipped into a working relationship
> and close friendship that is uncomplicated and easy.
> Remarkable in its ease and lack of complication. We have
> finished a day of interviewing for a project on the resilience
> of women who have a child with ASD or ADHD. So
> we both should be feeling that life is good, particularly as
> we are waiting for chai tea and cake in a sidewalk café on
> a warm, sunny afternoon in a tropical, seaside town.
>
> However, there is no joy at the completion of the day nor
> a feeling of accomplishment. Instead, elke and I both sit
> in silence, feeling exhausted and emotionally bereft. … (emerald and Carpenter 2015a, p. 741)
>
> elke's story
> It starts with a slight scar on my sight. Just a little
> blurring on the right, at about the 2 o'clock spot. And I
> hope that it doesn't spread. Then a little stab in my right
> temple, my neck tenses and a knife is slipped under my
> right shoulder blade. An ache spreads gently down my
> right arm, travelling slowly, like treacle, but it is nothing
> sweet. And then a clamp tightens on my head. All the
> while a creeping sense of sickness rises; dizziness; and a
> swimming stomach. Then the lights start flashing, a jagged
> line of electricity across the top right of my vision
> and the churning, rolling sickness starts.
> All this is familiar, or close enough to familiar, for
> people who get migraines. It's a pretty standard sort of
> migraine really, and actually not that severe in the
> scheme of things… [but] I am in the middle on an interview,
> and *I* am supposed to be the in-control researcher! … (emerald and Carpenter 2015a, p. 745)

Rather than *starting out* as an investigation of vulnerability, these explorations *became* an investigation into researcher vulnerability.

Autoethnography is not for the faint-hearted. As an autoethnographer you have decisions to make about self-exposure and vulnerability. We make ourselves vulnerable on many fronts. As an autoethnographer you expose yourself to yourself—but also to the world as you transgress the anonymity of scientific research and identify your self. Autoethnographers have written about addiction, domestic violence, abortion, relationships and failure. We must place considerable trust in our readers as rejection and criticism will have an added edge: it might feel like rejection and invalidation of you and your experience rather than rejection of the work. Thankfully our forebears have paved the way for us, as articulated in Douglas & Carless' history of autoethnography (2013), and we need no longer make a case for our existence. We have excellent associations such as the International Institute of Qualitative Inquiry (IIQI), the Association for Contemporary Ethnographies Across the Disciples (CEAD), the International Association of Qualitative Research (AQR), journals such as *Qualitative Research Journal*, *Qualitative Inquiry*, and *Creative*

Approaches to Research, and conferences such as the annual International Congress of Qualitative Inquiry, the biennial CEAD Hui, and the annual AQR conference, that welcome autoethnography and engage with what it offers. The sharp rejections that Holt (2003) and Carless (Douglas and Carless 2013) experienced (and wrote about) should be in the past now—and at the least we have their example to draw on if we are unlucky enough to present our work in the 'wrong' context (see also Ellis (2009) and Ellis and Bochner (2014) on 'defensiveness).

The question of why autoethnography seems to be often situated in painful contexts is certainly one that has been raised. But if understanding the social world for the purposes of transformation is our goal as social researchers, we must admit that social change is most often in challenging contexts. So, for Marilyn Metta (2013) revealing herself and her life through poetry and drawing, portraying herself as both embodied subject and silenced object cannot have been comfortable at a personal level—and yet by doing so, she is able to powerfully talk back to disempowering constructions of herself the 'battered woman' and 'victim' and move our understandings of domestic violence. Likewise Jackie Smith (2015), in her 'Beginnings Narrative' positions herself in the midst of addiction research as a mother supporting teenage children in addiction recovery; again, a courageous move that enables a shift in understandings of addiction recovery programs. This reminds us of Ruth Behar; "...anthropology that doesn't break your heart just isn't worth doing anymore" (Behar 1996, p. 177).

So while there have been calls for research into joy and pleasure (see Pringle et al. 2015), and there is a growing body of such work, understandably, social researchers are often drawn to contexts of pain (Ellis and Bochner 2014), as these are where we perceive there is work to be done, understanding to be sought and transformation enabled.

Interim Texts

So, now you have plumbed the depths and soared the heights and have a rich and interesting story? What next? As for all research, the 'analysis' question is the pivotal one in transforming 'data' or 'evidence' into research. It is here that we fashion and craft our experience, not to fabricate it, but to hone the point for the reader. An autoethnographer may have almost any theoretical lens, which, of course is driven by the research purpose, question or puzzle. For example:

- Laurel Richardson (2013) *After a fall: A sociomedical sojourn*, does not dictate the theoretical lens, trusting the reader; elke read it as commentary on the US health care system at the time, Lorelei read it as a meditation on retirement.
- In our article about vulnerability (emerald and Carpenter 2015a) we explored our experiences through the lenses of discussions of vulnerability (Behar 1996; Bloor et al. 2010; Ellis 2009) and explored the concepts of emotions in research

including discussion of emotional labor (Hochschild 1983), emotions as data (Hubbard et al. 2001) and emotionally sensed knowledge.
- Rachael Lambin-Hunter and Kahurangi Dey (2016) explored the politics of food and motherhood in reference to their own experiences as working mothers.
- In emerald and Carpenter (2015b) we used our autoethnographies, together with stories from others, to examine the pressures on researchers of modern market-driven academia (Fitzgerald et al. 2012).

In Lorelei's text featured in this chapter, we see how the text is itself therapeutic, supporting Lorelei as she sat in real time in a Breast Screening clinic, and at the same time, it documents a significant emotional and extraordinary experience. Lorelei's experience alerts us to a human side of modern medical care, the apparently sterile uncontaminated statistical or diagnostic procedure that determines who is, and who is not, called back for second diagnostic screenings, has a very human face, and body. The personal is political.

Research Texts

When we consider research texts we are thinking about questions of *representation*—the question of *how* we present our research to our audience. Ethnographers, autoethnographers and narrative inquirers have explored the boundaries of representation; including art (Dahlsen 2016), drama (Mienczakowski 2001), dance (Barbour 2013), poetry (Williams-Witherspoon 2015) and novel (Ellis 2004; Richardson, 2013; and see the Sense Social Fictions Series http://www.springer.com/series/10493), and the standard journal article. When devising a research paper, two common forms in autoethnography, similarly to narrative inquiry, are 1) to weave commentary, analysis and discussion through the autoethnography, and 2) to alternate vignettes with discussion, commentary, analysis. For example, Melissa Carey (2016) poetically weaves the scholarly with self exploration as she explores the discovery of her Maori heritage, and healing of the cultural loss she didn't know she had. In doing this she informs us as readers both of the personal journey for her and the research in this field—all in a captivating way. This is her abstract:

> When the ancestors call for us to take action to reconnect to our cultural past, how do we respond? Ruptures of self can occur through sudden discoveries of once hidden family traumas and secrets (Sztompka 2000). Autoethnography seeks to uncloak a secret past, and amplify muted voices (Denzin et al. 2008; Ellis et al. 2011; Reed-Danahay 1997; Smith 2012). This chapter charts a transformational journey of cultural healing through a Kaupapa Māori immersion (Pihama et al. 2002; Walker et al. 2006). It traces my healing of self through a process of cultural recovery. This is my answer to the ancestors call for action. Through Kaupapa Māori I embody the knowledge of my ancestors who guide and support my transformations, awakening the sleeping Māori self and lighting the fire of knowledge.

Similarly, emerald and Ewing (2015) explore Fe's experience of life at sea as 'stories to live by' (Clandinin and Connelly 1998). They interweave narrative theory and Bourdieuian theory within elke emerald's narration of a weekend of story-telling around Fe's kitchen table and in the context of 30 years friendship often emplaced at this same kitchen table:

> Thus, just as Fe is conscious that she steps on to a boat in the midst of its story, I am conscious that I hear Fe's stories in their midst; that is, Fe's meaning making through storying these events does not begin the day I arrive nor end as I leave (Clandinin and Connelly 2000). Meanings are not fixed. Murray Orr and Olsen remind us that it is in the telling and retelling that stories take on meaning and enable growth and change (Murray Orr and Olsen 2007, p. 822–823).
>
> Fe knows this too. She is not a sociologist or ethnographer, she is a marine scientist. Fe is by training and character a 'meaning maker'—she searches for meaning and she is fearlessly self-reflective. She does not shy away from self critique. As her laughter eased over that 'blast' of a trip she says: 'well I didn't behave too well on that occasion—I am not too proud of some of my behaviours then.' More than reflective, Fe is reflexive. She actively seeks to understand and expose the filters through which she makes meaning. She engages in the reflexive practice of 'objectivation of the knowing subject' (Deer 2008, p. 201). Perhaps she embodies the 'flexible or reflexive habitus' that Adkins (2003) and Sweetman (2003) propose. (emerald and Ewing 2015, p. 176)

Carolyn Ellis (2004) and Laurel Richardson (2013) both present ethnographic novels. Carolyn Ellis' *The Ethnographic I* is an exploration of autoethnography as a method and how to teach and assess it. Laurel Richardson *After a fall: A sociomedical sojourn*, is a novel length memoir that documents her treatment and recovery after surgery. Carolyn Ellis' novel guides the reader through theoretical, methodological, pedagogical and ethical concerns. Laurel Richardson's novel is more of a 'story', but as a reader we know this is the story from the point of view of a learned and thoughtful scholar and, knowing that, we may well contemplate her world through a similar lens. As we noted above, one of us read it as commentary on the US health care system at the time, the other read it as a meditation on retirement.

A Note About Ethics

When we write about ourselves, we write about others, and sometimes we just cannot. Many a rich and juicy research text has had to be set aside as it implicates others who have not given permission. Carolyn Ellis (1998, 2009) discovered this in painful ways during her early ethnography in a remote fishing village. She wrote about the community, thinking that no one in the village would read her text. When they did, or rather, had it read to them, the consequences were painful disruptions to relationships and a deep sense of betrayal as members of the community felt her representation of them was negative. She later documented the rupture and consequences, providing a courageous object lesson to all ethnographers and autoethnographers. Conversely, sometimes we are surprised by the insouciance of those we implicate. Douglas (2009) discovered this. Having been worried that her sister would object to her representation in Douglas' writing, she discovered that her sister was unconcerned. Sometimes we forget that not everyone is as passionately interested in our research as we are! In writing about our research experiences as you saw above (emerald and Carpenter 2015a), we were concerned for the participants in the project, wondering, how will it be for them if they read how it was for us to research with them. To help us decide on whether our texts were ethical, we shared them with colleagues, tabled our concerns at research fora and shared the writing with one of the research participants, herself an academic. There is no 100 % guaranteed formula in making ethical decisions. For example, you may be faced with a choice between risking a breech in anonymity and exposing institutional racism, sexism or bullying. Ethics advisors and colleagues are a point of reference here.

There is also the wider ethical concern of the possible misreadings of your text. While we cannot always control possible readings, counter readings and misreadings of our work, and indeed we may not want to, there are times when we are concerned to mitigate possible readings. In the story we present in this chapter, Lorelei, in real time, diarizes her experience of having 'second round' tests and waiting in a Breast Screening Clinic waiting room for results. We are concerned as authors that this story might be misread as a case against breast examinations and early detection procedures, as it highlights the considerable angst of 'false positive' results. As authors then, when publishing this story, we weigh up the rupture to form that a disclaimer would cause, against the harm of possible misreadings—and choose to err on the side of extra care and attach some form of disclaimer—perhaps as a footnote, or forenote. Consider your audience too when discussing sensitive and possibly distressing topics; a 'trigger warning' may be called for. Similarly, some cultures call for a warning if your story mentions people now deceased.

Lorelei's Story

In Lorelei's autoethnography below, you will see the choices she has made in presenting her autoethnography. Interestingly, and unusually, this was written, in its raw form, *in situ*. Lorelei wrote as she sat, waiting for the results of a 'call-back' breast screening. She storied her experience, making sense of the moment, using her writing to anchor her 'self', which was under threat at that time. We see her fighting for control of herself and her situation as each of her strategies falters and her confidence is relentlessly chipped away. After the fact, Lorelei revisited the text, tightened up some prose, perhaps choosing a more evocative word here and there, and then provided her reflection. In this second wave, Lorelei moves out from her experience to consider the social, cultural and political world that surrounds her experience. You'll see how her reading of her writing led her to ponder how her experience of time and control led her to consider questions of how the practicalities of medical care provision are sometimes in uneasy relation to the health and wellbeing needs of individuals. Lorelei explores this to some degree in this text. Our main purpose in this chapter is to demonstrate how an autoethnography can provide a unique insight and entree into a topic. At a later time, we will revisit this text to explore these issues in depth to create a further research text for a nursing, healthcare or medical audience. These two texts are, together, Lorelei's autoethnography. We hand this text to you now with no further commentary, inviting you to read it against the discussion above and consider how this narrative could be integral to a narrative inquiry of medical provision, for example. And we invite you to read beyond Lorelei's story—into the social, cultural and political context.

My Story Waiting on Medical Science. Why Didn't I Support Her[1]?

The phone rings and a cheerful voice on the other end says "Good morning. Could I speak to Dr Carpenter."

"Speaking", I reply.

"Good morning, Dr Carpenter. I am calling from the breast clinic. We need to recall you for another breast examination because of your recent mammogram results."

I feel fear. I am reminded that the distance between contentment and anguish is but a hair's breadth, or in this case, a short phone call. My future could change because of that phone call. My life is on the line.

Suddenly I am swept by confidence. My breast screen recall is sure to be an example of incompetence and over diagnosis! After all, I have previous reports and films that identified some potential problems, but concluded all was clear. This time would be a repeat.

I resist all offers by friends to accompany me, after all, nothing will be found and it will be a waste of time.

I have nothing to worry about.

Am I really that confident?

What if??

Somewhere in my mind, I wonder if my bravado is denial and an attempt to calm myself.

I steadfastly refuse to think about the event during the 7 days between the phone call and the appointment.

I reflect on the stressful time *other* women could have during this waiting period:

Other women, not me.

I do denial well.

On the night before my appointment, I busily arm myself for the defence of my body. I equip myself for battle.

[1]This story acknowledges and respects the research around breast examinations and the early detection of cancer. It acknowledges the positive contribution that breast screening can have on early detection of breast cancer. This article does not take an anti-mammogram stance. Rather it is simply an authentic expression of the writer's feelings and thoughts about a social experience that invites the reader to engage both affectively and cognitively. The author is subjectively involved both as participant and observer. The author makes no claim other than writing to comment on her personal, lived experience of a culture.

I am 30 min early for my appointment. I have been warned that the whole procedure could take up to 4 h. I hate being early for appointments. I am the traveller who prefers to walk on to the plane or train as it is about to leave. I do not like to sit in waiting rooms as it is a waste of precious time.

Time, time, do I have time to waste?

I sit in my car and realize I am nervous.

How can I be nervous with so much proof that all is well?

I walk into the breast clinic 15 min early. The reception area contains two men who I realize have come along to support their partners through this recall process. But there is little chance for anyone to provide support. A very cheerful receptionist ushers me quickly to a door that proclaims "Next room for females only." I qualify to be admitted to this exclusionary zone.

I wonder what the men must be feeling/thinking as their partners engage in secret women's business.

I enter a room where I had been some weeks ago when I began the initial process of a breast screen. At that time the process from entry to exit took less than 15 min. I was elated that the process was so rapid; uneasy that only two x-rays had been taken, and sceptical about the accuracy of the screening process.

Now I am back. I am alert and my senses are sharpened. I am ready to do battle with the enemy that wants to take over my body.

I am immediately overwhelmed by the sight of nine women sitting in a drab waiting room—a holding pen of identical shapeless white gowns. My mind flashes to the anonymity of people herded into the holocaust gas chambers; chosen to be there for the defining attribute of race; markers of ability, age, occupation, wealth becoming inconsequential. Similarly there is no space for difference here. We are reduced to a monotone sameness—mammogram recall—and a monotonous waiting.

We are united in this room by one question: 'Do I have breast cancer?'

There, I said it.

Cancer

Medical science has robbed us all of our distinctiveness. We have lost our individuality to a medical procedure. I feel my confidence shaking.

I am given two cards to read that explain what will happen today. Another shot across my bow of confidence. There is the possibility of a fine needle aspiration.

No! I have difficulties even looking at images of needles. Nobody will be putting a needle into my breast!

The ground beneath me shifts again, it's less secure.

We all read the same lifeless dog-eared laminated cards that describe the procedures we may endure today. Is this meant to educate the consumer? I am unprepared for these procedures.

I don't want to be here.

Is this the first step into the unknown for me? My future depends on what could happen today. It is a future that I must face alone despite being in a group of similar women. No sisterhood here. We are all alone. Shut off from the outside world by a sign on the other side of the entrance door excluding any type of support from family or friends.

Each of us here contributes to the statistic of the 10 % of women who are recalled for further investigation after their initial mammogram. Which of us in the group today will tick the more fateful exclusive statistical box of being the one in ten identified with breast cancer?

I was the tenth to arrive!!!!

I join the white clad group and barely have time to open my iPad, my sole support to help me wile away the time, when I am summoned into a room.

Good, things are moving. This isn't too bad.

The room is labelled 'Counsellor'. Megan the counsellor greets me and immediately inquires if I understand what will happen today.

Of course I do. I can read.

"Good now you need to sign a consent form to agree to all these procedures".

Another blow.

"Why do I have to agree to fine needle aspiration? I am unsure about that".

"Don't worry" she says "we can discuss that later if it needs to occur."

No it will not occur.

Things are moving too fast.

I am a researcher. I need to understand procedures and what they entail. I need to ensure I am with professionals who are the best in their field. What qualifications do these people have apart from the assumption that this service is staffed by practitioners who excel in their work?

Nobody is providing me with the type of information that would set my mind at ease. My confidence is further diminished as I lose more control of what is happening to me.

I leave Megan. I hope that my short time with her doesn't constitute counselling. My background is in counselling. I am sceptical that she engaged in a counselling relationship with me. Little can be done in a 5 min interview.

Back in the white clad pen I barely have time to settle in my seat when I am called into another room by a radiographer. At last I can defend myself. I have come prepared.

"Here are my reports from previous mammograms. See, they detected lumps that were benign."

"Yes but we have detected another small spot that concerns us."

Confidence disintegrates further. My defence is brushed away in a few seconds, making me vulnerable and weakened.

More x-rays are taken.

Back into the pen.

A few minutes later Doctor Kate ushers me into another room. She explains a breast examination is required because a small lump has been detected. I am up against a wall. I have to fight for my life. My defence comes out again. "Here are the results from my last scan", I say as I push my last bargaining chip towards her. She looks at the report and copies it and the x-rays.

"I'll need to show these to the other doctors and they can decide whether any further screening is required", she says.

Who are these faceless doctors who hold my future in their hands? Where are they? What else do I need to do?

My confidence wavers further.

Will my evidence be enough to convince these anonymous people that no further investigation is required?

This is fighting a battle in the dark against unknown opponents.

Back out in the holding pen I wait—I sit—I wait—I read.

What do I read? I don't know

I wait—I don't want to think—I wait.

As I wait, the place begins to empty. Relieved women are given the news that their results are clear. They escape. Quite soon there are only two of us left. We are two left of ten.

The tired, dusty dried flower arrangement hovering in the corner is the lifelessness of this room. It's a failed attempt to hide the ugliness of a reality I am unwilling to accept. The washed out purple of the chairs attempts to soften the blow of a verdict that could suddenly negate what their original colour intended to convey—sensitivity, compassion, support. Nothing in this room soothes my spirit or nurtures and comforts me.

Waiting—waiting—waiting—not knowing.

The purple chairs get harder and less accommodating—the dried flower arrangement becomes uglier and more lifeless—the room becomes even less comforting.

I am stifled.

Where is self-assured, self-directed Lorelei —where is she when I need her? Did I leave her behind when I walked into this room?

Did this room begin its life as a welcoming and soothing place, becoming more depressed and forlorn with each adverse verdict handed out to the white clad inmates?

Now I'm angry. I hate purple! Who decorated this room? It is ugly! I hate it! I want to leave. I feel imprisoned. I am unable to escape. There are no windows. My back hurts. I have been sitting too long. I have been here for over 3 h.

Purple has many meanings—feminism, power, respect, energy. Or richness, respect, luxury and wealth. None of those qualities are here: what is the colour of loss, suffering, aloneness, mortality?

My companion and I have silently shared this space for the last hour. Two left out of ten. Now she is back talking with counsellor Megan. The words, "We will need to do a needle biopsy" slither along the lifeless silence of the corridor. No privacy here; bad news is received in isolation, yet shared; overpowering silence in this underwhelming environment. Then, muffled laughter.

What could there possibly be to laugh about?

How is she feeling? What is she thinking? What would I do if I heard those words? Will I hear those words?

She returns composed, unconcerned. Or is she just too numb to register any emotion? She is alone; nobody to talk to or sit with her and murmur words of reassurance and comfort.

Ten women, one diagnosis. Or will it be two. Will I be the outlier?

Waiting—time is shuffling by. Yesterday in my free world, the hours briskly slipped by, smoothly, painlessly. Today time has warped further with the liberation of each absolved woman.

My bonhomie is waning.

I feel like it disappeared some time ago.

My bargaining power is diminishing with the waiting. My traits of friendliness, warmth, conviviality, guile and insight, which have served me well in the past, have little currency in this environment.

I feel an overwhelming tiredness. I want to sleep. I want to escape. I want to burst out to the sunshine and fresh air. Life is at a standstill.

I wait.

Time can ease us into our environment as we gradually become familiar with our new surroundings and begin to accept change. Yet I am becoming more uncomfortable and anxious. Time is not easing me in. Time is pressing down on me.

Suddenly there is a change in the room. A new receptionist arrives. As she walks in she brings a whiff of the freedom and lightness of the outside world. My silent companion and I look towards the door, straining for a glimpse beyond.

We wait.

In silence.

There is not much to talk about anyway. We are both weighed down by the unspoken possibility of being handed a life sentence today. What can we talk about? It seems absurd to discuss the trivialities of the outside world. The television that has relentlessly presented the beaming arctic-white toothed presenters of the "women's shows" since I arrived do little else except sharply juxtapose the oddness of this surreal environment with the outside world.

The outside world seems improbable compared to the private battle ground that each one of us has been thrown into today. Both of us are hanging on to hope. Swapping recipes and commenting on TV shows would be inane.

But, we both maintain a stoic façade. All that is left is our dignity.

Tears begin to well up and my feelings threaten to overwhelm me.

I must work hard to hang on to hope.

But the waiting chips away relentlessly at my façade and weakens any tenuous threads of hope that may be left.

Women don't do well at comforting each other.

We should be united.

Perhaps our solitariness is our strength.

What happens if I am the last one?

The doctor appears and calls my name. A rather bizarre thing to do when there are only two of us left. She smiles at me and instantly erases the agony of the day, "Your results are clear. You can go now." —all this in the presence of the woman awaiting the needle biopsy.

I can't move fast enough, I strip off my prison garb, throw it down and pull on my comforting real world clothes. I rush out the door. As I hurry through the waiting room my eyes meet those of the sole remaining inmate.

The one left of ten.

In that half second I try to convey to her my unspoken message of compassion and concern.

In the outer reception area a solitary male faithfully keeps vigil for his partner on the other side of the door: both separated and isolated by a door with a sign.

The sun and fresh air greet me, warm and comforting. As I drive home, my jubilant liberation is suddenly floored:

What happened to the woman who remained?
Why didn't I sit with her and offer her my support?

*****

Lorelei's Reflection

The craft of writing autoethnography is difficult and risky because it gives the reader permission to trespass upon the writer's life. While the autoethnographer voluntarily exposes themselves to the reader, their story risks being dismissed as an exercise in self-indulgence or one that reveals the writer's defective and flawed character. This is the challenge understood and acknowledged by autoethnographers including Richardson, Ellis, Behar and Stewart, and it is a challenge the autoethnographer must be prepared to face. Yet, responding to and writing ourselves into the middle of real life conflicts of everyday life allows the researcher an insider's view of the warp and weft of ordinary life. It is the insider's view that empowers the autoethnographer to expose the social/cultural/political in ordinary experiences.

According to Ellis et al. (2011), autoethnography is usually written retrospectively as a way of reflecting on a moment of significance. This autoethnography, in the main, written in real time, was of an experience that profoundly shattered my taken for granted existence: the controlled life of a white, well-educated woman. An experience that I was unprepared for. Because it occurred to me for the first time as I wrote, I knew I was looking through innocent eyes: but eyes that were alert enough to expose and reveal the hidden texts of a situation. In her writing about writing, Laurel Richardson (2001) makes the point that writing-stories (stories about our writing) are both personal and political; "Writing is always done in specific, local and historical contexts" (p. 35).

My physical context was apparent:

I am immediately overwhelmed by the sight of nine women sitting in a drab waiting room—a holding pen, made more overwhelming and intimidating by the identical shapeless white gowns that each woman wears.

I first became alerted to the political and gendered context upon entering the clinic.

I walk into the breast clinic 15 minutes early. The reception area contains two men who I realize have come along to support their partners through this recall process. But there is little chance for anyone to provide support. A very cheerful receptionist ushers me quickly to a door that proclaims "Next room for females only." I qualify to be admitted to this exclusionary zone. I wonder what the men must be feeling/thinking as their partners engage in secret women's business.

As time progressed I became further aware of the political nature of the process we were involved in: both patients and family.

We are all alone. Shut off from the outside world by a sign on the other side of the entrance door excluding any type of support from family or friends...

In the outer reception area a solitary male faithfully keeps vigil for his partner on the other side of the door: both separated and isolated by a door with a sign.

It is the isolation of the woman and the exclusion of the partner that is political. Both are rendered powerless and made vulnerable by an administrative process. The woman is robbed of her identity by being required to wear a shapeless gown that emphasizes anonymity and vulnerability. She is denied access to social support. The partner, who is excluded, is denied the opportunity to discuss the procedure or participate in any decision making and is made powerless. These processes separate and isolate. They are not democratic, they are not built around the wellbeing of the patient, but rather around administrative efficiencies.

Time acted as an impetus for me to continue writing as I sat in the waiting room; the absence of action and surplus of time that provided an opportunity for me to reflect on what was occurring.

More waiting—time is shuffling by. Yesterday in my free world the hours briskly slipped by smoothly and painlessly. Today time warps further with the liberation of each absolved woman.

When I reread my story I am struck by the repetition of the theme of time. This led me to an investigation of time and a study of people living with cancer by Mulcahy, Parry and Glover (2010). They used a Foucauldian understanding of power/knowledge to argue that some medical professionals expect their patients to be passive, while discounting the fact that patients who have extended times of waiting for knowledge or treatment can experience feelings of powerlessness, anxiety and depression. They concluded that the good patient was a "patient patient" (p. 1062). However, Mulcahy et al suggest that patients who are more involved in their treatment and decision making have a more positive experience of coping with illness. Hence, ironically, the patient, passive patient is at a health care disadvantage. I am neither patient nor passive by nature, my only resistance was to write as I sat. Partners are also disadvantaged. Like fathers in the twentieth century who were excluded from participating in childbirth their role is one of a helpless and powerless bystander who feels more worry and concern as time passes.

More specifically, the concerns related to women's emotional reactions to breast screening have been widely researched. Yasunaga et al. (2007) found that women who have false positive mammograms can experience anxiety. Blow et al. (2011) point out that many women find that they lose control of their lives and health care when they encounter the medical system and they concluded that all women who confront a cancer scare endure some degree of "existential, physical and emotional distress" (p. 1332). They recommend that women be allowed to discuss and reflect on their experience to improve their lives.

I could sense both my rapidly diminishing control as well as my struggle to maintain some sense of influence over what was happening to me. My existential, physical and emotional distress can be clearly heard in my words:

> Waiting—waiting—waiting—not knowing.
> The purple chairs get harder and less accommodating—the dried flower arrangement becomes uglier and more lifeless—the room becomes even less comforting.
> I am stifled.
> *Where is self-assured, self-directed Lorelei —where is she when I need her? Did I leave her behind when I walked into this room?*

Writing my story in real time was my attempt take back control and alleviate my increasing distress.

Did writing in real time make my story more emotional and reactive to the particular situation? I would argue "No". I recognized that the 'doing' of writing was my way to hold back from the seduction of emotionality. Writing in real time was my anchor in rationality. I could rationally plot my emotional distress. I wrote *my* story as researcher and a woman afraid of illness.

> *I am full of confidence…*
> *Nothing in this room soothes my spirit or nurtures and comforts me…*
> *I feel an overwhelming tiredness…*
> *We both hang on to a stoic façade…*
> *Tears begin to well up and my feelings threaten to overwhelm me.*

Woman and researcher: the two parts are intertwined, they are part of my complex self and will always influence the way I construct my world. To attempt to separate one part from the other in how I view the world would render me a dupe. To claim that my subjectivity as a woman afraid of illness contaminated my story, risks ignoring my skills as a researcher, able to recognise the cultural/social/political issues of the moments of my experience and speak for the unprotected. It would be a lie to write of this experience without acknowledging my presence.

In my case, I used writing in an attempt to reconnect with the familiar in an unfamiliar context: to engage in a familiar physical and cognitive activity that spoke against the passive and emotionally charged context that confronted me. I acknowledge the storying work that I engaged in gave me an anchor that allowed me to avoid losing myself in the emotional aspect of my situation. The independent, objective researcher that is so much a part of me, stepped in to support me in the emotional and subjective situation that was threatening me. For me, this is the interconnectedness of writing which Richardson (2001) refers to when she claims that "writing about your life in life stories can be a sacrament" (p. 36).

Now I am alert and my senses are sharpened as if I am ready to do battle with the enemy that wants to take over my body.

……My mind flashes to the anonymity of people herded into the holocaust gas chambers

…… As I hurry through the waiting room my eyes meet those of the sole remaining inmate.

There is a lot yet for me to explore in this autoethnography: the spectre of the questions that remain unspoken. Questions that are laden with social/political/cultural implications and which have the power to frame and construct my life—if I pursue them further.

Why didn't I support the sole woman left waiting at the clinic?

Why did I leave her there?

The one in ten.

Why did I breeze past and leave her partner sitting outside without communicating with him?

I fled to safety

I left them there.

Each alone.

Regardless of my writing and reflection, I continue to grieve.

Once again I reflect "What you write and how you write it shapes your life" (Richardson 2001, p.30).

Discussion Questions

1. We often enter a research topic because of something in our own experience – what is your story? How might your story of your interest contribute to your research?
2. What are the ethical concerns in your project for either including your autoethnography or asking your participants to produce autoethnographies as field or research texts.

References

Adkins, L. (2003). Reflexivity: Freedom or habit of gender? Theory. *Culture & Society, 20*(6), 21–42.

Barbour, K. N. (2013). Acts of representation: A labour of love. In R. Rinehart, K. N. Barbour, & C. Pope (Eds.), *Ethnographic worldviews: Transformations and social justice* (pp. 173–185). London: Springer.

Behar, R. (1993). *Translated woman: Crossing the border with Esperanza's story*. Boston: Beacon Press.

Behar, R. (1996). *The vulnerable observer: Anthropology that breaks your heart*. Boston: Beacon Press.

Bloor, M., Fincham, B., & Sampson, H. (2010). Unprepared for the worst: Risks of harm for qualitative researchers. *Methodological Innovations Online, 5*(1), 45–55.

Blow, A. J., Swiecicki, P., Haan, P., Osuch, J. R., Symonds, L. L., Smith, S. S., & Boivin, M. J. (2011). The emotional journey of women experiencing a breast abnormality. *Qualitative Health Research, 21*(10), 1316–1334.

Britton, J. (1971). What's the use: A schematic account of language functions. *Educational Review, 23*, 205–219.
Carey, M. (2016). The transformative experiences of cultural healing: An autoethnography of Kaupapa Māori. In R. Rinehart & e. emerald (Eds.), *Global South ethnographies: Minding the senses* (pp. 209–220). Amsterdam: Sense.
Clandinin, J., & Connelly, M. (1998). Stories to live by: Narrative understandings of school reform. *Curriculum Inquiry, 28*(2), 149–164.
Clandinin, D. J., & Connelly, M. (2000). *Narrative inquiry: Experience and story in qualitative research*. San Francisco: Jossey-Bass Publishers.
Clandinin, D. J., Huber, J., Huber, M., Murphy, M. S., Orr, A. M., Pearce, M., & Steeves, P. (2006). *Composing diverse identities: Narrative inquiries into the interwoven lives of children and teachers*. New York: Routledge.
Colyar, J. (2013). Reflections on writing. In S. Holman Jones, T. E. Adams, & C. Ellis (Eds.), *The handbook of autoethnography* (pp. 363–383). Walnut Creek: Left Coast Press Inc.
Dahlsen, J. (2016). Environmental art: A creative response to economic catastrophe. In R. Rinehart & e. emerald (Eds.), *Global South ethnographies: Minding the senses* (pp. 71–85). Amsterdam: Sense.
Deer, C. (2008). Reflexivity. In M. Grenfell (Ed.), *Pierre Bourdieu: Key concepts* (pp. 199–212). Stocksfield: Acumen Publishing.
Denzin, N. K., Lincoln, Y. S., & Tuhiwai Smith, L. (2008). *Handbook of critical and indigenous methodologies*. Thousand Oaks: Sage.
Douglas, K. (2009). Storying myself: Negotiating a relational identity in professional sport. *Qualitative Research in Sport and Exercise, 1*(2), 176–190.
Douglas, K., & Carless, D. (2013). A history of autoethographic inquiry. In S. Holman Jones, T. E. Adams, & C. Ellis (Eds.), *The handbook of autoethnography* (pp. 84–106). Walnut Creek: Left Coast Press Inc.
Ellis, C. (1998). Exploring loss through autoethnographic inquiry: Autoethnographic stories, co-constructed narratives, and interactive interviews. In J. Harvey (Ed.), *Perspectives on loss: A sourcebook* (pp. 49–61). Philadelphia: Taylor & Francis.
Ellis, C. (2004). *The ethnographic I: A methodological novel about autoethnography*. Walnut Creek: Alta Mira Press.
Ellis, C. (2009). Fighting back or moving on: An autoethnographic response to critics. *International Review of Qualitative Research, 2*(3), 371–378.
Ellis, C. & Bochner, A. (2014). *Auto ethnography in qualitative inquiry*. Retrieved from https://youtu.be/FKZ-wuJ_vnQ
Ellis, C., Adams, T. E., & Bochner, A. P. (2011). Autoethnography: An overview. *Forum: Qualitative Social Research, 12*(1). http://search.proquest.com/docview/870465772?accountid=13380
emerald, e., & Carpenter, L. (2015a, October). Vulnerability and emotions in research: Risks, dilemmas and doubts. *Qualitative Inquiry*, 21(8), 741–750.
emerald, e., & Carpenter, L (2015b). Researching the researcher: The heart and mind in sub-prime times. *Qualitative Research Journal*, 15(2):178–188.
emerald, e., & Ewing, F. (2015). "Shall we keel haul the little %$#@, or chuck him in the Chain locker?": How life at sea becomes 'stories to live by' for a woman on a fishing vessel. In M. Brown & B. Humberstone (Eds.), Seascapes: Shaped by the sea (pp. 173–186). Farham: AshGate Press.
Farham Surrey: AshGate Press Fitzgerald, T., White, J., & Gunter, H. (2012). *Hard Labour? Academic work and the changing landscape of higher education*. Bingly: Author.
Hochschild, A. (1983). *The managed heart: Commercialization of human feeling*. Berkeley: University of California Press.
Holt, N. L. (2003). Representation, legitimation, and autoethnography: An autoethnographic writing story. *International Journal of Qualitative Methods, 2*(1), 1–22.

Hubbard, G., Backett-Milburn, K., & Kemmer, D. (2001). Working with emotion: Issues for the researcher in fieldwork and teamwork. *International Journal of Social Research Methodology, 4*, 119–137. doi:10.1080/13645570116992.

Lamdin-Hunter, R., & Dey, K. (2016). Mothers and food: Performing the family mealtime. In R. Rinehart & e. emerald (Eds.), *Global South ethnographies: Minding the senses* (pp. 103–112). Amsterdam: Sense Publishers.

Metta, M. (2013). Putting the body on the line: Embodied recovery through domestic Violence. In S. Holman Jones, T. E. Adams, & C. Ellis (Eds.), *The handbook of autoethnography* (pp. 84–106). Walnut Creek: Left Coast Press Inc.

Mienczakowsk, J. (2001). Ethnodrama: Performed research—limitations and potential. In P. Atkinson, A. Coffey, S. Delamont, J. Lofland, & L. Lofland (Eds.), *Handbook of ethnography* (pp. 468–476). London: Sage.

Mulcahy, C. M., Parry, D. C., & Glover, T. D. (2010). The "patient patient": The trauma of waiting and the power of resistance for people living with cancer. *Qualitative Health Research, 20*(8), 1062–1075.

Murray Orr, A., & Olsen, M. (2007). Transforming narrative encounters. *Canadian Journal of Education, 30*(3), 819–838.

Pelias, R. J. (2011). *Leaning: A poetics of personal relations*. Walnut Creek: Left Coast Press.

Pihama, L., Cram, F., & Walker, S. (2002). Creating methodological space: A literature review of Kaupapa Maori research. *Canadian Journal of Native Education, 26*(1), 30. http://search.proquest.com.ezp01.library.qut.edu.au/docview/230302719?pq-origsite=summon

Pringle, R., Rinehart, R., & Caudwell, J. (Eds.). (2015). *Sport and the social significance of pleasure*. London: Routledge.

Reed-Danahay, D. (1997). *Auto/ethnography: Rewriting the self and the social*. Oxford: Berg.

Richardson, L. (1994). Writing: A method of inquiry. In N. K. Denzin & Y. S. Lincoln (Eds.), *Handbook of qualitative research* (pp. 516–529). Thousand Oaks: Sage.

Richardson, L. (1997). *Fields of play: Constructing an academic life*. New Brunswick: Rutgers University Press.

Richardson, L. (2001). Getting personal: Writing stories. *International Journal of Qualitative Studies in Education, 14*, 33–38. doi:10.1080/09518390010007647.

Richardson, L. (2013). *After a fall: A sociomedical sojourn*. Walnut Creek: Left Coast Press.

Smith, L. T. (2012). *Decolonizing methodologies: Research and indigenous peoples*. New York/London: Zed Books.

Smith, J. M. (2015). Recovering from silence. Composing self in time, spaces, and friendships: A narrative inquiry with four mothers supporting adolescent children through long-term addictions treatment. Unpublished doctoral thesis, University of Calgary: Canada.

Stewart, K. (1996). *A space on the side of the road: Cultural poetics in an "other" America*. Princeton: Princeton University Press.

Stewart, K. (2007). *Ordinary affects*. Durham: Duke University Press.

Sweetman, P. (2003). Twenty-first century dis-ease? Habitual reflexivity or the reflexive habitus. *The Sociological Review, 51*(4), 528–548.

Sztompka, P. (2000). Cultural trauma: The other face of social change. *European Journal of Social Theory, 3*(4), 449–466. doi:10.1177/136843100003004004.

Tedlock, B. (2013). Braiding evocative with analytic autoethnography. In S. Holman Jones, T. E. Adams, & C. Ellis (Eds.), *The handbook of autoethnography* (pp. 358–362). Walnut Creek: Left Coast Press Inc.

Tripp, D. (1990). Socially critical action research. *Theory Into Practice, 29*(3), 158–166.

Walker, S., Gibbs, A., & Eketone, A. (2006). An exploration of Kaupapa Maori research, its principles, processes and applications. *International Journal of Social Research Methodology, 9*(4), 331–344. doi:10.1080/13645570600916049.

Williams-Witherspoon, K. L. H. (2015). Performing 'SHOT': Personalizing North Philly, poverty and performance poetry. In R. Rinehart, e. emerald, & R. Matamua (Eds.), *Ethnographies in Pan Pacific research: Tensions and positionings* (pp. 36–55). New York: Taylor and Francis.

Yasunaga, H., Ide, H., Imamura, T., & Ohe, K. (2007). Women's anxieties caused by false positives in mammography screening: A contingent valuation survey. *Breast Cancer Research and Treatment, 101*(1), 59–64.

Chapter 3
Saying Goodbye to Mr Chips: Masculinity, Narrative and Identity Construction

Ian Davis and Greer Johnson

Abstract This paper provides a methodological demonstration, using a Ricoeurian analytic framework, to assess the impact of well-known fictional narratives on male teachers' *construction* of masculinities within educational settings. The analysis identifies a salient teacher type, *The Static Vocational*, as a durable professional identity in education. The alignment of key themes found in the teachers' survey data and interviews with those revealed in the novel *Goodbye Mr. Chips* demonstrates how literary tropes inform the enactment of social tropes in an educational setting. The findings have implications for new methods of reflective practice seeking deeper insights into *becoming* an education professional.

Keywords Masculinity • Ricoeur • Narrative • Teachers • Education

Introduction

In this chapter we explore the influence of fictional narratives on the construction and performance of masculinities within educational environments. We consider how fictional plotlines, characters and events impact notions of, in this case, masculine subjectivity and identity. To enable this we investigate how stories, narratives and literary tropes have become integrated into concepts of who we are, how we are and what we might *become*. The central question posed by the chapter is: Within educational environments are male teachers influenced by fictional narratives in the construction of masculinities; and how does this occur?

Using a Ricoeurian analytic framework the following chapter explores the way in which iconic literary tropes influence how professional identities are imagined and enacted. Firstly, we consider an innovative methodology based on a Ricoeurian narrative analysis, which explores the inter-relationship between the fictional teacher text and data gathered from a group of male teachers. This methodology

I. Davis (✉) • G. Johnson
Griffith Institute for Educational Research, Griffith University, Brisbane, Australia
e-mail: i.davis@griffith.edu.au

© Springer Science+Business Media Singapore 2017

R. Dwyer et al. (eds.), *Narrative Research in Practice*,
DOI 10.1007/978-981-10-1579-3_3

aims to identify specific characteristics attributed to teacher identity construction that align with consistent tropes found in fictional teacher narratives. Secondly, using data drawn from interviews with male teachers, we consider how specific expressions of *desire* influence male teachers in how they construct their own professional identities. We discover that the desire for *legacy*, *belonging* and *longevity*, which appear as key tropes in the fictional texts are still dominant in how male teachers describe themselves within an educational setting today. In identifying connections between research data and fictional texts we can explore the place of fictional tropes in strategic gender identity construction within education, mapping how the stories and tropes surrounding male teachers influence the choices they make in the enactment of their professional identities.

Situating Narrative, Masculinities & Education

This chapter considers what we believe to be a previously unexplored intersection found between the literature attached to *narrative studies* and *gender studies* and *education*. The following provides a brief critique of the salient debates inherent in the three bodies of literature. The aim is to highlight and discuss key gaps in the literature pertinent to our central question.

Narrative studies is a varied area of enquiry which encompasses many sociological and historical perspectives, some of which aim to further understand issues relating to identity and subjectivity. As previous chapters in this book have identified, these perspectives range from the literary, philosophical, to the ethnographic and anthropological. For example, a literary narrative focus is demonstrated in the work of Propp (1968) and more recently Bal (2006), an anthropological or cultural studies narrative focus is explicated in the work of Plummer (2001) and an educational narrative inquiry focus has been developed through the ongoing work of Connelly and Clandinin (1990, 2007). Each of these perspectives on the study of narrative methods offers a range of research techniques used to generate, assess and analyse different types of data. However, a common analytical approach across the disciplines focuses on structural elements within narratives, exploring how stories are told and how time and space are designed within a storied environment. To focus on the philosophical concept of narrative, time and identity we will be considering the ideas developed by Paul Ricoeur in his three-volume work *Time and Narrative* (1984, 1988, 1990).

The conceptualisation of *Masculinities* used within this study is derived from an historical and sociological form of analysis drawn from Connell's (1995, 2000) concept of hegemonic masculinities. Connell employed the concept of hegemony, as described by Gramsci, to explore "how particular groups of men inhabit positions of power and wealth … reproduc[ing] the social relationships that generate their dominance" (Carrigan et al. 1985, p. 599). Conceptualising masculinities as constructs that are socially and historically produced assists the focus of this study and our consideration of the professional and social performance of male teachers within the teaching profession. As the model of *hegemonic masculinity* dictates, that masculine ideal is experienced only by very few since "[t]here is a distance and a tension between the collective ideal and actual lives" (Carrigan et al. 1985, p. 601), meaning that most men fail to achieve the hegemonic ideal. If this is the case why does hegemony succeed as strategy that supports masculine constructions? As Carrigan et al. (1985) assert it is because male hegemony perpetuates the subordination of women and operates through persuasive techniques to demonstrate the strategic division of labour that becomes normalised between men and women. Therefore although hegemonic masculinity is achieved only by the few, its male beneficiaries are many.

Although the concept of hegemonic masculinities has been regularly contested (Connell and Messerschmidt 2005) the practical influence of the theory has persisted. Connell's early work on masculinity "offers a systematic account of gender … as a social practice" (Petersen 1998, p. 116), rather than as fixed entity. However, one of the more persuasive critiques of hegemonic masculinity points to an over reliance on a socially focused hegemonic system that excludes the site of the body and of critical psychology as elements in male sex difference. Hegemonic systems refer solely to cultural and social systems of analysis, excluding an analysis of how the "materialisation of men's bodies as biologically sexed bodies is effected through historically and socially specific discourses …" (Petersen 1998, p. 117). Despite the limitations of a hegemonic system, the promotion of an idealistic masculine type provides a starting point from which we can explore how tropes and representations of masculine identities can be valorised strategically by individuals and institutions.

There is a body of literature that explores the relationship between teaching, masculinity and popular narratives; though none sustain an analysis of all three subject areas simultaneously. Studies such as *The Hollywood Curriculum: Teaching and Teachers in the Movies* (Dalton 1999), *Carry On Teachers* (Ellsmore 2005), *Education on Popular Culture* (Fisher et al. 2008) and, more recently, *The Celluloid Teacher* (Breault 2009) present detailed examinations of how teaching has been portrayed within popular culture. In her study of how teaching is depicted by Hollywood cinema, Dalton makes the claim that "We borrow from the stories of films we see to help us create ourselves as characters and organize the plotlines of our lives" (1999, p. 3).

Other studies with a gender focus such as: *Big Bad Wolves: Masculinity in American Film* (Mellen 1977) *Teaching Men and Film* (Hall 2005) and *Cinematic Symptoms of Masculinity in Transition* (Bainbridge and Yates 2005) opened up a discussion of how men and masculinity are depicted within popular culture, primarily cinema. Although the respective works of Mellen and Bainbridge and Yates discuss how filmic representation impacts hegemonic ideas, neither of these otherwise detailed studies address these issues within educational settings. Hall has produced an important study that discusses how to use film within a classroom environment to discuss issues that surround gender and masculinity, but does not address how this might influence the teacher as a professional. Some relatively recent research (Mottart 2009) has used fictional narratives, namely Frank McCourt's

Teacher Man (2005), within teacher education to exemplify teaching practices around classroom management, giving pre-service teachers "opportunit[ies] to link this (fictional) narrative with personal narratives" (Mottart 2009, p. 500). However this study does not specifically focus on gender as a potential point of reflection on becoming a professional.

Finally, Raewyn Connell suggests that considering how masculinities have been considered within education is an almost silent pursuit where, "We don't seem to hear much small-arms fire or smell much grease paint here … we [are] making a morning coffee call on the man without qualities, the organizational man …" (Connell 2008, p. 237). A majority of the literature in this area springs from the *feminization of education* argument and is dealt with in two ways: firstly by considering the moral panic around boys' education, and secondly from the perspective of the teacher and the institution.

Focusing on teachers and masculinities, Martino and Meyenn (2002) argue it is often the teacher's 'normalizing assumptions about boys that drive the pedagogy' (2002, p. 264). Martino and Meyenn suggest that a teacher's own models of practicing masculinities are largely based on an anxiety as to how their own gender performance will be read and responded to within the institution. Male teachers "attempt[ed] to distance themselves from any association with the feminine in terms of their own embodied social practices of masculinity" (2002, p. 319). As well as a male teacher's anxiety as to how their gender performance might be read, the researchers also highlighted an anxiety, expressed by teachers, as to how their sexual identities might be interpreted if "male teachers start to encourage boys to interrogate hegemonic heterosexual masculinity their own sexuality may be brought into question" (2002, p. 319). It is of little surprise therefore that considering the fear and threat that can be generated by even suggesting multiple masculinities may exist within the classroom, or indeed the staff room, male teachers understandably resort to, as one teacher in their study put it, trying to be 'just one of the boys' (2002, p. 311).

In summary, this chapter focuses on the inter-relationship of the three fields of research explored above, namely: *narrative studies*, *gender studies* and *education studies*. We develop a methodology to consider how fictional representations of male teachers impact on the construction of professional identities within an educational setting.

Developing a Methodology

This analysis aims to reveal the major fictional tropes described within the narrative structure and language of a well-known fictional text, in this case the novel *Goodbye Mr Chips* (Hilton 1939), alongside descriptions from biographical interviews of male teachers. The textual analysis and resulting taxonomy provides a theoretical framework from which to compare and contrast the results of a literary analysis, alongside a consideration of research interviews with male teachers. The aim is to demonstrate how fictional tropes and themes become entangled and embodied in the biographical narratives of male teachers and in the construction of male teachers' professional identities.

The biographical interview data used here was collected as part of the *Teaching Men* project. The focus of this project were male teachers in Australia working in Technical and Further Education (TAFE) organizations, and their counterparts in Further Education (FE) in the United Kingdom. The research was conducted within TAFE and FE environments where the subjects taught were considered traditionally *masculine* such as gas fitting, carpentry, electronics. The student population and the teaching staff, within in these specific TAFE/FE environments were, with very few exceptions, entirely male. The *Teaching Men* project was carried out at a site of *situated intensity* in terms of maleness and masculinity. Ethical permission having been given and institutional partnerships forged, the interviews took place between the winter of 2010 and the summer of 2011.

As referred to earlier, our working approach to the analysis of fictional text employs a philosophical and literary process drawn from Paul Ricoeur's notion of storied temporality, as outlined in his three-volume work *Time and Narrative* (1984, 1988, 1990). Ricoeur uses a hermeneutic approach to explain how we use narrative to make sense of our experience of time and the resulting *narrated identity*. This article describes the application of Ricoeur's concept of *three-fold mimesis* in the analysis of fictional text. The purpose of this form of literary analysis is to identify what Riessman (2008), after Bakhtin, calls the "hidden internal politics, historical discourses and ambiguities beyond the author's voice" (p. 46).

The three-stage process of textual analysis used here begins with an initial thematic analysis, which informs the development of a working taxonomy, and finally the consideration of the text using a Ricoeurian system. The analysis therefore begins with an investigation of four thematic factors. Firstly, what was the original form of the text, for example, a novel, play, film; secondly, what is the identity of the principle teacher character within the text, including their, race, gender, class position, sexuality and heritage; third, what is the outcome of the narrative, what was the result of the exposition; and finally, how has each text dealt with notions of sex and sexuality.

Due to the advent of compulsory education framed within the Education Act 1918 (UK), notions of the teacher and of teaching became a subject of public and institutional interest from the 1920s onwards. Since 1934 there has been a consistent surge of texts that depict teachers and teaching within developing a genre, described in this study as *the teacher text*. Twenty-two of these texts were selected for the *Teaching Men* project, depicting the teacher text genre across a seventy year period, ranging from an early example, *Goodbye Mr Chips* (1934) to the modern and controversial *Half Nelson* (2006). Specifically, each of the 22 texts was chosen for its narrative focus: that of teachers and teaching, rather than schools and students. Therefore texts such as *Tom Brown's School Days* (1857) or *Grease* (1984) have been omitted, due to their narrative focus being the student body. The initial thematic analysis of these texts has enabled an excavation of distinguishing professional attributes that shape each exposition and drive the narrative outcomes. This

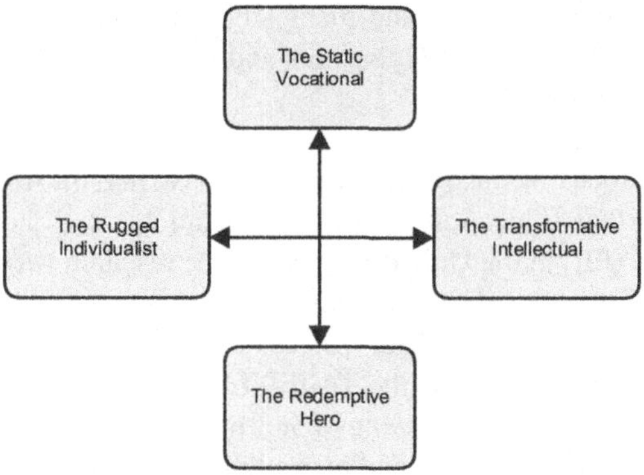

Fig. 3.1 Teacher text taxonomy

process identified distinct narrative patterns and tropes, which were developed into a taxonomy in order to describe this specific aspect of the teacher text genre. The taxonomy is an expression of four fictional types of teacher which recurs across the genre (see Fig. 3.1). Explicitly these are: *The Redemptive Hero*, *The Transformative Intellectual*, *The Static Vocational* and *The Rugged Individualist*.

This chapter focuses on one of the oldest of these teacher texts, *Goodbye Mr Chips* (Hilton 1939) and the allied teacher type, *The Static Vocational*. However, to provide context, a brief explanation of all four teacher types is provided here.

The Rugged Individualist and *The Transformative Intellectual*, although conceptualised here as part of the taxonomy, are terms drawn from Deborah Britzman's (1986) work on cultural mythology identified within teacher biographies. *The Rugged Individualist*, originally coined by Waller (1938), is described as a teacher who autonomously challenges the institution on behalf of the pupil, works successfully outside the given curriculum and is able to focus on the individual student with previously untold insight and energy. Because popular fictional texts such as *The History Boys* (Bennett 2006) and *Dead Poets Society* (Weir 1998) valorise and exemplify the attributes of *The Rugged Individualist*, this narrated identity becomes a powerful discursive stance and fictional trope to be used by teachers for identity work.

As an antithesis to *The Rugged Individualist*, Britzman uses the term *The Transformative Intellectual* to describe a professional educator positioned as a "significant counter framework" (1986, p. 454). This teacher, having been trained as a professional, is able to work in accordance with the institution, the student body and the academy. Fictional narratives such as *Dangerous Minds* (Smith and Johnson 1995), *Freedom Fighters* (LaGravenese 2007), and *Teacher Man* (McCourt 2005) expound the virtues of *The Transformative Intellectual*.

Adjacent to *The Rugged Individualist* and *The Transformative Intellectual* are two further mythological systems, which emerged from the thematic analysis of the fictional texts. These are *The Redemptive Hero* and the subject of this analysis, *The Static Vocational*.

The Redemptive Hero trope describes a teacher who uses their vocation to redeem and rehabilitate themselves. Texts such as *Pay it Forward* (Leder 2000), *To Serve them All my Days* (Delderfield 1972) and more recently the controversial *Half*

Nelson (Boden and Fleck 2006) depict broken or damaged teacher characters who use an educational career to rebuild themselves emotionally and spiritually. Accordingly educational institutions are presented as safe havens that require little professional skill and can manage personal projects of physical, vocational and spiritual rehabilitation.

Finally, the subject of this analysis: *The Static Vocational*; a popular and influential figure within the teacher text genre. Famous examples include two classic teacher texts, *Goodbye Mr Chips* (Hilton 1939) and *Mr Holland's Opus* (Herek 1996). *The Static Vocational* is a stable force usually closely aligned to a single institution, is often viewed as having never matured or left school and is often depicted with heightened pathos. The creation of a taxonomy to categorise the vast area of literary fiction about teachers and teaching was completed with an awareness of the dangers of using models that mimic positivist schemes and offer easy over-generalisations. Therefore, the taxonomy drawn from the analysis is referred to as a working tool rather than an analytical outcome, specifically used to provide an entry into deeper analysis, not to delimit it.

The methodological approaches used within our analysis are quantitative and narrative in nature. The analysis of fictional texts such as *Goodbye Mr Chips* (Hilton 1939), the identification of key fictional tropes within these, the development of the working taxonomy and the collection of live narrative data are research elements designed to enhance the quality of the analysis and enrich the scope of the findings.

The interviews that took place as part of the *Teaching Men* project provided an opportunity for participants to reflect critically on how they work with constructions of gender within the teaching profession. The interview process encouraged participants to deliberate on how as professionals, like authors of our own text, they are constantly writing and re-writing their professional identities. As Connelly and Clandinin suggest we are "… all of us lead[ing] storied lives on storied landscapes…" (1990, p. 107), we are agents of historical and cultural discourse that shapes ambiguous and unique identity constructions, some of which we might be unaware.

The following sections test the methodological framework using a triangulation of: (a) the fictional text, namely *Goodbye Mr Chips*, against; (b) the allied teacher type *The Static Vocational* in relation to; (c) the biographical interview data. The resulting analysis addresses the central question: (How) are male teachers influenced by fictional narratives in the construction of masculinities within education?

Case Study: The Static Vocational & Goodbye Mr Chips

As detailed above, the analysis of the fictional teacher texts identified a set of key characteristics. As part of this process *The Static Vocational* teacher type was established as an influential archetype and trope within the teacher text genre. Famous examples of *The Static Vocational* include two classic texts, *Goodbye Mr Chips*

(Hilton 1939) and *Mr Holland's Opus* (Herek 1996). Due to their popularity both texts have become influential in our understanding of the genre.

Characteristically, *The Static Vocational* fictional teacher type is depicted as having remained a stable force within a single institution for his entire career, often rising to positions of power but never to the top of his profession. This type is consistently characterised by an undercurrent of sadness and pathos within the narratives; the principle characters are often constructed as failed men having never fully left, or been able to leave, the safety of the one particular institution or school environment. Students have come and gone, developed and improved, yet the teacher has remained apparently static within the institution. Viewed as good and fair teachers, they were never seen to achieve their own ambitions in terms of leadership within academia but have managed to survive the professional world, and their personal situation, by sheltering within the institution.

To further explore the character of *The Static Vocational* we examine *Goodbye Mr Chips* as a key text within the teacher text genre, and analyse the novella alongside interview data generated during the recent *Teaching Men* project.

Goodbye Mr Chips has become a cultural franchise. Written by James Hilton (1934) based on his former Latin teacher, the text, published as a novella, has since undergone numerous transformations. Various versions of the text have in turn become re-readings aligned purposefully to the preoccupations of subsequent generations. Hilton's novel became a film starring Robert Donat (1939), and a stage and film musical by Leslie Bricusse (1967), and has inspired numerous television and radio productions (1939, 1984, 2002, 2010). As with many teacher texts the proliferation of Hilton's original text means that generations of teachers and readers will have encountered the story, or parts of it, in one of its many forms. As a hegemonic figure Mr Chips provides a demonstration of a number of tropes that would be considered ideal both in terms of masculinity and as an educator. Although the original text would now be perhaps less known to younger generations of readers and teachers, its wide distribution and access has assured the text's place as a dominant feature in the discourse of teaching and has provided a model from which other more recent texts have been created, such as *Mr Holland's Opus* (Herek 1996) and *The Prime of Miss Jean Brodie* (Spark 1965). The character of Mr Chips is also often referred to eponymously away from the context of the narrative from which it belongs, as with one interviewee who referred to a colleague as a 'bit of a Mr Chips—you know!'.

The novella by James Hilton (1934) was written between the World Wars. The narrative scheme is highly complex, readers being guided by an omniscient narrator who describes how the character of an old retired teacher, Mr Chips, sits by his fire place in a boarding house opposite his old school, 'Brookfield', drifting in and out of sleep. Each time Mr Chips falls asleep he encounters memories from a different era of his life. The unique style of disturbed temporality used in the novella creates a playfulness with time that develops a complexity as the narrative unfolds.

It is the narrator's ability to focalise intimately on the character of Mr Chips, both when he is awake and asleep, that binds the text and facilitates our understanding of the people, places and events that are described. Hilton's (1939) novella is a very brief, direct and a characteristically un-sentimentalised documentation of a teacher's life. Transformations or readings of the story have exploited the potential for sentimentality within the text, making Mr Chips synonymous as a figure who exudes pathos; this is a characterisation that is never explicitly developed within the original text. What is often overlooked in more modern readings of the story is how the text is evocative of the trauma and distress evident in post-World War One Britain through its exploration of themes of loss, grief, memory and ghosts. By the end of the text many of Mr Chips' *boys* had been killed at the front and remain only as ghosts in his memory. Though often referring to different evocations of the text, the teachers interviewed during the *Teaching Men* study often confirmed that, for them, *Goodbye Mr Chips* remains one of the most influential texts within the genre.

The Analytic Process

The final step in the analysis of the fictional text is based on Paul Ricoeur's concept of time and narrative, and his reading of desire and semantics. The aim is to provide a well-theorised alternative to current less interpretive readings of masculinity in education. This research seeks to reach beyond what is shown by participants and to interpret, within Ricoeur's theoretical framework, teachers' talk about identity in such a way that might even be outside of their own awareness. The Ricoeurian framework addresses four key areas of concern (see Fig. 3.2.) within the narrative scheme, namely: *language and desire*, *time*, the process of *circular mimesis* and the resulting construction of a *narrative identity*. This four-part level of analysis facilitates an interpretation of the narrative elements within the text in order to understand how they might become a point of reference in the construction of professional identities. This section will focus on a stage-by-stage account of the four–part Ricoeurian analytical process, enabling an alignment of theme and content between the fictional text *Goodbye Mr Chips*, and interview narratives generated by the *Teaching Men* project. This process will further our inquiry into how influential fictional tropes might be in how we construct *narrative identities* as males involved in the profession of teaching.

The analysis based on the Ricoeurian scheme of *three-fold mimesis* begins firstly with a focus on *Language and Desire*. Hilton's (1939) text promotes two primary areas of desire, namely *belonging* and *legacy*. First, the notion of *belonging* to an

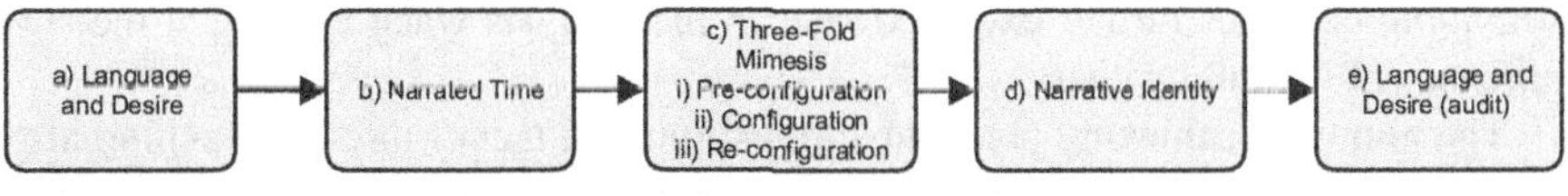

Fig. 3.2 Ricoeur's analytical framework

institution as if it was an extended family is promoted in various forms throughout Hilton's text. This notion of a school presents a counter discourse to that traditionally associated with English Victorian schools public. Until Hilton's text was published schools were often depicted as places of terror, violence and isolation, as represented in Thomas Hughes's (1857) novel *Tom Brown's School Days*, Bronte's *Jane Eyre* (1847) as well as in numerous instances in the novels of Charles Dickens. As a counter discourse Hilton's text presents the concept of *belonging* in a reciprocal sense, firstly in terms of Mr Chips belonging to the school, Brookfield, and secondly in terms of the boys' sense of belonging to Brookfield, supported by the accommodating character of Mr Chips.

Mr Chips' sense of belonging to Brookfield is depicted as a matter of lifelong acculturation, which, although spanning decades, is presented as a process that is achieved with relative ease and without apparent conflict: "About 1880 after he had been at Brookfield a decade … the possibility of staying where he was began to fill a comfortable niche in his mind" (Hilton 1939, p. 14). Later Mr Chips is shown being coaxed out of retirement during the war years because of his ability to promote a sense of belonging at Brookfield: "what I would like you for, more than anything else … your help in … just belonging here" (p. 96).

The second instance of *belonging* involves the students' *belonging* to Brookfield facilitated through the character of Mr Chips. This is a more complex construction of belonging expressed through the idea of Mr Chips acting as the repository of school-day memories.

The boys' belongingness is described dichotomously; either as an indifferent transient population belonging to, but passing through the school, or as a cohesive cohort of students whom Mr Chips eventually considers as his own offspring, albeit in his memories only. In response to an ex-student mentioning how sad it is that Mr Chips never had children he replies, "Yes—umph—I have … Thousands of'em … thousands of 'em … and all boys" (Hilton 1939, p. 131). This perspective of belonging is further consolidated through the depiction of the brutality of the Great War. Mr. Chips becomes the keeper of memories of many children who have been killed and live now only as ghosts or memories: "1916…. The Somme Battle, twenty-three names read out one Sunday evening" (p. 94).

Within the interview data, themes of *belonging*, linking to institutional and interpersonal relationships, are positioned as significant factors in how male teachers constructed their identities themselves. The interview data produces multiple references to an owned period of time: *my school days* and *my school life*, a time and place described as an existence separate from the general life of childhood. The data consistently refer to the significant influence of teachers that enabled a sense of belonging: 'made me feel part of the school' and 'brought me into the school', 'helped me fit in'. As will be demonstrated in the following, the importance of *belonging* becomes further extended later in the analysis when looking at the significance of institutionalism.

The notion of achieving personal and institutional *legacy* through teaching also relates to the idea of teachers as the repository of institutional and personal memories. Mr Chips is portrayed throughout the text as the guardian of his students' childhood memories. He is seen to remember the slightest of details regarding his students and their families, across many generations: "…the thin line of boys filing past the bench … new names but the old ones still remained … Jefferson, Jennings, Jolyon, Jupp, Kingsley Primus, Kingsley Secundus, Kingsley Tertius, Kingston … where have you all gone" (p. 112). Once again this is reciprocal in nature: as Mr Chips in turn becomes a fixture in the memory of his students, he begins to represent the school and his students' memory of it: "At sixty … he was Brookfield" (p. 14).

The reciprocal nature of this sharing of memories is where the ability to achieve *legacy* lies, as a pact between Chips' students and himself to remember. Hilton's text (1939) describes the complexities of such a pact: "Did any emotion really matter when the last trace of it had vanished from human memory … what crowd of emotions clung to him … He must be kind to them must treasure them in his mind before their long sleep" (p. 50).

The idea of *legacy* is one of the most surprising yet consistent themes drawn from the interview data. The idea of *legacy*, that is, with participants, remembering, and being remembered, was reported as a key motivating factor within the teachers' professional lives. An interviewee Mr Terry stated he wanted to be remembered forever as 'the extra mile guy'. Another interviewee, Mr Harley, said 'I like the idea that in 15 years' time they will be saying 'that Mr Harley bloke at college yes he was all right' … I think that is making a difference that they remember who you are'. Mr Drew offers a more nuanced approach to the idea of legacy. He reflects that 'it is not the self-glorification … but the legacy I hope to leave behind is um the realisation that um even though some things in life look difficult very often it is the things we have left undone that we regret on our death bed … I hope my legacy is helping to make them feel things were not so difficult … I love the fact that I have fired something in them that is my legacy'. These responses link the concept of *legacy* within teaching in different ways to ideas of memory and also to mortality.

Legacy within a profession like teaching and within an institution like a school can facilitate a level of immortality through the memories and achievements of students and colleagues as well as in the fabric of the institution. As the interview data has illustrated, like the portraits of headmasters that hung on the hallowed halls at Mr Chips' Brookfield, *legacy* is a motivating factor in the identity construction of many of the male teachers who participated in the *Teaching Men* project.

The section above shows that both the research data and Hilton's (1939) text highlight two primary areas of desire, expressed as *belonging* and *legacy*, consistent with the first point in the Ricoeurian analytical scheme, namely *Language and Desire*. When considering the research data, we see that there are crossovers and similarities in how *belonging* and *legacy* are described and expressed. Across the fictional and interview narratives to this point the analysis shows that issues illustrated by Hilton's text feature in how male teachers design and construct their professional or narrated identities.

The second stage of analysis in Ricoeur's scheme *Narrated Time* extends the ideas developed in the first stage, by setting the notions of *belonging and legacy* against the concept of how time is constructed within the narrative scheme.

Narrated Time

Amongst other themes, *Goodbye Mr Chips* explores the seductive power of institutions to capture its inhabitants. This view is in concert with the manner in which *The Static Vocational* is depicted as never really leaving the school environment, but rather surviving life by hiding within the institution of education. Hilton's (1939) text creates an alternative institutional world within the text by suggesting that Brookfield maintained its own time: "It was Brookfield far more than Greenwich mean-time that both he and his landlady kept … the school bell sounding dinner, call-over, prep and lights-out" (p. 4).

The institutionalisation of the teaching professional is a key feature in the chracterisation of *The Static Vocational* teacher type. Throughout the text Hilton (1939) never questions whether this level of institutionalisation is healthy or not. He promotes Brookfield as a safe harbour whilst hinting at the darker practices, such as petty politics within the staff and bullying amongst the boys, which institutions can sustain and conceal as form of alienation from general society.

Unlike other teacher texts, which obediently follow the academic yearly cycle, *Goodbye Mr Chips* (Hilton 1939) and other texts such as *Mr. Holland's Opus* (Herek 1996), whose characters fall within *The Static Vocational* category, differ from this temporal scheme. Instead these texts refer to the longevity of teaching as a vocation, and to time as spanning an entire career. Time is depicted through the inevitable passing of generations and the fate of the one who is represented as being forced to stay and watch as time passes him by.

As mentioned earlier the narrative scheme within Hilton's (1939) novella is highly complex in the treatment of time. As Mr Chips sits by his fire, drifting in and out of sleep, passing through different eras of his life:

> And there he was, dreaming again before the fire, dreaming of times and incidents … they all mixed up in his mind and someday however hard it proved to be he would sort them out and make a book of them … (Hilton 1939, p. 53)

The disturbed temporality creates an intricate system of narrated time that becomes more complicated as the text continues. Texts that depict *The Static Vocational* trope illustrate a specific management of narrative time. In texts such as *Goodbye Mr Chips* and *Mr Holland's Opus*, time is shown as spanning a career or lifetime, whereas other texts in this category, for example *The Prime of Miss Jean Brodie* (Spark 1965) and *187* (Reynolds and Yagemann 1997), denote time as a crisis point in a professional career. Either way, this category departs from the usual portrayal of time as mirroring the scheme of an academic year that in turn is indebted to the *bildungsroman* or *coming-of-age* genre in relation to those undergoing education.

An analysis of the interview data reflects this specific treatment of narrative temporality. Highlighting teachers' concerns with *longevity*, participants referred to the need for teachers to remain committed not only to their environment or institution but also to their subject or discipline. One participant noted his admiration for his old teacher because 'After all his years he had not lost his dedication for teaching his students the art of cabinet making'; whilst another referred to a teacher he saw as an influential teacher having ‘the strength to see it through … not giving up’. Echoing the sentiments portrayed in the fictional text there is a definite value attached to being able to survive and prove longevity within the role of the professional educator. Like Mr Chips there is also a sense of flattery at being asked to stay or being brought back. For example, Mr Yusef, who after an entire career in one role states ‘the view from all the teachers and the student seem to be there’s no way they are going to let you go … because I have put the yards in and changed a lot of formats here’.

So far this analysis has identified *belonging*, *legacy* and *longevity* as three key themes, or expressions of desire, that are shared between an analysis of the fictional teacher text *Goodbye Mr Chips* (Hilton 1939) and interview data generated by a cohort of male teachers. In the following we continue to argue that the thematic links between the two text types help constitute the identifiable teacher trope *The Static Vocational.*

The third level of the Ricoeurian analytic scheme enables a theoretically robust response to the question: Could the fictional text simply be reflecting the themes that exist within the educational profession, or has this fictional depiction shaped how those themes are developed by male teachers?

Three-fold Mimesis: Pre-configuration, Configuration, Re-configuration

There are three parts to the third analytic stage *three-fold mimesis.* Mimetic or mimesis like mimic, a literary and philosophical term, refers to a representation or imitation of human action; Ricoeur suggested that mimesis was a cyclical or circular process and event. Firstly, *pre-configuration*, what influences the construction of the narratives in question; secondly, *configuration*, an examination of how the narrative was constructed; and finally *re-configuration*, an exploration of how what is created by the narrative is exported into other narrative constructions. This view of narrative strategy and structure depicts a cycle within which narratives are able to generate and regenerate themselves across time and cultures. Central to the analysis at this stage is the notion of memory. Each of our three key desires—*belonging*, *legacy* and *longevity*—relates wholly or tentatively back to the idea of memory, and more specifically to who has the memories, how are they created and who guards them.

Pre-configuration

Pre-configuration considers what influences the imaginative construction of the narrative in question and how notions of *legacy*, *belonging* and *longevity*, have been addressed in Hilton’s (1939) novel. There are numerous examples of earlier texts that promote these themes. Texts such as *Tom Brown’s School Days*, *Jane Eyre*,

Dombey and Son, and *Oliver Twist*, all feature these themes within the narrative scheme. Therefore, in the beginning of how Hilton's text was imagined in a pre-configurative state, we can identify that *legacy*, *belonging* and *longevity* were all expressions of desire that existed within the narrative environment of texts about teaching and schooling.

We argue that *legacy*, *belonging* and *longevity* are features of desire that are realistically reflected from within educational institutions and their professional identities.

Configuration

Having identified pre-configuratively that expressions of *legacy*, *belonging* and *longevity* emerge from within the narrative environment of the teacher genre in general, what becomes significant now is how Hilton's (1939) text treats these themes. The power of his novella comes from his fusing of our identified expressions of desire—*legacy*, *belonging* and *longevity*—alongside a complex exploration of memory.

The manner in which Hilton (1939) uses the Great War as a backdrop to the novella forces us to consider the idea of memories differently: Who has them, who holds onto them and how do they die away eventually? In Hilton's text the teacher figure becomes the static holder of childhood memories, the holder of ghosts and souls as well as the arbiter of nostalgia. Having been set within a milieu of war, death, loss and mortality, this particular narrative *configuration* underscores the themes of *legacy*, *belonging* and *longevity* in a profound, powerful and heightened manner.

Hilton's (1939) focus on memory in relation to desire is further consolidated by the manner in which the narrative scheme drops in and out of episodes of time in a non-chronological manner. Important events, such as the death of Chips' wife, occur outside of any clear chronological progression. There is no obvious cohesion in the story line. Rather readers are introduced to fragments of memory that build to form an identifiable whole.

Within this fragmented scheme the themes of *legacy*, *belonging* and *longevity* take on a new character. These powerful facets of desire are depicted as essential and akin to a teacher's responsibility for being the keeper of memories. *Belonging* is viewed as quite intangible in terms of how it can be acquired. However, the manner in which Hilton positions *time* and *memory* against *desire* provides *Goodbye Mr Chips* with the textual richness that has helped it remain a classic literary text relevant, through its transformations perhaps, to a current generation of male teachers.

Re-configuration

Re-configuration, the third level of analysis, is a methodological means of understanding the capacity of a narrative's construction to influence subsequent narratives over time and across cultures. Central to the analysis at this stage is the notion of *memory*. More specifically, at this point our analytic aim is to enquire into what Hilton's (1939) narrative scheme offers, and to consider how it might impact on the *pre-configuration* of subsequent narratives, both fictional and biographical.

A critical point in our argument to this point is that the expressions of desire on which we have been focused, namely *legacy*, *belonging* and *longevity*, could be simply reflected from within the educational profession itself. Hilton as a writer of fiction offers something beyond a mere reflection of institutional issues. Instead Hilton's character constructions not only express the key desires we have discussed, but do so alongside a complex exploration of memory. The text *Goodbye Mr Chips* demonstrates, through the use of intrinsic and extrinsic character development, how as teaching professionals we might use narrativised identities to survive and flourish within a professional environment.

A highly complex system of construction and configuration exists beyond a simple reflection of a given place or situation. It is the strength and complexity of the masculinity depicted in characters like Mr Chips that have impacted on the construction of the masculine teacher fictional narratives that followed, *Mr Holland's Opus* being a good example.

The alignment of identity constituted through the desire for *legacy*, *belonging* and *longevity* was shared by Mr Chips as well as with participants in the *Teaching Men* study. The participants preconfigured their personal narrative identities based on notions of how they can survive as men in their profession and be perceived as successful within it—notions that are aligned with features identified in *Goodbye Mr Chips* and in the taxonomic type *The Static Vocational*.

The analytic stages presented so far open up arguments as to how influential fictional narratives are on teachers' constructions of narrated professional identities. This concern is the focus of the fourth stage of the Ricoeurian scheme, *Narrative Identities*.

Narrative Identities

As a taxonomic teacher trope, *The Static Vocational* is characteristically seen to measure the calibre and value of their teaching in their ability to survive within the institution rather than through any reflection on the quality of pedagogy. The successful achievement of identified key desires, namely *legacy*, *belonging* and *longevity*, is at the core of how Hilton's (1934) Mr Chips narrative identity is constructed and what appears to motivate such identities within the profession.

But how can we transpose knowledge from our analysis of fictional identities into actual teaching environments and against real teaching subjects? Within his philosophical approach Ricoeur (1988) asserts that we use *narrative* as a strategy to bridge what he identifies as the fracture between our phenomenological notion of time, that is, our subjective experience of how time passes, and our cosmological notion of time, that is, the scientific numerical concept of time denoting years, days, hours and seconds. Ricoeur describes a conceptual fissure that exists between these two competing methods of positioning ourselves within any given framework of time. His reading of *narrative identities* contains a similar polemic; Ricoeur sees the narrative identity as the "poetic resolution of the hermeneutic circle" (Ricoeur 1988, p. 248), referring to the cyclical nature of the *three-fold mimesis* and how in the *pre-configurative* state narrators are using information from *reconfigured* narratives to make sense of themselves within a place in time.

Ricoeur claims that *narrative identity* "becomes the name of a problem at least as much as it is that of a solution" (Ricoeur 1988, p. 249). He highlights that *narrative identity* is not a stable state or a place of completion, but is instead the expression of a struggle taking place at the site of turmoil and conflict which narrative appears to temporarily resolve, or rationalise. For example, interview data demonstrates that there is often confusion between memories of our actual schooling and what is narrated to us through stories and fictional representations of teaching. The interview data from the *Teaching Men* project bears this out. For example, Mr Harley's statement:

> Umm—Martin Clunes in second world war—That was Mr Chips, Please Sir, Mind Your Language … when I went to my first secondary school—which was a grammar school—it was very much cap and gowns. Thinking about it the Bash Street Kids—it was very different from my primary school.

Mr Harley's statement is evidence of the persistent overlap between the impressions made through readings of fiction and our actual memory. This view supports Ricouer's (1984, 1988, 1990) view that *narrative identity* is not a stable entity. Rather he sees it as a struggle or conflict which narrative only appears to solve, leaving what cannot be actually remembered to be lived vicariously through fiction.

Ricoeur (1984, 1988, 1990) argues for narrative as an enabling force. Such an understanding facilitates a reconsideration of how multiple narrative identities exist within any single environment or profession. This perspective "illustrates how narrative identity mediates between two extremes: harmony and dissonance, lived and told, innovation and sedimentation, fact and fiction …" (Hutten 2002, p. 58). This view supports our differentiation of our four teacher tropes from their virtual environments and reconsiders how they might exist as influential and useful narrative strategies within an actual educational environment. As Ricoeur argues, "The fragile offshoot issuing from … fiction is the assignment to an individual or community of a specific identity that we can call their narrative identity" (Ricoeur 1988, p. 246).

Our working taxonomy therefore is not only supported by the analysis of the fictional texts, but also explains how we as professionals might represent and shape different narrative identities at different times to suit the needs of current situations or events.

Language and Desire (Audit)

The final stage returns to *Language and Desire* as an audit of what has been achieved through the analytical process. There were three common themes highlighted in both the construction of the fictional texts and in the interview data— *legacy*, *belonging* and *longevity*—all of which were associated with the idea of *memory* and ultimately *time* as experienced by teaching professionals.

Throughout the analysis we have seen how a *narrative identity*, be it fictional as with Hilton's text, or generated from biographical interview data, regularly constructs teachers as the guardians of childhood, school day *memories*. The guardianship role further consolidates the notion of cultivating personal and institutional *legacy* and is reflected in the interview data as a key motivator for male teachers to remain in the teaching profession. The concept of *legacy* in turn refers to notions of mortality and to teaching as a vocational career, or lifetime commitment. The fictional text and interview data alike highlight the participants' desire to attain a level of immortality in the memories of students and colleagues, as well as by contributing to the academic institution and profession.

Fictional teacher texts and the interview data also highlight themes of *belonging* linked to institutionalisation as a state that perpetuates *longevity* as a desired goal and measure of success. Expressed also is a desire for individual and professional immersion within an institution that will work to protect and nurture the individual. As exemplified by Mr Chips, there is professional currency associated with being able to survive and prove *longevity* as a professional educator.

This claim was borne out in the interview data: survival and a desire for a sustained nurturing environment are highlighted as key professional motivators for the male teachers who were interviewed.

Concluding Comments

In an era when the time that teachers remain in the profession is relatively short it is all the more important that they have robust tools at hand for interrogating who they are and who they might become within the profession. The methodology outlined in this paper is research based and has shown how teachers might use their alignment with fictional and biographical stories to investigate through critical reflection how they approach their own identity work.

A consideration of the final point of analysis, *Language and Desire* (*audit*), enables a short summary of the analysis presented above using the Ricoeurian analytical system. Within this summary we confirm how major themes of *memory*, *legacy*, *belonging* and *longevity* are associated with how male teachers construct narrative identities and manage the notion of *time* over the duration of a professional life. We can also identify how professionals might use information from fictional narrative identities not only to inform how they might *become* within their profession but furthermore how they might survive within it.

As Connelly and Clandinin (2007) remind us, we are all engaged in living, constructing and being constructed into storied lives and storied landscapes. This paper has contributed a theoretical support to such a view. The above analysis offers a demonstration of how *fictional* and *real identities* can become integrated into concepts of who we are, and what we might *become*. By exploring the place of fictional narratives in how gendered identities are constructed within educational institutions we have addressed a central question: How are male teachers influenced by fictional narratives in the construction of masculinities within education? In our analysis we have considered how literary tropes inform how professional identities can be both imagined and enacted.

This analytical demonstration, using a Ricoeurian scheme, has charted the development of a working taxonomy. It has also provided a new and rigorous theoretical methodology for assisting researchers in reading fictional texts as cultural artefacts alongside biographical narratives.

This research has implications for initial teacher education as well as for ongoing professional development, by offering an innovative means of delivering and doing critical reflective practice. The methodology outlined above provides a robust qualitative demonstration of how teachers as critically reflective practitioners might move to a more explicit understanding of how fragments of stories—fictional and lived—are accumulated, acculturated, and integrated into concepts of who we are and how they might provide stability for how and what we might *become*. Further work is necessary to assess how the use of critical reflective practice in teacher education might be implicated in the narratisation of professional identities, but also how we might encompass the use of this methodology in how we work with professional reflection, to bridge the notion of idealised teacher types and every day practice. The final word to Mr Harley:

> Becoming a teacher … I still get excited by it I never want to lose it, this thing I think one day someone is going to tap me on the shoulder and say, 'right you're not a teacher … get back to welding' … even though I am one I am still in awe of teachers.

Discussion Questions

1. In what way do you think the fictional characters you have encountered in books, film and television are significant in how you have developed your identity either as a professional or in your personal life.
2. When collecting narratives from research participants what do you think are the key considerations in terms of how you might read the story in light of an understanding of how fiction narrative structures might influence the ways in which stories are constructed?

References

Bainbridge, C., & Yates, C. (2005). Cinematic symptoms of masculinity in transition: Memory, history and mythology in contemporary film. *Psychoanalysis, Culture and Society, 10*(3), 299–318.

Bal, M. (2006). *A Mieke Bal reader*. London: University of Chicago Press.

Bennett, A. (2006). *The history boys*. New York: Faber and Faber.

Boden, A., & Fleck, R. (Writers). (2006). *Half Nelson*. In A. Boden (Producer). New York: ThinkFilm.

Breault, R. (2009). The celluloid teacher. *The Educational Forum, 73*(4), 306–317.

Britzman, D. (1986). Cultural myths in the making of a teacher. *Havard Educational Review, 56*(4), 442–456.

Carrigan, T., Connell, B., & Lee, J. (1985). Towards a new sociology of masculinity. *Theory and Society, 14*(5), 551–604.

Connell, R. (1995). *Masculinities*. Berkeley: University of California Press.

Connell, R. (2000). *The men and the boys*. Berkeley: University of California Press.

Connell, R. (2008). A thousand miles from kind: Men, masculinities and modern institutions. *Journal of Men's Studies, 16*(3), 237–249.

Connell, R., & Messerschmidt, J. W. (2005). Hegemonic masculinity: Rethinking the concept. *Gender & Society, 19*(6), 829–859.

Connelly, M., & Clandinin, J. (1990). Stories of experience and narrative inquiry. *Educational Researcher, 19*(5), 2–14.

Connelly, M., & Clandinin, J. (2007). *Handbook of narrative inquiry: Mapping a methodology*. Thousand Oaks: Sage.

Dalton, M. M. (1999). *The Hollywood curriculum : Teachers and teaching in the movies*. New York: Peter Lang.

Delderfield, R. F. (1972). *To serve them all my days*. New York: Simon and Schuster.

Ellsmore, S. (2005). *Carry on teachers: Representations of the teaching profession in screen culture*. Stoke on Trent: Trentham Books.

Fisher, R., Harris, A., & Jarvis, C. (2008). *Education and popular culture: Telling tales on teachers and learners*. Abingdon: Routledge.

Hall, M. (2005). *Teaching: Men and film*. London: British Film Institute.

Herek, S. (Writer). (1996). *Mr Holland's Opus* [videorecording]. Universal City: Polygram Entertainment.

Hilton, J. (1934). *Goodbye, Mr Chips*. London: Hodder & Stoughton.

Hilton, J. (1939). *Goodbye, Mr. Chips*. London: Hodder & Stoughton.

Hutten, R. (Ed.). (2002). *Narrative research: Voices of teachers and philosophers*. Jyvaskyla: SoPhi.

LaGravenese, R. (Writer). (2007). *Freedom writers*. Hollywood: Paramount Pictures.

Leder, M. (Writer). (2000). *Pay it forward*. In M. McLaglen, J. Treisman, S. Reuther, & P. Abrams (Producer). Hollywood: Warner Bros.

Martino, W., & Meyenn, B. (2002). War, guns, and cool, tough things: Interrogating single sex classes as a strategy for engaging boys in English. *Journal of Education, 32*(3), 304–323.

McCourt, F. (2005). *Teacher man*. New York: Scribner.

Mellen, J. (1977). *Big bad wolves: Masculinity in American film*. London: Elm Tree Books.

Mottart, A. (2009). Fictional narratives as didactical tools: Using Frank McCourt's Teacher Man in pre-service teacher education. *Educational Studies, 35*(5), 493–502.

Petersen, A. R. (1998). *Unmasking the masculine: 'Men' and 'identity' in a sceptical age*. London: Sage.

Plummer, K. (2001). *Documents of life 2: An invitation to a critical humanism* (2nd ed.). London: Sage.

Propp, V. (1968). *Morphology of the folktale*. Austin: University of Texas Press.

Reynolds, K., & Yagemann, S. (Writers). (1997). *187*. In B. Davey & S. McEveety (Producer). Hollywood: Warner Bros.
Ricoeur, P. (1984). *Time and narrative* (Vol. 2). Chicago: University of Chicago Press.
Ricoeur, P. (1988). *Time and narrative* (Vol. 3). Chicago: University of Chicago Press.
Ricoeur, P. (1990). *Time and narrative* (Vol. 1). Chicago: University of Chicago Press.
Riessman, C. K. (2008). *Narrative methods for the human sciences*. Los Angeles: Sage.
Smith, J., & Johnson, L. (Writers). (1995). *Dangerous minds*. Hollywood: Hollywood Picture.
Spark, M. (1965). *The prime of Miss Jean Brodie*. Harmondsworth: Penguin.
Waller, W. (1938). *The sociology of education*. Hobeken: Wiley.
Weir, P. (Writer). (1998). *Dead poets society*. In S. Haft (Producer). Burbank: Warner Home Video.

Chapter 4
Critical Junctures in Narrative Research: Collaborative Reflections on Methodological Issues

Jeanette Kennelly, Alison Ledger, and Libby Flynn

Abstract The co-creation of narratives can be a complex and intricate process where findings are shaped and molded by the interactions between researcher and study participants. From the moment the researcher enters the field of inquiry through to the writings of each story, and often beyond the final storytelling, there are poignant moments or junctures that the researcher may face in relation to methodology and ethical practice. The authors present three narratives about their experience of conducting narrative research within the field of music therapy. Each author tells her story in relation to the methodological and ethical challenges and considerations encountered. Looking both within and across these three stories, the authors highlight five critical junctures that may arise during the research process. Common strategies for negotiating these challenges are identified to assist narrative researchers in any discipline who may be experiencing their own pivotal junctures.

Keywords Research methodology • Narrative design • Anonymization • Reflexivity • Ethics

Introduction

Narrative researchers grounded in transactional and subjectivist epistemologies understand research findings as a co-creation between researchers and participants (Lincoln et al. 2011). From this perspective, findings are developed through interactions between the researcher and study participants, with the values and beliefs held by the researcher shaping the findings that emerge (Daly 2007). In narrative research,

J. Kennelly (✉) • L. Flynn
The University of Queensland, St Lucia, QLD, Australia
e-mail: jkennelly1@optusnet.com.au

A. Ledger
The University of Leeds, Leeds, UK

© Springer Science+Business Media Singapore 2017

R. Dwyer et al. (eds.), *Narrative Research in Practice*,
DOI 10.1007/978-981-10-1579-3_4

the relationship between researcher and participants is crucial and requires ongoing consideration and negotiation. This may be particularly the case when the researcher chooses to study a topic that involves vulnerable participants or professionals within their own discipline. The dynamics between the researcher and participant may be impacted by issues such as multiple roles, blurring of boundaries, conflicts of interest, and concerns about faithful representation (Rosenblatt 1995).

In this chapter, we present three narratives about undertaking narrative research with music therapy clients or colleagues. In these narratives, we each reflect on the methodological and ethical challenges we encountered as we worked to co-create meaningful and respectful narratives and maintain professional relationships with participants. We also compare the ways in which we navigated challenges, made difficult decisions, and changed our methodological approach to protect the participants and the developing narrative. Through bringing these narratives together, we highlight five critical junctures in narrative research and identify common strategies for negotiating unexpected challenges in the research process. Though our narratives are about music therapy research, our strategies are presented to assist narrative researchers in any discipline who are facing critical junctures of their own.

"How Do We Best Tell Their Story?" Our Narrative Research Stories

Prelude

Prior to undertaking narrative research, all three of us were practicing music therapists. When it came to choosing a topic for our PhDs, we decided to study under-researched aspects of our practice. Narrative research held appeal for its potential for exploring participants' experiences of situations we knew little about and the developments or changes in these experiences over time (Clandinin and Connelly 2000).

As therapists, we were experienced in negotiating interactions with a wide range of people in complex environments. However, narrative research brought up a whole new set of challenges that we had not anticipated as early career researchers. We underestimated the amount of consideration and reconsideration needed to preserve relationships, reputations, and participants' (and our own) wellbeing.

When the opportunity to contribute to this book arose, we were keen to write the chapter we wished we had read when starting out in narrative research. We had all read narrative research textbooks and publications of narrative research findings, but felt ill-prepared for the challenges and complexities of undertaking narrative research within our own small helping profession. We agreed that we wanted to write a chapter that revealed such challenges. Rather than presenting a polished set of narrative research findings, we wanted to demonstrate the practicalities of undertaking narrative research and to provide more detailed explanations of our methodological decisions.

We started out by each writing a narrative about our experience of the narrative research process. These narratives highlighted the methodological issues we encountered and the ways that we resolved challenges along the way. After sharing our narratives with each other, we each made revisions to our own narratives, removing unnecessary details and adding further recollections, explanations, or emphases. We then brought the three revised narratives together to identify commonalities and differences in our experiences. This work led to the identification of five critical junctures, namely:

1. Enacting a narrative research design
2. Approaches to Analysis
3. Concerns about Anonymisation
4. Reflexivity and the Self
5. Situating narrative in a mixed methods design

By examining and reflecting on these points in the research process, we hoped to highlight some of the complexities in undertaking narrative research and provide a range of strategies for researchers who find themselves at similar junctures in the research process.

Here, we present the three revised narratives, before discussing the five critical junctures and associated strategies. Consistent with understandings of narratives as a way of ordering, organizing, and making sense of experiences (Clandinin 2007; Daiute 2014; Polkinghorne 1995), it was important for us to present each narrative as a whole. That way, readers could understand how we arrived at the various junctures and evaluate the relevance of our experiences for their own narrative research.

Libby's Story: The Road Taken: Ethical Considerations in Narrative Research with Vulnerable Groups

After running a music therapy session for bereaved parents, it took a year and a half of reflection and chance encounters with music used from the session for me to arrive at the topic for my PhD. As a result of this process, my PhD aimed to explore the way music therapy for five bereaved parents shaped their engagement with music in their lives, specifically focusing on the role of song parody. To attempt to unveil these bereaved parents' experiences, I conducted in-depth interviews at 1 or 2 years post therapy, during which, music that was used in the therapy session was played to participants. In order to address the overarching aim of the research, three main questions were explored during the interviews: (1) What are bereaved parents' lived experiences of music therapy? (2) How do bereaved parents' lived experiences of music therapy affect their ongoing relationship with music? and (3) In what ways does the song parody technique shape a bereaved parent's meaning of the song? Adopting a constructivist lens, the methodology of narrative inquiry was employed as it allowed the storied lives of the bereaved parents as well as the music to be told in a way that acknowledged the existence of multiple realities, accounted for the individual nature of grief and recognized the dual import of researcher and participant.

The process of working with and then retrospectively researching bereaved parents' lived experience of music used in therapy proved to be a steep learning curve. I found myself stumbling into unforeseen junctures in which I had to make critical decisions for the ethical and emotional safety of not just my participants but also of myself. As with many questions of an ethical nature, there were no concrete answers; no guarantee that the route I chose would be the same route another researcher would choose.

There is always increased concern when conducting research with participants who are vulnerable; a category into which bereaved parents can fall (Hynson et al. 2006). As a therapist and researcher, I was acutely aware of the possibility of causing psychological distress due to the personal and reflective nature of the interview process. As Elliott (2005) suggests, the interview process can prompt participants to reflect on topics and aspects of their lives that they had never previously considered; a phenomenon that I witnessed in a number of the interviews I conducted. Although there is a natural reflex to want to take away a person's pain, which is largely driven by "researcher guilt", it is also acknowledged in the literature that these difficult moments can be therapeutic (Postmus 2013).

Despite the potential vulnerability of this client group, I was reassured going into this research by the fact that previous to conducting the interviews, I had also briefly worked with the participants as a therapist during music therapy sessions. Although the issue of inhabiting multiple roles as researcher and therapist can require complex navigation, for this particular project, my experience was that by having past insight into the participants and where they were at in their grieving process, helped to not only strengthen the interview process but also ensure greater emotional safety for participants. Possibly as a result of the already pre-established therapeutic relationship I had with the participants, the interviews were very deep, honest, confronting and humbling; thus, it was at this point I realised the narratives also needed to have the breadth and space to capture and honour the full richness of their stories and memories.

Following the interviews, member checking was implemented and participants received a full verbatim copy of the interview transcript, including any discussion that occurred during the tea break. Views on the use of member checking within the field of qualitative research are divided, with some advocating its use based on its ability to add a further layer to the research (Dickson-Swift et al. 2007, 2009; Forbat and Henderson 2005; Koelsch 2013); others however highlight the contentiousness due to aspects such as changed perceptions over time, defensive reactions from participants or difficulty in adopting a critical stance due to the researcher-participant relationship (Holloway and Wheeler 2010; Sands 2013). Despite these considerations, I decided to include member checking in my research design as it would allow the participants the opportunity to add, clarify in further depth or most importantly, remove any information they felt uncomfortable including. This final point was particularly pertinent in my decision making process as I felt that it would assist in giving the participants more power in the research process by allowing them the opportunity to choose what aspects of their voice would be heard in the forthcoming narratives. Upon receiving the member-checked copies of the transcript, it became clear to me that for a number of participants, the act of re-reading their story was an emotionally difficult one, the weight of which is captured in the following excerpt from Francine's story:

> *I placed the weighty interview transcript and a copy of the group recording of the song from the bereaved parents' retreat in the mail and anxiously awaited a response. Months went by. There were unanswered emails and voice mail messages from me gently checking in with Francine to see if she had even received the package in the mail. Time started to run short so I tried to ring again, and this time Francine answered. She was brief in her responses. She had found member checking the interview transcript difficult, but was nearly finished. When I tentatively asked her if she'd had a chance to listen to the recording, she became very quiet before affirming that she had. I became worried as I questioned, 'how was that for you?' There was silence on the other end of the line until finally she whispered 'not good'* (Flynn 2014).

The ramifications of this encounter and how it informed future decision making in the research process will be discussed later in the section.

Analyzing the interview transcripts, I implemented a five-step approach which primarily utilized Aldridge's (2005) Therapeutic Narrative Analysis (TNA) model. This approach was initially developed as a way of explicating meaning through a constructivist lens, centered heavily around the concept of identifying episodes which the resulting narrative helps bring together. The steps of analysis applied were as follows:

1. Pictorial representation of the 3 dimensional narrative inquiry space
2. Identify episodes of relevance
3. Submit episodes to analysis
4. Generate themes
5. Story creation

In hindsight, one of the most critical steps in the analysis process was the use of pictorial representation, a step that was not originally included in Aldridge's TNA model. The addition of this step was initially in reaction to the interview transcripts, which were so large and rich with information, when it became apparent that each story could adopt many different focuses. I found myself struggling to identify what parts of their story were not as relevant to my study and realized at this point I needed to find the 'big picture'; the heart of the story. The use of Clandinin and Connelly's (2000; Clandinin 2006) three dimensional narrative inquiry space allowed me to approach the data with a focus on three broad elements: first, temporality, which encompassed the constant temporal transitions and state of flux that people and events are constantly engaged in; second, sociality, which bridges the personal and social conditions of a person's life world, including the relationship of the narrative inquirer to the participants; and third, place, which encompasses the physical space where the event and/or inquiry takes place and how this can impact on the experience (Clandinin et al. 2007). The pictorial representation of these three

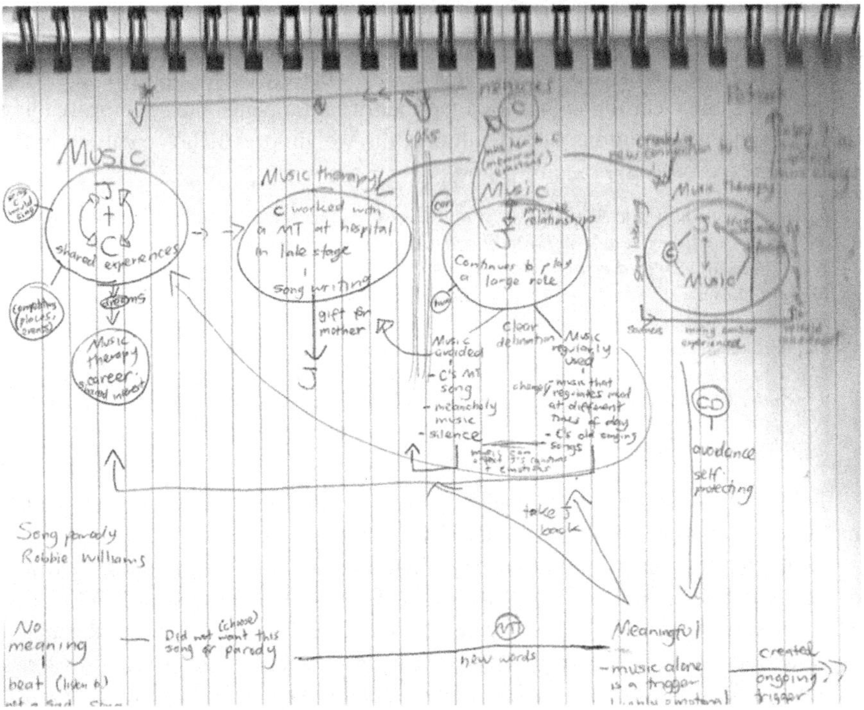

Fig. 4.1 Pictorial representation of the narrative inquiry space

elements within each participant's story provided the opportunity to not only see the 'big picture', but to view if and how all these elements were interacting and if there was a certain part of the story which held particular focus (see Fig. 4.1). Although pictorial representation was only the first step of a five-stage analysis process, I found myself revisiting these pictures often during the writing process as this visual 'snapshot' helped to bring clarity to aspects of genre, structure and voice for the forthcoming narratives.

After completing my first pictorial representation, it became apparent to me that the 'shape' of my analysis process aligned with my choice of methodology. I viewed the narrative inquiry process as a two-way funnel; starting broadly with the whole story (step 1 of the analysis process), then slowly becoming more and more specific in details through stages 2–4, with the final step bringing it back out again, with a narrative that captured the full richness of these bereaved parents' experiences with music used in therapy.

In order to account for the humanness of qualitative research, with all its messiness and moments of intricate subjectivity, the act of reflexivity became integral to all stages of the research process described above. Dickson-Swift et al. (2009) discuss in their examination of researching sensitive topics that given the emotional labor this type of research can have, it is important that researchers pay due attention to management of the self throughout the process. This became particularly apparent to me as I started to recognize the many points where my personal story intersected with aspects of my participants' stories. Depending on where in the process these moments of counterpoint occurred, I engaged in different forms of reflexive practice which included:

1. In-depth reflexive notes embedded within the interview transcripts that were revisited at multiple points throughout the research process. By revisiting these notes, I was able to reflect on whether my opinions, understanding and analysis of the interviews had developed over time and if so, how.
2. Sharing of personal written stories with my supervisors. These stories were written at my own perceived critical junctures throughout the research process and served as a way for my supervisors to understand *my* story better. By providing this background information, my supervisors were able to provide more informed feedback in regards to whether my own subjective interpretation was becoming too dominant throughout the analysis and resultant narratives.
3. The most critical point of reflexivity throughout this research project was the decision to undergo psychotherapy to explore my own understanding of death and the losses in my own life: a process that lasted for 18 months. Aside from my own personal exploration during this time, the therapy process became a critical resource for exploring issues of ethics, relationships, boundaries, and professional supervision.

As a result of engaging in the above reflexive practices, I was able to ensure greater transparency, clarity and acknowledgement of moments of countertransference throughout the research process. Furthermore, it equipped me with greater insight to handle all the foreseen and unforeseen junctures that arise when researching vulnerable populations which I believe allowed me to make decisions that were ethically sound, with my participants and their well-being at the core of the decision making process.

As a final note extending on the above discussion, although member checking of narratives was not part of the design submitted to ethical clearance, it was still a topic often discussed in supervision sessions as the narratives started to take their final form. The question weighed heavily on my mind; I needed to know that the decision I ended up making was one with the participants in mind and not driven by my own fear of the participants' reactions to the narratives. Having written the final narrative, I came to the decision to not pursue member checking; a decision largely guided by a combination of my knowledge of grief theories and my view of temporality in which we are engaged in constant temporal transitions. A large amount of time had passed since I had seen all of the participants; there was no way of knowing where they were at in their grieving process and I had already witnessed with Francine the powerful and potentially negative effect member checking can have on participants. The final narratives were powerful pieces filled with raw emotions, painful memories, sometimes words of hope but mostly of loss; ethically, I could not take the risk of bringing the participants back to those dark places.

Alison's Story: Bringing Emotions to the Fore: Communicating Therapists' Stories Through Poetry

My PhD aimed to address a gap in music therapy research and training—a need for further reflection about the challenges of developing new music therapy services. I had three main aims:

1. to learn more about music therapist's experiences of developing new services in healthcare organizations,
2. to uncover effective strategies for introducing and establishing new music therapy services, and
3. to further explore the contribution of qualitative research approaches to understand facets of music therapy development (Ledger 2010).

To meet these aims, I collected narratives from expert music therapists about their experiences of developing new positions in hospitals. I recruited eleven music therapists from a range of countries (Australia, Canada, Ireland, the United Kingdom, and the United States), using my and my PhD supervisor Jane's contacts. Potential participants included people whose work I had read or seen presented at conferences, as well as people who were well known to me as close colleagues or past coursework or fieldwork students. After considering several methods of data analysis, I settled on an arts-based approach in which I wrote poetry in response to the narratives I received. This approach helped me to identify seven themes in relation to the music therapists' experiences.

When beginning my PhD adventure, I read about other narrative researchers' experiences and considered some of the challenges I might encounter. I wrote my own autobiographical accounts of service development, to explore my assumptions about music therapy service development and to gain a sense of what the process of contributing a narrative might be like for participants in my research. This heightened my awareness of the partial and situated nature of narratives, which I reflected on in my thesis:

> I was struck by the way in which I constructed my narratives to suit my audience. My awareness that my doctoral supervisor would read the narratives influenced some of the details I included and the details I omitted. I left out some aspects of my experience, knowing that my doctoral supervisor had pre-existing and ongoing relationships with some of the people in my narratives… Another thing that occurred to me was the role of memory in constructing an autobiographical narrative. There were times when I tried to imagine being back in a scene physically and emotionally, but could not recall the full details of a given situation. (Ledger 2010, p. 106)

The experience of writing my own narratives was extremely helpful in the research design phase. I decided to request that participants contribute narratives in written form, to allow them the time and space to edit their narratives until they were happy to share their stories. After writing my own narrative, I was aware that participants may face decisions about what to include and what to leave out and that these decisions may take some time to consider and resolve. Giving participants time to prepare their narrative would allow them time to make considered choices and to check the details of their stories if they so wished. (Here it was not my intention to obtain "true" accounts, but I foresaw that checking details may be helpful to the participants in ascribing meaning to their experiences and achieving coherence). I also planned to be deliberately open-ended in my request for narratives, to allow participants to include whatever aspects of their experiences they deemed important and appropriate to share. As a music therapy colleague with experience of service development pressures, I anticipated that it was important the research requirements were not perceived as demanding or threatening.

My considered approach to the collection of narratives was reinforced when three potential participants emailed to ask further questions about the research. These music therapists wanted to know what should be included in the narrative, how the narratives would be analysed, how confidentiality would be ensured and how much time the creation of a narrative should take. These questions were difficult to answer, as I wanted to avoid being too prescriptive about what should be included in the narrative and how much time each participant should spend. Furthermore, I was yet to make final decisions about what my analysis and findings would look like. I responded to questions by explaining that I had been deliberately open-ended to elicit a range of responses and reassured participants that I was looking for a selective account based on current perceptions and viewpoints (rather than a fact-based account of all relevant events). I also indicated that I would be reading narratives closely, comparing them to others' and my own service development experiences, and developing a composite story of music therapists' experiences. Although I was unsure of my exact methods of analysis at this point, I promised potential participants that I would make efforts to disguise their identities. Only one potential participant decided not to proceed with the research at this point, citing time constraints as the reason she would not be returning her consent form.

Two music therapists felt unable to commit to providing a written narrative and asked if they could provide a narrative verbally instead. One agreed to provide a service development narrative over the phone, while the other offered to record her narrative onto compact disc (recorded over two sittings). Although I favoured a written narrative (for reasons explained above), I decided to remain flexible with regard to data collection methods to allow these music therapists to participate (and obtain these music therapists' stories). It was later interesting to note the differences between the verbal and written narratives I had received. I perceived that the spoken narratives were more evocative and powerful, as you could hear the therapist's tone of voice and any hesitations in the telling of the story. In future research, I may prioritise this advantage of spoken narratives in decisions about data collection methods.

As the narratives came in, I was impressed by the music therapists' honesty and felt privileged to be reading their accounts. The music therapists were very open in sharing difficult work encounters and expressed strong emotions such as insecurity, isolation, frustration, and disappointment. It was also interesting to note the differences in language use and style. Whilst all of the narratives were revealing, I noted that participants who were less known to me wrote in a more distanced way, using academic conventions and even citing academic publications. Previous students tended to convey an optimistic outlook and portrayed themselves as rising to the demands of introducing new music therapy services. Participants who were previous colleagues were the most frank in telling their stories and wrote in a more personal way. Colleagues' narratives were particularly honest when I was already familiar with aspects of their work and I sensed that these narratives had undergone less refinement and revision. I therefore considered that close relationships may have increased my access to subjective experiences and that the information provided in the narratives should be treated with special care.

When I read the email messages that accompanied the narratives, it became clear that writing (or verbally telling) a narrative was not a trivial nor inconsequential act. One of the participants reflected on writing her narrative at "the right time", after a period of instability in her work had settled, while another indicated that writing a narrative had been a "trigger" for making changes to her work circumstances. A further participant wrote to me some time after she had submitted her original narrative, asking for further clarification about my intentions for concealing participants' identities. I explained my plans to use pseudonyms and mix up participants' stories, but at that stage could not guarantee that readers would not try to guess the identities of the music therapists involved. The participant then decided to amend her narrative to remove some statements which she deemed too sensitive for inclusion. I respected this participant's wishes and only used the amended narrative in my analysis.

At the outset of my research, I was unsure how I would analyse and present the music therapists' narratives. I knew that I wanted to develop qualitative research skills and had read about different approaches to narrative analysis (Elliot 2005; Polkinghorne 1995), but I was uncertain about which particular way I should turn. I therefore kept my ethics application and information sheet fairly open, stating that I would be using qualitative analysis to "explore potential influences" or "identify critical issues" in music therapy service development. Though this had disadvantages in terms of informing my participants how their narratives would be "used", this approach allowed me to remain open to a range of analytic possibilities.

When it later came time to decide on my exact strategies for analysis and presentation, four main concerns arose. First, I wished to keep the music therapists' identities secret. Due to the small nature of the music therapy profession, it was possible to identify the music therapists from the details in their stories (details such as client group or length of practice). As the music therapists had been so honest in sharing their stories, I perceived that there were risks to presenting the therapists' stories as a whole. I considered the possibility that the stories could be damaging to the music therapists themselves, to their relationships with colleagues, or to the reputation of the hospitals where they were working. For this reason, it did not seem possible for me to present the individual stories without changing details within the music therapists' stories. At the same time, I felt the context of the work was crucial for understanding the music therapists' experiences and was opposed to breaking up or mixing up the narratives. I anticipated that breaking up the narratives would disrupt the meaning given to the experiences by the music therapists.

Second, I cared that the narratives were treated with utmost respect. The music therapy participants were colleagues, whose experiences I recognised and appreciated. It was important to me that I portrayed them authentically and that I did not abuse the trust they had given me in sharing their stories. It was possible that I would continue to work with the music therapists in the future, and I wished to avoid any damage to effective partnerships. It was therefore important to me that I not only portrayed the challenges that music therapist experienced, but also the passion and determination that music therapists displayed in developing their services.

Third, I struggled to find an appropriate way to bring together multiple sources of data—the narratives, my fieldwork observations of a music therapist starting up a new service, my service development training, and my own experiences as a music therapist. I tried a number of conventional techniques for dealing with narratives, such as content analysis, Labov and Waletzky's (1967/1997) structural analysis, and Polkinghorne's (1995) narrative-type narrative analysis. These were helpful in exploring the participants' telling of their service development experiences, but I wished to develop an approach in which I could further explore my own experiences and responses as a music therapist.

Fourth, I wanted to develop an analytic strategy which would capture the strong emotions that the music therapists communicated through their narratives. This was when my research supervisor, Professor Jane Edwards, suggested I consider arts-based research methods. At the time of the research, the use of arts-based methods in healthcare research was growing and was reported to be effective in exploring subjective experiences and strong emotions (Ledger and Edwards 2011). Jane and I discussed a range of possibilities, including the development of a musical based on the narratives I had collected, but I began by writing a poem in response to one of the narratives (as I usually start with writing the lyrics when songwriting).

Over time, I developed the following procedure for analysing the narratives through poetry:

1. re-read a music therapist's narrative,
2. identify significant words or phrases in the narrative,
3. write a poem around the words or phrases identified (Ledger and Edwards 2011, pp. 315–316).

In all, I wrote twelve poems (one narrative yielded two poems). From there, I was able to group certain poems together and identify seven themes in the music therapists' narratives (going solo, looking for a home, building relationships, accepting the challenge, insecurity, investment, and development takes time). I included excerpts from the poems in the findings section of my thesis to aid in describing the themes and the full poems were included in the appendix. The following poem is one which expressed the insecurity experienced by new music therapists.

Where do I stand?
I'm like a girl who feels neglected
Giving much without return
Longing only to be noticed
For security I yearn

Tell me that you rate me
Tell me why you keep me here
Tell me what it is you value
How can I keep in the clear?

You broke another promise
Built me up then cut me down
I gave you my submission
But no funding this time 'round

Should I stay or should I go?
Can't go on fighting any more
I think I could do better and
I'm tired of this war. (Ledger 2010, pp. 297–298)

Analysing narratives through poetry served my needs to anonymise the narrative data, to treat the narratives carefully, and to include my own experiences in the analytic process. The poems were also highly effective in communicating the music therapists' emotions, such as "isolation, insecurity, and uncertainty in their development work" (Ledger and Edwards 2011, p. 316). However, there were further benefits of the poems in terms of communicating the research findings. During the course of my PhD studies, I included a number of poems in a newsletter update to research participants and other interested colleagues. Although I perceived a danger that the poems would not be well-received, several music therapists emailed to comment on how powerful the poems were and how the poems reminded them of their own experiences. Some music therapists contributed further reflections on their service development experiences, which provided useful additional data. The poems were also valuable when presenting research findings in teaching and at academic conferences. Not only were the poems engaging and evocative, but they were also effective in getting a story across in a few words and in a short space of time. For further detail about the benefits and challenges of my arts-based approach, see Ledger and Edwards (2011) and Ledger and McCaffrey (2015).

Jeanette's Story: The Use of Narrative Summaries When Researching One's Own Profession

My PhD used a four-phased mixed methods design (sequential explanatory) to explore the views, experiences and practices regarding professional supervision for Australian-based music therapists. I felt the topic of professional supervision was generally under-researched in music therapy and, particularly for my own profession in Australia, there was little evidence to support its use. I selected a design which could explore views, experiences and practice, and while priority was given to the qualitative data collection and analysis, the sequencing of quantitative and qualitative data and the selection of methods and tools impacted on the creation of the final narratives.

My narratives investigated therapists' experiences of professional supervision and the themes that characterize their experiences; the influence of the supervisor's professional background on these experiences; the outcomes of supervision described in their experiences and the role of the employer, the Australian Music Therapy Association and the tertiary sector, in particular Australian Universities, in relation to supervision. Seven music therapists who ranged from 2 to over 20 years' experience within the music therapy profession provided interview data for analysis. Some participants completed drawings during the interview and these were digitally photographed and included in the data analysis. Through a lengthy period of reflexive thinking and planning which was primarily guided by the methodological requirements of my mixed methods design and the issue of identification, I used four stages of narrative analysis to produce the final narrative summaries.

From the moment I prepared my application to enroll as a PhD student through to the submission of my final thesis for examination, I was deeply aware of the ways I engaged with music therapists and my past interactions with music therapy students. Many of these experiences involved the use of professional supervision, either through providing this service to others or receiving it myself. Over the past 21 years, I have supervised music therapists and music therapy students and lectured and published on the topic of supervision. I have held committee positions within our professional association and today, continue to engage in national representation in support of professional supervision practice. During my study, I became acutely aware of my conduct in relation to practical and theoretical issues along the research continuum and this revealed another layer of my identity to the Australian music therapy profession. Each role and relationship had the potential to impact on my role as a researcher in this study and this was particularly evident in the analysis of data and presentation of the narrative findings. The academic supervision I received from two music therapists with whom I had prior and current relationships was also impacted by these multiple roles. I was a music therapist researching my own profession and at times researching colleagues with whom I had developed different types of relationships. All of these experiences profoundly influenced my thinking, behaviours, actions and my writing during the course of this study. At the heart of these multiple connections and relational layers was the topic of professional supervision and the search for an authentic and confidential way of presenting each participant's supervision story while maintaining the rigor of a mixed methods design.

To research one's own profession was an exciting and at the same time a daunting task. Expectations within the profession about researching professional supervision were also high and given the paucity of evidence in this area, (sometimes conflicting) recommendations, guidance and opinions relating to my study's research design were provided to me from many music therapy researchers in Australia. Researching a community which is small in size and known to the researcher requires an examination of ethical considerations and actions throughout every phase of the study (Damianakis and Woodford 2012) and this was particularly highlighted to me as I searched for methods to analyse the interview data and create the narratives. As these narratives formed one phase of my mixed methods design,

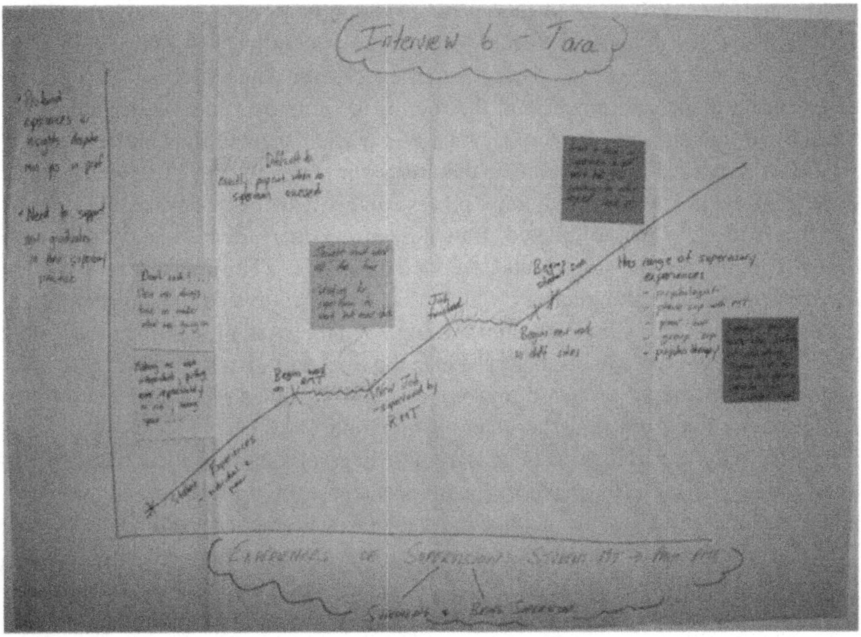

Fig. 4.2 Tara's life course graph

I needed to use methods of analysis which were rigorous and transferrable across the other phases of the study. This was particularly important in a) the final stage of narrative analysis when the seven narrative summaries were integrated in order to compare and contrast the themes within each supervision story, and b) the final integration of all quantitative and qualitative findings as phase 4 of my study. Combined with the issue of identification in the retelling of supervision stories within the small profession of music therapy in Australia, I was faced with the lengthy task of searching for ways to do this appropriately.

In stage one, I began by using life course graph analysis to create a visual representation of each music therapist's supervision journey. Informed by the analytical approach used by Lieblich et al. (1998) and more recently in music therapy research by Ledger (2010), the life course graph in my study presented the overall view of the supervision story. The narratives described the music therapists' experiences of student supervision and their transition to professional supervision. The use of the life course graph enabled a clearer understanding of the trajectory or chapters of these experiences, including the starts and stops of the supervision process, the use of different supervisors, and important moments of the experience. This outline allowed me to focus on the narrative as a whole, and more specifically, the form and direction taken by the content of the narrative and the development of the story over time (Elliot 2005; Lieblich et al. 1998). Figure 4.2 provides an example of one participant's life course graph.

Table 4.1 The "Images of Supervision Question" (Interview Question 3)

Chapter/phase of supervision journey	Narrative tone	Imagery	Themes
Professional supervision	None found	"Two separate people"	Separate but unified
		"A channel"	Characteristics of a good supervisor

In stage two, I used a method called narrative psychological analysis to examine the meaning systems and structures associated with human behaviour and experience (Polkinghorne 1988). Previous research has adopted this form of analysis in understanding significant events related to identity construction and the exploration of self in relation to these events (Crossley 2000b, 2003; Crossley and Crossley 2001; Davies 1997). I wanted to explore in more depth the meaning systems and structures around the supervision experiences and did this by examining three elements of the interviews: *tone*, *imagery* and *theme*. *Narrative tone* was defined as the content and form, or manner, in which the story is told (Crossley 2000a; McAdams 1993), for example an optimistic or pessimistic tone. Metaphors, images and symbols used by the therapists were analysed and any drawings created by respondents in relation to *imagery* or feelings associated with supervision were used to confirm the findings. Guided by the research questions and results of the life course graphs, I then inductively analysed the text and highlighted the *themes*.

The combined use of the life course graph and narrative psychological analysis provided for a wider breadth of perspective in relation to each supervision trajectory, including the different types and forms of phenomena which impacted this journey. Table 4.1 presents an example of this second stage of analysis, where narrative psychological findings were categorised according to the interview question and the chapters identified from each life course graph.

In stage three, I met the critical juncture of deciding how to create the supervision narrative. Mindful of maintaining the de-identified story for each therapist and the required rigor pertaining to mixed methods research, I searched for analytical methods which could achieve this. I came across two types of methods: component story framework (Nuttgens 1997) and narrative analysis (Polkinghorne 1995). I used both methods to synthesise the emerging findings into one cohesive narrative account for each therapist. Adopting this framework allowed for multiple stories to be told which were impacted by each other (Clark 2009; Nuttgens 1997). Component stories in my study were constructed using four steps of narrative analysis (Polkinghorne 1995):

1. Stage 2 findings were arranged chronologically
2. elements (tone, imagery and theme) that occurred at the same time were identified
3. the links of cause and influence within these elements were ascertained through a search for connections among the events to produce a descriptive account. The

goal of descriptive narrative research is to tell the current story, not create a new narrative (Polkinghorne 1988)
4. the story was written with minimal interpretation and to reinforce and highlight the experience of the interviewee (Nuttgens 1997). However, unlike the process used by Nuttgens, I wrote each component story as influenced by both the content revealed in each section of the interview and the ways in which their reflections were recalled. This process presents a multi-lensed view of the journeys recounted in the interviews which is supported by the constructivist stance I adopted throughout this study (Riessman 1993).

I was now faced with a first narrative which was rather lengthy (almost 7000 words) and the current structure (component story with particular sub-titles) presented potential opportunities for participant identification. Given there were six remaining stories to be analysed, created and integrated, together with the presentation of quantitative and qualitative findings from other phases of this study, word count quickly became an issue.

I decided to use a fourth stage of analysis in order to address not only the issue of word count but also reduce the opportunity for identification. In stage four, each set of component stories was analysed using Polkinghorne's (1995) analysis of narratives in order to provide a narrative summary. I deductively analysed each longer version of the narrative using terms from the study's research questions and restructured the narrative using different subheadings (rather than those used in the component stories) to provide a consistent and flowing narrative. Segments of the music therapist's responses were interspersed with supportive descriptions linking back to the study's research questions. This stage of analysis resulted in a shorter narrative, which maintained the study's methodological rigor and most importantly reduced the opportunity for identification. These sequential methods of narrative analysis and analysis of narratives (stages 1–4) also provided for an increased level of understanding and depth of phenomena rather than the use of one method alone (Simons et al. 2008). The following is an excerpt from one of the shorter narratives:

History of Supervision for Tara

Supervisors (MT and non MT) who presented a structured and flexible approach in their sessions provided optimal learning experiences for Tara **[impact of supervision on practice; issues and themes of the supervisory experience].**

> T: *I remember my favourite supervisor as a student and what made it stand out was that style. The supervision was what I liked or what I worked really well with and it made me perform. It was probably making me more independent like putting more responsibility on me, having space to do whatever it was I had to do as opposed to my previous supervisor who was very very structured. Not giving you the chance to just explore it. You need to be creative and do your thing but you get too scared to do that if someone has a set.*

A non-MT supervisor also provided new opportunities for learning and guidance during an independent placement. These included *'stuff that was non-musical'* – understanding the use of appropriate clinical language in a psychotherapeutic setting **[impact of supervision on practice; issues and themes of the supervisory experience; influence of supervisor's professional background]** (Kennelly 2013).

As I constructed the seventh and final narrative summary, I remember feeling exhausted but relieved. A solution had been found in relation to my analysis dilemma and one that had hopefully protected the narrative while meeting the demands for rigor. However to this day I still wonder what these narratives could have looked like if more creative analytical methods were adopted (similar to Alison's and Libby's) – ones that could have preserved the essence of each therapist's story which in my opinion became sometimes lost in these narrative summaries. Alas, this has given me something to ponder on further – the appropriateness of using narrative analysis within a mixed methods design and what the researcher may need to "give up" in creating the participant's story.

Discussion

On revisiting our stories, it was clear that critical junctures emerged throughout the entire narrative research process. Some junctures were common to all three studies, while others were more particular to the research topic, the nature of the relationship between researcher and participants, and the precise methods chosen. In this discussion, we tease out junctures which other researchers may experience and suggest strategies for progressing narrative research in considerate and careful ways.

Juncture 1: Enacting a Narrative Research Design

Critical junctures emerged right from the start of the research process, as evident in Alison and Libby's stories. For Alison, her preferred mode of data collection was not necessarily the preferred mode for her research participants and recruitment proved more challenging than she had anticipated. In response to this, Alison highlighted the importance in remaining flexible in relation to the mode through which narratives are collected and to allow participants to tell their stories in ways that are most comfortable and convenient to them. From an ethical point of view, Alison found it was also important to remain open about what participants should include in their narratives and how the final results would be presented. This approach had limitations in terms of providing assurances of confidentiality, but remaining open to possibilities during data collection and subsequent analysis allowed Alison to develop analytic methods that could convey music therapists' emotions honorably.

In Libby's story, a different set of considerations in relation to data collection was apparent. Any form of research that occurs with populations that are considered vulnerable requires considered and detailed planning by the researcher to ensure the safety of the participants. In the initial planning phase, Libby searched the bereavement literature for publications that looked at the specific ethical considerations when researching bereaved parents. This literature helped guide the early phases of the research process (recruitment and data collection) while providing Libby with assurances that the way she was approaching and working with the participants was in alignment with ethical research practice. During the actual interviews for data collection, Libby made the point that participants did become emotional, however, she felt able to ensure their emotional safety due to her experience as a therapist as well as her pre-existing relationship with the participants. Although this was Libby's experience, it must be acknowledged that each researcher approaches their work inhabiting different skill sets and relationships with their participants. For people researching vulnerable populations where this type of emotional tension and/or fluctuation is likely, it is each researcher's personal and ethical responsibility to ensure that they have the knowledge and skills to appropriately respond to any strong and/or negative emotions from participants. Researchers who are not comfortable in managing these situations should seek out appropriate supervision and training prior to commencing any form of data collection.

Juncture 2: Approaches to Analysis

We all experienced critical junctures during the analysis phase. Challenges arose when we attempted to reduce rich and detailed stories to a shorter text that could be shared readily, was faithful to participants' experiences and retained something of the depth of the original stories. In each case, trying out different modes of representation was helpful. Jeanette and Libby found visual representation helpful in identifying the heart of participants' stories and Alison found poetry writing helpful for identifying the powerful emotions that music therapists expressed. We therefore recommend that other researchers experiment with creative ways of sense-making, to help them in ordering, prioritizing, and reconstructing their narrative data.

Libby's study raised questions as to the extent to which participants should be included in the analytic process. As she was working with participants who are normally considered vulnerable, she felt it was important to allow them opportunities for member-checking. However, her experience suggested that reading detailed narrative transcripts could be demanding for participants, particularly when it meant revisiting stories that were emotionally difficult or even painful. Although each research project will encompass its own set of unique considerations when deciding whether to pursue member-checking, general considerations for researchers include: What is the potential time lapse between the interview and participants receiving either the transcript or narrative to member-check? Is it emotionally safe for participants to revisit the content of the interview? What purpose would member-checking serve in the research process?

Juncture 3: Concerns About Anonymisation

Keeping participants' identities anonymous was a particular concern of both Alison and Jeanette, who were undertaking narrative research about the experiences of close colleagues. As music therapy is a small profession, in which most members have a profile and niche area of practice, it was difficult to reproduce detailed stories without identifying research participants. However, it was important to keep participants' identities secret, due to the domain of study (music therapists' personal and professional development), the risk to reputations and ongoing relationships, and because of assurances made during the recruitment process. Neither Alison nor Jeanette felt able to present the participants' narratives in their original form and both needed to develop new ways of analysing the data and presenting the findings. This was not a simple task, and developing appropriate methods took trial and error and considerable time.

To address concerns about anonymisation, what was most helpful was repeatedly engaging with the initial ethics proposal and discussing decisions about analysis and presentation with others. Alison consulted her participants before settling on changes to the presentation of data (from composite stories to poems and disguising the gender of participants who could easily be identified). In her case, maintaining relationships with participants for the duration of data collection and analysis was essential and commensurate with her constructivist research design. Jeanette was expected to maintain a more distanced relationship with participants within her mixed method design and associated demands for rigor. As she moved from one stage of analysis to the next, close consultations took place with her supervisors and the issue of anonymity was a constant theme in these discussions.

Juncture 4: Reflexivity and the 'Self'

Critical junctures also arose in respect to the extent to which the self was included in analysis and representation. Each author had different orientations with regard to inclusion of themselves in the analytic process: Jeanette wished to produce narratives with minimal interpretation, Libby wanted to avoid a situation where her interpretations were too dominant, while Alison wanted to integrate her own story with the narratives she had received. Regardless of our orientation with regard to the self, we all learned the value of reflexivity for considering our roles in the research process. Helpful reflexive strategies included making reflexive notes, writing our own stories, talking with research supervisors, external supervisors, and undergoing psychotherapy. We suggest that researchers carefully consider the ways they wish to include or represent themselves in the creation of the narratives and be attentive to this throughout the research trajectory. It is important that this consideration is reviewed consistently during the course of the research as changes regarding the choice of analysis methods and the narrative's mode of representation may be impacted by the researcher's epistemological stance.

Juncture 5: Situating Narrative in a Mixed Methods Design

A concern unique to Jeanette's story was the integration of narrative data within a mixed methods approach. This meant that Jeanette met junctures in which she had to balance demands for rigor with her desire to communicate therapists' stories authentically. The priority or weighting given to the qualitative component of a mixed methods study can impact on the selection of analysis methods and representation of the stories (Ivankova et al. 2006). In this case, Jeanette prioritized the supervision experiences over the survey data and systematic review of the evidence, which meant that a fine balance needed to be achieved between rigor and authenticity. Using four stages of narrative analysis provided this rigor and facilitated for a smoother integration of all findings in the final phase of the study. These stages also allowed Jeanette to explore in depth the supervisory experiences, and particularly through the combined use of the life course graph and narrative psychological analysis, provided a creative means to shape and present the stories. We recommend that researchers who are considering the use of narrative methods within mixed methods studies carefully examine the placement of the narrative within the overall study, the priority or weighting given to this phase of the study and be guided by the literature and collaborative discussions with research supervisors, in order to find the most appropriate methods to satisfy both the demands of rigor and the integrity of the participant's story.

Conclusion

Our role as narrative researchers allowed us to take a step into the world of our participants, to sit alongside them and not just listen and record their experience but also become part of the storytelling. We used different methods of narrative analysis to shape and tell their stories and most importantly, our participants' stories helped shape and guide the selection of these methods and the decision processes around each one. The critical junctures we have presented highlight the ongoing negotiation required in narrative research. In documenting the difficult decisions we faced and the steps we took before resolving on an approach, we hope that we have helped other researchers in anticipating challenges and making their own decisions with regard to research methods. We encourage other narrative researchers to document their decision-making processes fully, to help others out there who are navigating tricky terrain. Based on our experiences, remaining flexible and reflexive throughout each stage of the research process is crucial to ensuring that participants' voices are represented with safety, respect, and authenticity.

Discussion Questions

1. Consider the critical junctures that the authors identify in this chapter. How might those same junctures be encountered in your own research? Are there others that you can predict?
2. Are there particular ethical considerations that are unique to your research context? How do you plan to address them? Are there steps you could take in your design that would help to avoid or alleviate problems later?

References

Aldridge, G. (2005). Therapeutic narrative analysis as a narrative case study approach. In D. Aldridge (Ed.), *Case study designs in music therapy* (pp. 31–52). London: Jessica Kingsley.

Clandinin, D. J. (2006). Narrative inquiry: A methodology for studying lived experience. *Research Studies in Music Education, 27*, 44–54. doi:10.1177/1321103X060270010301.

Clandinin, D. J. (2007). *Handbook of narrative inquiry: Mapping a methodology*. Thousand Oaks: Sage.

Clandinin, D. J., & Connelly, F. M. (2000). *Narrative inquiry: Experience and story within qualitative research*. San Francisco: Jossey-Bass.

Clandinin, D. J., Pushor, D., & Orr, A. M. (2007). Navigating sites for narrative inquiry. *Journal of Teacher Education, 58*(1), 21–35. doi:10.1177/0022487106296218.

Clark, J. (2009). Clinical supervision after suicide: Panacea or pretence? *Psychotherapy in Australia, 16*(1), 16–23. Retrieved from http://search.informit.com.au.ezproxy.library.uq.edu.au/fullText;dn=673700376615634;res=IELHEA

Crossley, M. (2000a). *Introducing narrative psychology—Self, trauma and the construction of meaning*. Philadelphia: Open University Press.

Crossley, M. (2000b). Narrative psychology, trauma and the study of self/identity. *Theory and Psychology, 10*(4), 527–546. doi:10.1177/0959354300104005.

Crossley, M. (2003). 'Let me explain': Narrative emplotment and one patient's experience of oral cancer. *Social Science and Medicine, 56*(3), 439–448. doi:10.1016/S0277-9536(01)00362-8.

Crossley, M., & Crossley, N. (2001). 'Patient' voices, social movements and the habitus; How psychiatric survivors 'speak out'. *Social Science and Medicine, 52*, 1477–1489. doi:10.1016/S0277-9536(00)00257-4.

Daiute, C. (2014). *Narrative inquiry: A dynamic approach*. Thousand Oaks: Sage.

Daly, K. (2007). *Qualitative methods for family studies and human development*. Thousand Oaks: Sage.

Damianakis, T., & Woodford, M. R. (2012). Qualitative research with small connected communities: Generating new knowledge while upholding research ethics. *Qualitative Health Research, 22*(5), 708–718. doi:10.1177/1049732311431444.

Davies, M. (1997). Shattered assumptions: Time and the experience of long-term HIV positivity. *Social Science and Medicine, 44*(5), 561–571. doi:10.1016/S0277-9536(96)00177-3.

Dickson-Swift, V., James, E. L., Kippen, S., & Liamputtong, P. (2007). Doing sensitive research: What challenges do qualitative researchers face? *Qualitative Research, 7*(3), 327–353. doi:10.1177/1468794107078515.

Dickson-Swift, V., James, E. L., Kippen, S., & Liamputtong, P. (2009). Researching sensitive topics: Qualitative research as emotion work. *Qualitative Research, 9*(1), 61–79. doi:10.1177/1468794108098031.

Elliott, J. (2005). *Using narrative in social research: Qualitative and quantitative approaches*. London: Sage.

Flynn, L. (2014). *The stories we haven't told: The lived experience of music used in therapy for bereaved parents*. Unpublished doctoral thesis, University of Queensland, Australia.

Forbat, L., & Henderson, J. (2005). Theoretical and practical reflections on sharing transcripts with participants. *Qualitative Health Research, 15*, 1114–1128. doi:10.1177/1049732305279065.

Holloway, I., & Wheeler, S. (2010). *Qualitative research in nursing and healthcare*. Chichester: Wiley-Blackwell.

Hynson, J. L., Aroni, R., Bauld, C., & Sawyer, S. M. (2006). Research with bereaved parents: A question of how not why. *Palliative Medicine, 20*, 805–811.

Ivankova, N., Creswell, J., & Stick, S. (2006). Using mixed-methods sequential explanatory design: From theory to practice. *Field Methods, 18*(1), 3–20. doi:10.1177/1525822X05282260.

Kennelly, J. (2013). *Sight, sounds and feelings: The views, experiences and practices regarding professional supervision for Australian-based music therapists*. Unpublished doctoral thesis, University of Queensland, Australia. Available at https://espace.library.uq.edu.au/view/UQ:319389

Koelsch, L. E. (2013). Reconceptualizing the member check interview. *International Journal of Qualitative Methods, 12*, 168–171.

Labov, W., & Waletzky, J. (1997). Narrative analysis: Oral versions of personal experience. *Journal of Narrative and Life History, 7*, 3–38. (Original work published 1967)

Ledger, A. J. (2010). *Am I a founder or am I a fraud? Music therapists' experiences of developing services in healthcare organizations*. Doctoral thesis, University of Limerick, Ireland. URI: https://ulir.ul.ie/handle/10344/1131

Ledger, A., & Edwards, J. (2011). Arts-based research practices in music therapy research: Existing and potential developments. *Arts in Psychotherapy, 38*(5), 312–317. doi:10.1016/j.aip.2011.09.001.

Ledger, A., & McCaffrey, T. (2015). Performative, arts-based, or arts-informed? Reflections on the development of arts-based research in music therapy. *Journal of Music Therapy, 52*(4), 441–456.

Lieblich, A., Tuval-Mashiach, R., & Zilber, T. (1998). *Narrative research–Reading, analysis and interpretation*. Thousand Oaks: Sage.

Lincoln, Y. S., Lynham, S. A., & Guba, E. G. (2011). Paradigmatic controversies, contradictions, and emerging confluences, revisited. In N. K. Denzin & Y. S. Lincoln (Eds.), *The Sage handbook of qualitative research* (pp. 97–128). Thousand Oaks: Sage.

McAdams, D. (1993). *The stories we live by—Personal myths and the making of the self*. New York: William Morrow & Co.

Nuttgens, S. (1997). *Bereavement following suicide: A narrative study*. Doctoral thesis, University of Alberta (UMI No. 304390339).

Polkinghorne, D. (1988). *Narrative knowing and the human sciences*. Albany: State University of New York Press.

Polkinghorne, D. E. (1995). Narrative configuration in qualitative analysis. *International Journal of Qualitative Studies in Education, 8*(1), 5–23.

Postmus, J. L. (2013). Qualitative interviewing. In A. E. Fortune, W. J. Reid, & R. L. Miller Jr. (Eds.), *Qualitative research in social work* (pp. 241–263). New York: Columbia University Press.

Riessman, C. (1993). *Narrative analysis*. Thousand Oaks: Sage.

Rosenblatt, P. C. (1995). Ethics of qualitative interviewing with grieving families. *Death Studies, 19*, 139–155.

Sands, R. G. (2013). Ethnography. In A. E. Fortune, W. J. Reid, & R. L. Miller Jr. (Eds.), *Qualitative research in social work* (pp. 136–167). New York: Columbia University Press.

Simons, L., Lathlean, J., & Squire, C. (2008). Shifting the focus: Sequential methods of analysis with qualitative data. *Qualitative Health Research, 18*(1), 120–132. doi:10.1177/1049732307310264.

Chapter 5
If You See What I Mean? Visual Narratives – Stories Told Through, With And By Visual Images

lisahunter

Abstract Visual field texts, visual methods, and representation of research using visual genres have had a long history and at times a close relationship with narrative research. Visual methods can contribute particular depth to what we can understand from a story and a teller: Visual diaries to tell personal stories; found images and participatory/researcher constructed images act as representations of narratives; photo elicitation can be used to stimulate stories; documentaries capture personal and cultural stories; and, storytelling may be captured visually as a representation and non-representation. Drawing on the work of scholars in visual traditions, including visual narrative and my own visual work, I will illustrate (in visual and textual modes) how the visual may be harnessed in three research spaces: during field text creation, as interim research texts or analysis, and as research texts for dissemination (Clandinin and Connelly 2000). I conclude with some of the issues and challenges for those wanting to employ visual narrative.

Keywords Visuality • Image • Visual narrative • Visual methodology

Introduction

> More and more people look back, using devices ranging from traditional cameras to camcorders and Webcams. At the same time, work and leisure are increasingly centred on visual media, from computers to Digital Video Disks. Human experience is now more visual and visualized than ever before from the satellite picture to medical images of the interior of the body. In the era of the visual screen, your viewpoint is crucial…In this swirl of imagery, seeing is much more than believing. It is not just a part of everyday life, it is everyday life. (Mirzoeff 1999. p. 1)

lisahunter (✉)
Freelance Academic, Independent Scholar, Hamilton, New Zealand
e-mail: lisahunteracademic@gmail.com

© Springer Science+Business Media Singapore 2017

R. Dwyer et al. (eds.), *Narrative Research in Practice*,
DOI 10.1007/978-981-10-1579-3_5

Visual field texts, visual methods, and representation of research using visual genres have had a long history and a close relationship with narrative research. They are a way for us to communicate and make meaning, if you see what I mean! Berger claims that 'seeing comes before words' (1972, p. 7) while Fyfe and Law argue 'depiction, picturing and seeing are ubiquitous features of the process by which most human beings come to know the world as it really *is* for them' (1988, p. 2), although there is much to be learned from those who live without sight. Visual methods can contribute particular depth to what we can understand from a story and a teller: visual diaries to tell or retell personal stories, visuals as representations of narratives, photo elicitation to stimulate stories, documentaries that capture personal and cultural stories, and visually captured storytelling. Drawing on my own research and the work of scholars who have contributed to research associated with visual narrative I will illustrate (in visual and textual modes) how the visual may be harnessed in conjunction with narrative. As a frame to guide this exploration, I use Clandinin and Connelly's three research moment texts: field texts, interim texts and research texts (2000).

In 2007 Rose suggested researchers take images seriously to consider their effects. Prosser argued that visual research is potentially one of the most important qualitative research methodologies in this century (2011, p. 494) and Pink, that it is powerful in bringing together theory, technology and method (2012, p. 3). Their own scholarship has been important in the development of visual research, a relatively new area of study when compared with study of language and written text. The scholarship of visual culture studies and images studies emerged in the middle of the last century with important theoretical work being done by scholars such as Pierre Bourdieu, Roland Barthes, Stuart Hall, Rosalind Krauss, and Jean-François Lyotard. What is often termed the 'visual turn', a shift in emphasis towards an increasing importance of the image and the visual, was stimulated by the increasing use of visual technologies and their use in shaping our world around the turn of this century. Reissman (2008) identifies this visual turn as being significant in stimulating the more recent interest in visual narratives.

What stories do we learn or tell through our visual world? What part does visuality play in narrative? And how does the visual sensory mode interact with the spoken or written word as or for narrative? Our seeing is already deeply predetermined in our ocularcentric (Jay 1993) world, vision being western society's historically dominant and dominating sense where "looking, seeing and knowing have become perilously intertwined" (Jenks 1995, p. 1–2) (see also Hamburger 1997; Shohat and Stam 1998, who argue that visual images were also central to other times and places). As noted by MacDougall (2006), we gain much of our knowledge "through vision and our other senses, and the way we direct our seeing is highly organized. To a large extent this is not a matter of choice but of our cultural and even our neural conditioning" (2006, p. 2). Perception, conception and perspective are obvious and important factors to consider when researching the visual and significant work has informed scholarship in this area (for example see the early ethnographic work of Bourdieu, 1977 also captured in Schultheis and Frisinghelli 2012; early visual sociology by Barthes 1983; Becker 1981; Goffman 1979; Sontag 1977).

Both the affordances of visual research and issues raised by visual research have informed research beyond the visual, to written text for example, by bringing attention to the particular onto-epistemological, theoretical and methodological aspects of visual research. Further, visual mediums often operate in conjunction with other sensory modes or forms of communication—such as in digital narratives or audio-visual narratives—and are therefore an element in a multidimensional text, more complex than monomodal communication. As such, we need to be aware of the complexities of affordances and therefore what is possible for scholars in bringing visual and narrative together. For instance, Ewert (2000) examines *Maus*, a graphic novel with a Holocaust narrative by American cartoonist Art Spiegelman. Ewart argues that few scholars have focused on the visual narrative "its graphic arrangement of narrative layers and frames, its pictorial treatment of narrative time, and its efforts towards formal unity, exemplified by uses of visual metaphor and metonymy." (p. 87). As communication forms such as these, representational and nonrepresentational, are taken more seriously, different ways of seeing and being in the world, and their social effects will become apparent.

The claim that narratives, whether drawing from oral, textual or visual sources, in the form of individual stories or cultural frames, are integral to human expression and communication is commonly understood. Visual forms range from ancient paintings and hieroglyphics (Australian Aboriginal cave paintings, Egyptian hieroglyphics), to more recent artefacts (eg Roman Olympic pottery, the Bayeux Tapestry) and modern day magazines, graphic novels, films, websites and other forms of social media (Cohn 2013; McCloud 1993). Visual narratives have been shown to act as powerful vehicles for the transmission of collective memory and events (Zelizer 1998). Like Harper (2002) and Harrison (2002), Hoecker (2014) demonstrates how visuals create the building blocks of narrative: characters, setting, and plot, helping viewers construct narratives about past events. In her work creating visual narratives in trauma recovery she concludes:

> while these visual projects are understood as "popularized" versions of the official reports, they are by no means dumbed-down editions. On the contrary, these visual narratives produce complex depictions of the conflicts—the causes, the main actors, and the consequences. These visual projects provide important spaces where the general public interacts with the commissions' work and they deserve to be analyzed in their own right. The construction of narrative is a critical element in trauma recovery, so these visual narratives should be studied as a tool to help truth commissions achieve their goal of "never again" allowing such violence to occur. (p. 278)

Her work suggests the power of the visual in creating field texts that in themselves act as meaning-making processes, at once 'data' and 'research output'.

Visual narratives, or stories told through, by or with images can take a variety of forms: single image still photos and sketches; a sequence of either; film; other forms of mixed textual representation (for example websites, graphic novels, search engine image searches, visual specific sites such as Pinterest, Instagram, billboards and graffiti), and arguably, imaginings that fuel any narrative. Harper argues "[i]mages allow us to make statements which cannot be made by words" and these "images enlarge our consciousness" (1998, p. 38). For instance, picture the beach,

Image 5.1 'Apartheid' (1988). Michael Leunig's portrayal of a beach scene (Permission granted by Michael Leunig)

the surf, and the stories that are told about this geosociopolitical space. Below (Image 5.1) is one cultural 'narrative' caught in a single image where the 'beautiful' on the left are differentiated visually to those on the right, the 'ugly'. The author is suggesting that such visibility and visuality creates an 'apartheid' in our society:

The saying 'a picture paints a thousand words' is well known; pictures from which we make meaning and tell stories, or that represent individual and societal narratives. Even single frame images such as the cartoon communicates a narrative, through a visual grammar and visual perspective, in this instance portraying power relationships of economic wealth and body type.

In today's highly visually-mediated world there is an increase in the proportion of visual to text-based information for scholars to draw upon in order to understand and potentially influence our world. If you are a Facebook user you will most likely be familiar with *LOL cats* and the use of such images to drive human activity. The proliferation of YouTube, as entertainment, as documentation, and as pedagogy, has replaced earlier visual forms of television, cinema and even books and teachers in schools. Pinterest, Instagram and Twitter all heavily employ visuals to partially or fully 'tell a story'—these and many more social media offering a burgeoning field for research.

Barthes (1977) recognized the visual as holding a narrative: "Narrative is present in myth, legend, fable, tale, novella, epic, history, tragedy, drama, comedy, mime, painting,[...] stained glass windows, cinema, comics, news item, conversation [..]" (p. 79). However, Sontag (2003) reminds us that the relationship between text and the visual is not straight forward in that each does separate and distinctive work and the work they do together is different again, for example, she considers photographs a distinctive medium when depicting others' pain: "[Harrowing photographs] are not much help if the task is to understand. Narratives can make us understand. Photographs do something else: they haunt us" (2003, p. 89). The New London Group (1996) encouraged education to seriously consider the complex relationship between narrative and the visual, arguing for a pedagogy of multiliteracies some time ago. Such insight has manifested in work by Jacobs (2007), among others, who has worked with graphic narratives as serious multimodal texts which are increasingly becoming a major genre in the digitally mediated world:

> I wish to move beyond seeing the reading of comics as a debased or simplified word-based literacy. Instead, I want to advance two ideas: (1) reading comics involves a complex, multimodal literacy; and (2) by using comics in our classrooms, we can help students develop as critical and engaged readers of multimodal texts (p.19).

Some scholars have adopted the graphic form using graphic guides to many social theories and theorists—see Icon Books 'Introducing' series for example (http://www.iconbooks.com/introducing2/) and the now quite popular animated explanations for theories or concepts (for example, https://www.ted.com/talks/ken_robinson_changing_education_paradigms). Various grammars of the visual have been developed (for example Eisner 1985; Kress and van Leeuwen 2006) and literacy curricula quite routinely consider visual meaning making, for example, observations that picturing subjects from below makes them look more powerful.

We are accustomed to noting in narrative research that narrative may be part of the research in a variety of ways, as field, interim or research texts. Likewise, as a narrative researcher you may be considering the visual in many ways: creating visual narratives; documenting field texts in visual forms, using visuals to eliciting narratives from participants; using visual analysis, or disseminating research as visual representations. Using Clandinin and Connelly's (2000) three research moments of field text, interim/research analysis text, and research text, I will illustrate and explain visual narrative, concluding with a sideways glance at some of the issues, and a look to the future as we imagine visuality, research and its impact. This cannot be a comprehensive review of all visual methods or analytics, but certainly enough to fuel your journey as both a narrative researcher and a visual researcher.

The Visual as Field Text or Evidence of Narrative

Visual texts, as found or constructed field text, can come in many forms and have different functions in relation to research; we might 'gather' found images from the field (pre-existing photographs, drawings and so on), we might create a visual record of the field (take photographs, make drawings for example) and/or we might have participants make visual texts as a way of storying (make video diaries, photographs, painting, collages for example). The edited volume *Video methods: Social science research in motion* (Bates 2015) specifically explores the many options in the use of video alone: video diaries, 'go-alongs', time-lapse video, multi-angle video recording, video ethnography and installation—as field texts. O'Bryan demonstrates using video to gather and facilitate analysis of data in the chapter following this. Here, I will explore research that has utilized various visual texts in the field text moment, not to present a comprehensive review, but rather an overview that alerts you as a narrative researcher to fruitful collaborations of narrative and visual research and to some of the challenges and pitfalls.

Ethnographers have long employed the visual to create a record of what they frame as important. Schultheis and Frisinghelli (2012) archived photographs that Bourdieu took during his early ethnographic work in Algeria in the 1950's. This largely unpublished photographic archive recently became a record of Bourdieu's sociological and political view, Bourdieu's student and colleague Schultheis noting "[a]s Pierre Bourdieu emphasized on many occasions in our conversations, he saw his photographs not only as testimonies, but as a form of political commitment: seeing in order to make something visible, understanding in order to make something understandable" (2012, p. 5). Having taken thousands of photographs in his early work, only hundreds now remaining, the photographs were for the first time made public as a book and an exhibition in 2012. Schultheis worked with Bourdieu as the original photographer and ethnographic informer to "'frame' the photographs in their chronological, geographical, and thematic contexts, for a biographical reconstruction of the crucial years in his life" (p.6). The photographs are themselves a pivotal visual narrative, Calhoun (2012) concluding that "the images command the book [are not] mere illustrations but occasions for further thought" (p. viii).

In a study of student transition to high-school (Hunter 2002), I had students draw their experience of health and physical education (HPE) classes and of concepts such as body and health. These drawings were part of the students' stories of their experiences as they transitioned from primary to secondary school (see for example Image 5.2). These drawings and stories, together with still photographs (Image 5.3) and videos of the students' classes were my primary field texts and facilitated multiple (re)viewing, that enhanced my extensive field notes.

As well, the photographs, drawings and videos were elicitation material that students (re)viewed as I interviewed them to hear their story of transition. This form of memory-elicitation was highly productive in communicating events and for gaining different student perspectives. Today, all these visual field texts still act as powerful stimulation to my own memory—remembering that they, like all field texts, only capture what I had framed in the moment.

Framing, or what gets to be captured in the image or left out of the image, is an onto-epistemological and methodological topic that has had much scholarly attention (for recent summaries see Bekkers and Moody 2014; Greenwood and Jenkins

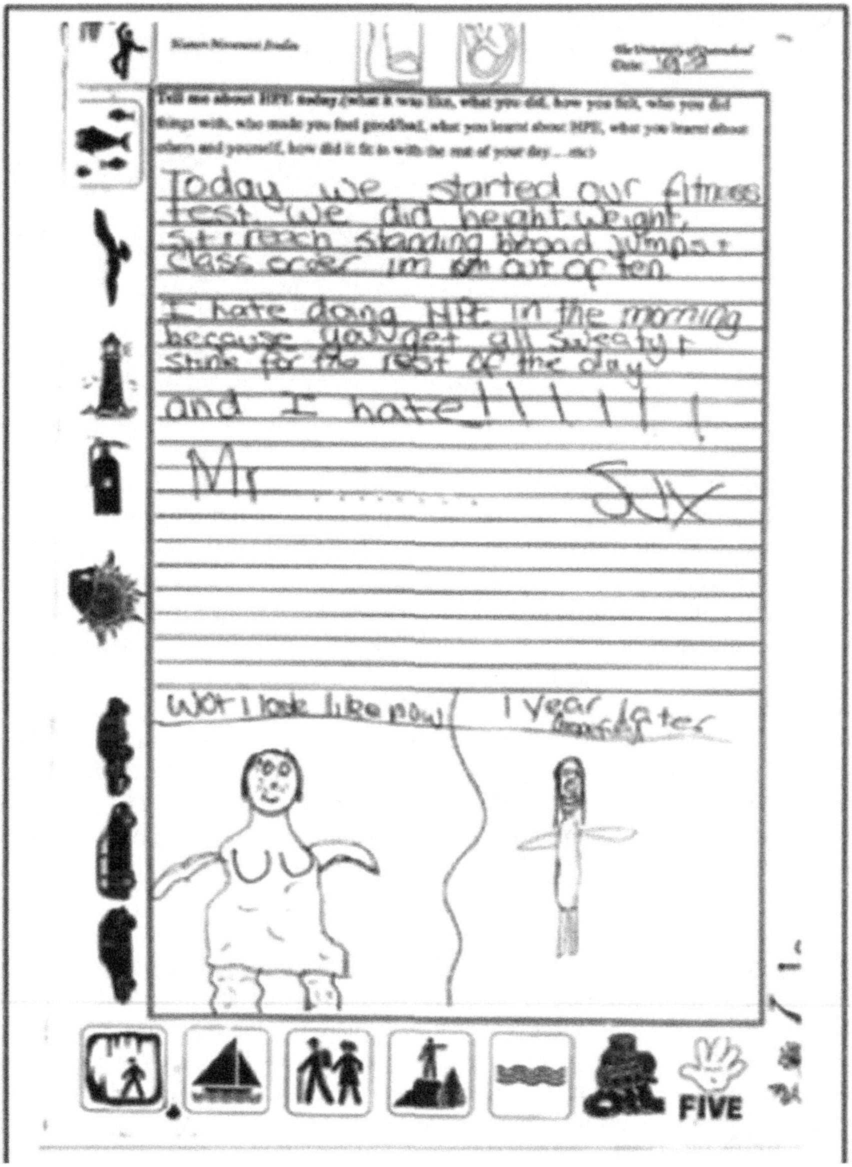

Image 5.2 Student drawing of HPE experiences

Image 5.3 Still photograph of height and weight measurement in HPE

2015; Kang and Lin 2015[1]). Just as we recognize that transcription is already analysis, we must be aware how our 'framing' is already filtered through our epistemological and ontological foundations—as notably demonstrated when Caine (2010) gave students cameras to photograph 'community' and one student produced photographs of the ghost that lived in his home, and who he considered 'community'. The student's onto-epistemology was evident in the ways he framed the photographs. A consideration of visual framing itself will give insight in how we understand what constitutes cultural narratives. For example, as fleshed out below, in my surfing research, I consider the ways that women as surfers have been firstly historically erased—i.e., left out of the frame altogether—as such left out of the cultural narrative of 'surfer'—and then later, if included, framed in objectified and sexualized ways (rather than competent surfer ways) including even appearing only as 'bits of women' (butts and breasts). This research used visuals already existing in the field as the texts of research.

The visual and narrative can also come together to enhance participatory methods of field text construction, for example in autoethnographies, or facilitate narrative therapy where participants as co-researchers create the images themselves. Everett (2015) asked students to create a visual narrative through Powerpoint, Prezi or Windows Movie Maker to facilitate telling the story of their experience in a well-being project. Drawing on narrative inquiry (Smith and Sparkes 2008) and the visual narratives that distance runners created, Busanich et al. (2016) explored the runners' embodied and disordered eating experiences with insights into their "processes of making meaning around the body, food and exercise while simultaneously illustrating a larger cultural picture of gender, power and resistance" (p. 98). Evers used film as a narration of his surfing experience (2015) and Azzarito (2012) ana-

[1] In 2014 the special issue *Framing Lives* (2014) employed visual life narratives (Chansky 2014), graphic memoirs (Refaie 2014), photo memoirs (Tamboukou 2014) and photographs in memoirs (Cantiello 2014) to "rigorously explore …'framing' [what is in and not in the picture] as it applies to presenting and displaying lives" (Arthur 2014, p. 2). What this issue makes clear is the key role of visual culture in creating and representing memories.

lyzed photographs with young females to capture how bodies were narrated and how they might change such narrations through their own photography. This move was a form of pedagogy in physical culture. Cashmore et al. (2010) used videos, video diaries and digital diaries to capture first-year university students' experiences while Carrington et al. (2007) used visual narrative techniques as a participatory method to enhance secondary students' contribution to the development of inclusive, socially just school environments. Such visual texts can be layered and enriched when an interview or exegesis that follows on the visual, and uses the visual as stimulus, acts as a cognitive mediation tool. In such instances, the image is at once dependent upon textual communication but also works beyond it. Interview or exegesis allows participants to communicate their interpretations of the visual text they created or viewed (eg Gillies et al. 2005; Luttrell 2003). These researchers all used a range of visual representations—photographs, pictures and/or text from magazines or newspapers, artwork, video, and/or any other tangible visual materials—both those in the environment and those constructed by participants—in creative ways.

Just as in our narrative research we understand that stories are not simple, unproblematic representations of realities, as researchers we must consider that images-as-texts, are produced (Riessman 2008). That is, they are products of human awareness and perception (Harrison 2002; Phoenix 2010), and as such not just an unproblematic documentation of an objective world. For example, in the context of the visual within the visual – photographs in comics, Pedri notes:

> Photography in comics does not fulfill a documentary function, corroborating the facts of the cartoon storyworld; it is not subordinated to the other verbal and visual elements that comprise the comics universe in which it is used. Instead, it joins those elements to advance the narrative and get the business of storytelling done. (2015: 2)

Visual narratives are prone to similar cognitive processes as written or oral texts. Walker (2005) reminds us that visuality refers to the socialization of vision as 'a network of cultural meanings generated from various discourses that shape the social practices of vision' (p.24). As narrative researchers and inquirers we are looking too to what visual texts can provide beyond what written or oral texts do or can. While visual texts are informed by media and other cultural texts, they are flexible, multimodal storytelling forms and 'produce(s) numerous codes to create meaning' (Postema 2013, p. xvi). The relationship between these codes is one that can enrich our narrative inquiry.

Construction of visual narratives has provided research participants with 'a new way to creatively express their embodiment', eliciting discussion and reflection:

> Creating the visual narratives allowed the participants of this study to express a deeper level of emotion and reflection on their embodied experiences as a male runner that they both enjoyed and appreciated. It also allowed us as researchers further insight into the narratives and resources that male athletes draw upon in the meaning-making process. (Busanich et al. 2016: 110)

Such active construction of the narrative that participants wish to tell has been used to aid participants in restorying their lives (McNutt 2013) or as a powerful pedagogical tool (Everett 2015). The relationship between the narrative and the visual in the evocative, therapeutic or remembering process is not fully understood, but it is one that Art Therapy explores, as do visual narrative inquirers.

In her autobiographical work and a project where schoolgirls photographed their curriculum, Bach used photographs as field texts (1999, 2001, 2007). As an early visual narrative inquirer she defined visual narrative inquiry as "an intentional, reflective, active human process in which researchers and participants explore and make meaning of experience both visually and narratively" (2007, p. 10). Storying around photographs, her own and her participants, she suggested that "[v]isual narrative inquiry allows another layer of meaning to narrative inquiry", continuing by noting that

> [o]ur experiences are always our own, but they are shaped by the social, cultural, and institutional narratives in which individuals are embedded' ... 'one of the ways in which individuals tell their stories is through the photographs that they take and through the photographs that others take of them. (2007, p. 282).

In some further examples you might pursue: Johnson (2004) worked with picture books and storying as critical reflection; Harrison (2002) drew on images in photo journals and video diaries, employing photo voice; Bell (1999) explored documentary film and still photographs; Radley (2004) used photo narratives; Walkerdine (1990) used video diaries; Frohmann (2005) employed photo elicitation; Rich et al. (2002) used Video Intervention Assessments; and, Jones used graphic narratives to teach critical literacy to (re) think orientalism (2015).

The Story of Surfing: An Example of Visual Field Texts Telling a Story

To provide a more fleshed example of the use of visual field texts, I draw on my recent work in surfing. In this example, I discuss the 'story of surfing' drawing on visual texts collected from the field (of surfing in Hawai'i) to consider the power of the visual narrative in maintaining dominant stories that become further legitimated as both history and present possibilities. My interest here is in the cultural story or meta-narrative of 'who can be a surfer'. I took up surfing in my early 40's and suddenly I wondered 'why now'—why not 30 years ago growing up on the beach, active in the surf and surf lifesaving and then as helicopter rescue crew—why did I not even *imagine* that surfing was available to me? My imaginary did not include surfing—why? Surfing is and has been heavily mediated through image. The field of surfing includes not just the surfers themselves, learning and visioning who they are as part of their identity, but also those who make this learning/visioning possible through constituting and legitimizing the social rules, beliefs, attitudes, relationships, participants, artefacts of history; this includes magazines, films, surf companies, festivals and competitions and all the associated epiphenomena of the surfing culture.

Image 5.4 Wallace Mackay's 'Maids on the Wave' "Kahele and I watched the surf-swimmers for some time, charmed with the spectacle." Engraving of surfers on the crest of a wave and swimmers within it. Used as the frontispiece of the book "Summer Cruising in the South Seas" by Charles Warren Stoddard, published in London by Chatto and Windus in 1874. Permission granted by copyright holder Bishop Museum Image ID SP_102955

Prior to photography and film, sketches and writing created a record of visibility for the past. Visual (re)presentations became pivotal in creating particular visions of surfing's past. An important record of this past is Wallace Mackay's 'Maids on the Wave' (Image 5.4) illustrating pre-colonial surfing in Hawai'i, and importantly featuring both females and males surfing. But when photography emerged as a common medium in the late 1800's-early 1900's, the images in circulation depicted Hawai'ian surfing's colonisation. Photographs were prominent in travel brochures and postcards and attracted Westerners initially to Hawai'i (Image 5.5) and then to other beach destinations around the world.

Postcards and the covers of magazines such as this provided a rich narrative of the identity of Honolulu as portrayed by the white patriocolonial males who produced the magazines, travel brochures and films (Brown 2006). Kānaka maoli wahine (native Hawai'an women) were absent from photographs from early 1900s onwards and haole women (white female Euro-American women) were presented as object of gaze, linked to fashion, and often represented as dependent upon males. These surfing images formed narratives of who could be imaged and imagined as a surfer, and also acting as a pedagogical device that teaches who is to be seen, recognized, acknowledged, and remembered. The story of the female at the surf as the beach-bound 'babe', passive and decorative (rather than athletic) and supporting the male surfer has held together the naturalized story of what is only a hundred-year-

Image 5.5 1938 Magazine cover of 'Paradise of the Pacific' 1938 (Permission granted by copyright holder Pacific Basin Communications)

old vision of surfing that all but erased the precolonial history and female participation. The babe is still a dominant trope in the visual representation of surfing. The subject position 'female surfer' became heavily bound to a particular 'look'—based on a particular version of 'beauty' that reified the nostalgia of the modern surfing myth, that is, as hegemonically active masculinity with absent or passive and subservient femininity… at least until very recently.

Turning to the visual record of the field of surfing to *see* the story it tells, demonstrates the erasure of active females from surfing history, politically positioning them as absent or at the margins of the field. This has further legitimized their marginalization and invisibility in the field and the waves, not so much in the oral narratives, but in the visual representations (sketches, photography, art, cartoons, film and now, the internet). These representations are artefacts that create the naturalized and orthodox meta-narrative of surfing. Now I understand why and how I was not able to imagine myself as 'surfer'—I literally could not *see* others like me, female, as surfer. As someone committed to movement and action, there was no role for me in that cultural narrative of surfing.

There has been movement at the edges of the story with voices of opposition starting as far back as the 'Gidget' story (Image 5.6) – the 1959 hit film, novel and film series that told the story of Kathy Kohner's early experiences of surfing (Comer 2010). Despite images and narratives that position females as surfers, the decorative beach babe, even AS surfer, is a resilient trope very evident in today's media (lisahunter in press a, b).

Image 5.6 The author's daughter, Katherine Kohner on the dust jacket of Frederick Kohner's novel "Gidget" (1957) that influenced the surfing imaginary (Photo by E. Lenart, permission granted by Katherine Kohner-Zuckerman)

In a very real way, images act as potent pedagogical devices—in this case of the patriocolonial frame, through which audiences learn to see and imagine participation in surfing. Whether heroic patriocolonial images of white male supremacy in modern surfing, or complimentary passive beach babes captured by white male photographers, alongside the visual erasure of female surfers in precolonial or postcolonial times, audiences have had limited opportunities to imagine and create a narrative of the female-surfer-athlete. Presently the legitimated image of female is still highly sexualised and, if athletic and competent, must often still be a 'babe'. This claim is littered through female surfer biographics and still today by a professional surfer, Silvana Lima,[2] who has been unable to secure sponsorship as she does not have the babe look—a claim legitimized by those who reap the benefits of heterofemininity.

With extensive internet and television images showing professional surfing (see for example the World Surf League—WSL the self proclaimed 'global home of surfing' http://www.worldsurfleague.com/), high-quality athletic performance is now highly visible. As female professional surfing has captured the eye of the public recently there is also more visibility as companies who stand to benefit from sales see new female markets for their wares. However, there is still a low of prevalence of non-dominant images in sport, the media or society of 'female-as-active participant'. Visual narratives of female surfers, even professionals, are still overwhelmingly made intelligible through fashion, sex, and appearance discourses. While new media and grassroots social media act as major disruptions to the narrow visioning of females in and by hegemonic mass media, we cannot forget that those who wish to maintain and/or re-establish narratives of white supremacy, heteronormative gender binaries, and cisgender hegemony as the vision of the past also populate and use new/social media. Using found and constructed images I have been able to show this narrative of absence, marginalization and sexualization—more of which I will discuss in the next two sections.

Visual Analysis and Interim Research Texts

While 'narrative' as verbal/text has a long history of analysis, the visual is more recent and less well established. As noted elsewhere in this book, the question of analysis sits firmly on onto-epistemological and methodological propositions. Rose (2012) is very clear about critical visual methodology underpinning her work. You may be using the visual in your field texts as a method, for example, in visual field notes/observations and photo elicitation, in which case you will be employing the narrative analytic that aligns with your onto-epistemological, theoretical, and methodological foundations, many of which are flagged in Chap. 1 of this volume. For example, plotting the 'landscape' in terms of the axes of sociality, temporality and place would be part of the analysis if drawing on a Clandinin and Connolly inspired narrative inquiry (2000). Or you may be unpacking Barkhuizen's (2008) model of three interconnected stories to frame your analysis (see Yucel and Iwashita, this volume) or drawing on Bamberg's small and big stories (2006, see Dwyer and emerald, this volume). In such cases you will bring all the usual imperatives of data interpretation (well documented in other parts of this volume) to bear on your visual record.

---

[2] See one opinion piece that includes the film made with Lima http://www.theinertia.com/surf/silvana-lima-says-she-wasnt-pretty-enough-to-sponsor/ as well as a response saying 'get over it' http://www.theinertia.com/surf/womens-surfing-doesnt-do-ugly-get-over-it/

Table 5.1 Count of images of females in magazines

Magazine	# images that include people	# images that include women
Australian Longboarding Issue 39, May/June 05	145	24 (16.6 %)
Australia's Surfing Life issue 200 May 2005	391	46 (5 %)
sg: surf, snow, skate, girl magazine April 2005	160	152 (95 %)

In this section I discuss some of the visual analytics that researchers have fruitfully employed and that can work alongside or within narrative research. As analytic methods are often complex and necessarily embedded in theory, here I can only alert you as a researcher to some of the possibilities, a thorough review of each being impossible in a single chapter.

My recent quantitative analysis of a Google Image search on the term 'surfer' in 2016 showed only two of the first one hundred images were of females and both in passive roles (lisahunter 2015a). This relatively straightforward quantitative and qualitative review is not unlike another study where we used a quantitative and qualitative analysis in image depiction of females in surf magazines (lisahunter and Austin 2006). Both tell a similar story firstly of female absence and then of objectification and sexualization—rather than athleticism or performance. In this study, the three publicly available surfing magazines at my local newsagent were analyzed for their image number and nature of representation of females (see Table 5.1).

A simple count of images revealed the low percentage of images of females in surfing magazines other than *sg* (Table 5.1) and a further qualitative analysis revealed that of the images of females a low percentage represented females as surfing participants—as compared to being in consumer or accessory roles, reflected as sexualized body parts or in model shots. This was the case even in the female participation focused magazine *sg*. Riessman (2008) notes that narrative researchers have mostly drawn upon both thematic and dialogic/performance analysis to interpret visual images alongside spoken and/or written text. The qualitative element of this analysis of images was akin to the thematic analysis—the 'themes' themselves arising from the field and shedding light on the story of surfing.

The analysis of visual texts must be just as diligent and rigorous as the interpretation of written or spoken texts. From other visual fields of research several visual grammars have been developed which themselves can be operationalised as an analytic tools, for example see Eisner's (1985) work on comics and sequential art, McCloud (1993) on comics, Kress and van Leeuwen (2006) on the grammar of visual design, and the more recent work of Cohn (2013) on narrative structure. Each of these reflect the growth and depth of analysis that has developed in a relatively short period of time. See also the developments by Reissman (2008) offering a fourth analytical level, that of visual narrative inquiry (see Chap. 6 in particular).

Using photographic research texts Bach (2007) considers 'reading' photographs to create a photographic research text that is a 'the visual narrative composite' (294). The forwards and back process between looking at the photographs, and perhaps between photographs and texts is one that many researchers use as a form of analysis. I have used this method to create possible narratives and counter-narratives of student positioning in HPE classes (lisahunter 2012), school transition (Hunter 2004), and the positioning of females in surfing events (lisahunter 2013). One of the criticisms of this form of analysis is that is too loose and allows for multiple interpretations. Multiple readings become possible because the constructor of the image may be associated with particular spaces and times that are different to the audience. Riessman cautions "Images may be composed to accomplish specific aims, but audiences can read the images differently than an artist intended" (2008, p. 102). Yet this caution applies to all forms of research including word-based research. It also offers spaces for new readings and counter-narratives. In her book *Visual Methodologies* Rose (2012) notes that "[i]nterpreting images is just that, interpretation"(xviii) not claiming they contain any one truth but requiring of the researcher an explicit methodology that positions onto-epistemological and theoretical perspectives from which one does that interpretation. In a comprehensive set of chapters Rose unpacks methodologies of compositional interpretation, content analysis, semiology, psychoanalysis, discourse analysis, ethnographic analyses and audience studies, all of which have their application with narrative.

The ordering of people and events in space and time has often been a characteristic of narrative research (for example, Bamberg 2006; Clandinin and Connelly 2000). In visual research, Cohn (2013) describes of a theory of narrative structure based on the ways that sequenced images create meaning. He proposes five basic elements of visual narrative grammar that create narrative arcs, that is, ordering of people and events in space and time: Establisher; Initial (tension or conflict); Prolongation; Peak; Release. He suggests "experimentation on structure and processing of sequential images can emulate paradigms for studying sentences." (p. 33). Images are another text to investigate, just as are words. An issue of the journal *Image & Narrative* (2015, volume 16 number 2), provides some interesting examples of the potential and dilemmas of visuality with narrative: the place of color photography in self-outing (Amihay 2015); authenticity in graphic memoirs (Ernst 2015), and photography in comics (Pedri 2015).

Images, found or constructed, can be representational or nonrepresentational, and they have potential for multiple forms of analysis depending on the research question and whether the purpose is to explore interpretation and meaning exchange, or the perceptual, experiential and sensory aspects of the image. The potential for analytical possibilities where narrative and the visual come together is extensive and as yet still relatively unexplored albeit drawing from a rich analytical history of visual analysis and narrative analysis.

Research Texts: Representation and Dissemination

As discussed throughout this book (see Dwyer and emerald, this volume) there are many pathways through a narrative inquiry—with 'narrative' itself featuring at any or all the research moments. Likewise, visual elements of the narrative inquiry may be apparent at many or any of the moments. Just as the proliferation and centralization of the visual within many societies led to new research methodologies and theories to understand visual and visual narratives, and new ways to analyze texts, there is also a growing sophistication in the dissemination of research through visual and multimodal texts. We have much to learn from the visual cultures that have to date been so successful in representation and in challenging ontological and epistemological perspectives. As I write, for instance, the narrative of a history of a shoe company is being constructed using the visual (see http://vans_hk.hk-dev.cmgrp.com/vans50anniversary/). The website surfersvillage.com describes the project thus:

> In a never before seen combination of techniques, The Story of Vans uses forced perspective drawings, traditional cell animation, paper cut outs and photos of Vans footwear, all stop motion animated in an intricately choreographed celebration of the brand. (http://www.surfersvillage.com/content/vans-introduces-its-campaign-honor-its-50th-anniversary/?utm_source=link-title&utm_medium=news-alert&utm_content=vans-introduces-its-campaign-honor-its-50th-anniversary&utm_campaign=20160317 accessed March 26, 2016).

As part of the website where the film is housed 'you' can share 'your own story', adding buy-in to interest in the brand, one of many techniques the academic world might consider employing (with cautions).

This 'story of the shoe' is at once a dissemination text for the company, and an informative field text. It can serve an inspiration to scholars to consider complementary and supplementary (to the written word) techniques to connect findings to different audiences, within and outside the academy, and in engaging ways. There is an increasing willingness and exploration in the use of multimodal research texts in scholarship, including creative PhDs, short audiovisual explanations of a paper by the author on journal sites, documentary films, graphic narratives, artistic installations, photographic essays, ethnographic dramas and a range of other 'outputs', at times called 'creative outputs', that extend or challenge the dominant textual modes. The use of the visual to tell the research story, as with the previous two research moments, meets resistance and challenges while also inviting new knowledges and ways of knowing. In a recent special issue of *Teaching And Teacher Education* designed to encourage epistemological shifts, embrace new ways of researching, be more inclusive of non-written text epistemologies and explore the boundaries of digital texts (lisahunter et al. 2014) several unforeseen challenges arose including complex ill-defined publisher permissions, difficulties with technology platforms, author ethics, technologies of reviewers, and even what constituted scholarship—all these issues took on a distinctive flavor in the digital and visual platform.

This section illustrates several studies that have, like the special issue, employed the visual to narrate research, blurring lines between what is often politically siloed as academic, artistic, and/or scientific. Through such media as film, installations, painting and photographic essay the visual is important in engaging senses beyond written text, as either the primary sense or as a synesthesia, designed to deliberately interrupt rational thought.

Film/Moving Image

As established earlier, the image was highly influential in the development of surfing over the last hundred years; in the commodification of the physical culture, and the constitution of a certain history of surfing. A great deal of my early surfing festival ethnographic research involved still photography and video and I noticed that photographers, surfing and media, would drop their cameras and take a break when the female competition heats began, but quickly lifting them again for a 'sexy babe' bikini shot on the beach—and when the males started surfing again. The photographers were mostly male, the industry was mostly male-focused, legitimizing one sex as skillful athlete and a naturalized second sex as something for heterosexual males to look at. In my ongoing and open ethnography of the past and contemporary practices of surfing (see for example lisahunter 2006, 2013, 2014a, b, 2015a, b, in press a, in press b; lisahunter and Austin 2006), I have become increasingly concerned about the narratives of symbolic and physical violence and what was being absented from surfing narratives in terms of who surfed, who could imagine surfing, and what surfing was about. Looking critically literally meant looking. So, to attempt to play in the media and tell a different story, I continued to photograph female surfers as active, athletic, in the pleasures of the surf as well as the difficult moments and what constituted 'field texts', also became an output, an action and a set of visual artefacts, fully visual, that required few words and looked nothing like a journal article in a scholarly text. Was it research dissemination? That is still up for debate! But if we look to the dissemination power of the audiovisual in the proliferation of YouTube and Vimeo among others, we might notice a relatively large research blind-spot. A recent film *Out in the Lineup* (2015) (Image 5.7) has perhaps done more to get the message of homophobia in surfing into the public eye than much of the sport-related scholarship.

So as a second response to the narrative of female participation that was unfolding in my research I constructed a short video from interviews with the first World Championship winner in 1964, Phyllis O'Donnell, interviews with museum curators and surfing field participants, and document collection from newspapers. It became apparent that although Phyl was announced World Champion *before* the male competitor for the male division was announced, Phyl was often erased from the records of 'First World Champion'. This was despite

Image 5.7 Out in the Lineup. Uncovering the taboo of homosexuality in surfing (2015) (Permissions by Producer Thomas Castets and participant Krista Coppedge)

literally being the first person to hold the title 'World Champion'. Some of this story, became the basis for my first foray into film-making: 'Who is Phyllis?' https://drive.google.com/file/d/0B33IBenn6xcBcUVqRk9hV0hVTWM/view?usp=sharing

The time it took to learn the skills, create this video, deal with maintaining links, and ensure all permissions were sought and received was considerable: an often reported disadvantage in employing the visual. Its impact was immediate to viewers at the conference and those who have since viewed it. By the end of the approximately ten-minute viewing, audiences 'got it'. While some film scholars and image critics are quick to question the filmic quality of entry level products such as this, I persevere with such techniques and make a point to teach visual literacy and video production in my undergraduate classes as this will not only strengthen our understandings/skills in the academic silo, but also trouble that silo and enrich it through the artistry and science of visual narrative. Now my sights are on a documentary of early and still living female pioneer surfers in a small island in the Pacific. Watch this space!

Installations

As my interest is not just on the visual aspects of narrative and ethnography but also the multimodal, sensorial and embodied experiences of human movement and physical culture, I have also explored my digital 'self' in the mundane everyday situation of doing academic work. In particular, one project focused on 'digital smarts': a group of colleagues met regularly to develop their own perspective of 'digital smarts' for a collaborative open access digital book (lisahunter 2015c). The common narrative at development meetings around this concept was noticeably positive. While I readily engaged with the digital world in teaching and research, I was also noticing a range of challenges: resistances by colleagues to employ elearning and digital pedagogies; structural difficulties in setting up course sites for students via the Learning Management System; personnel difficulties for mentoring staff taking on new approaches; software and hardware technological difficulties with simple tasks in programs leading to ongoing computer issues; difficulties in timetabling and incentive for professional development in elearning; financial barriers to accessing the technology needed to facilitate projects, and more. To explore these challenges, I revisited the digitally related 'smarting' or negative components of my academic work from my autoethnographic journal. Many of the field texts were screenshots or photos where words could not express my feelings at the time. But just writing about what I called 'digital bytes' (see open access version at http://www.waikato.ac.nz/wmier/publications/books/digital-smarts-enhancing-learning-and-teaching) was limiting my audience and was limited by my ability to evoke emotion through words. As the Contemporary Ethnography Conference Across the Disciplines (CEAD) encouraged creativity and experimentation in scholarship, I recreated the affect and emotion that I was trying to communicate in the digital chapter in an installation. Here is one delegate's response to the installation:

> I entered the dark, confined space warily, closing the door cut out all light and as claustrophobia set in I sat before the laptop on the desk and followed the instruction to hit the 'start' button. An earie (sic) voice began to sing a pretty song but it slowly gathered in pitch and speed and built to madness. Lights and sounds and the 'spinning wheel of death' circled around me, over the walls and the ceiling. As the sounds and lights built, my tension and anxiety built, becoming more claustrophobic and frustrated. I completely resonate with the distress, helplessness, anger, tension, anxiety of the installation – it so reflects my constant struggles with technology. The 'smashing' of the computer at the end was cathartic – and I hope I don't hurl my own computer out the window next time it crashes on me ... it would be so tempting... and sooo satisfying (anonymous audience response)

This multimodal installation represented one aspect of academic work and what it means for some people—being pro elearning in universities requires investment by one's embodied self and can be work that feels unsupported, blocked, frustrating, and dehumanizing with implications for individual and the profession's health, well-being and worker capacity. Do not get me wrong, there are many positive affordances and I have felt them too, but plenty of these had already been captured and promoted through the university research that supported implementation of elearning and digital pedagogies.

Some conference delegates loved the installation, resonating with their own visceral experiences; some did not understand how this was scholarship or what the point was; some disliked how it elicited senses and the unpleasantness of their work; and others said it made them think differently about doing and presenting their academic work. Even visually representing the experience in 'text' form creatively (see lisahunter 2016 where space, font, color, images, and text interact on the page to 'tell the story') will tell a different story to different people. Nevertheless, employment of visual techniques to tell the stories of research, beyond the written research text, stories like *Digital $%#@ smarts a lot*! are ones that are becoming more accessible to us all. This prompts discussions of complexity, embodiment, multidimensionality, multisensorial experiences, and our interaction with the digital, which includes the visual, in living and researching our lives.

Issues and Challenges in Visual Research

The usual imperatives of 'good' research practice and evaluating research outcomes apply to visual narrative research. There are however some concerns particular to the visual, or exacerbated by the visual. These include: ethical concerns and tensions including anonymity, ownership, permission to use images from public spaces, copyright consent and permissions to reproduce images; construction, storage and reproduction costs; editing time; publisher restrictions on number of images, costs of color; and release sites. I now discuss some of these.

While some suggest the construction of visual narratives are fraught with researcher bias—and particularly so in contemporary times where the production of high volumes of visual material is by neophytes—there is much to be said about the economics and accessibility of naive authorship. The ethical concerns of textual narrative research pertain also to visual—however there are important issues associated particularly with the ethics of visuality.[3] As Bach notes "How can I respond to ignorant, romantic, and even naïve or moralistic commentaries about these photographs? How can there be conversation around the silence? The illegal? The private? What becomes public?" (2007, p. 296). Drawing on Sontag's (1977) ethics of seeing, Bach notes that images modify and enhance our view of what we have a 'right' to observe and what is significant to look at. This inspires her to be sensitive to othering and careful on negotiating research relations.

This negotiated research relationship differs somewhat from the more public space of streets, beach, and festivals for example, raising the question of the ethical implications of using imagery without the explicit knowledge and agreement of the people involved. At several surf events, after getting organizer consent, I posted A3 sized laminated notices explaining the research project and including my contact details should anyone wish to discuss issues associated with the ethics of filming and photographing the site. To date I have only had one discussion—related to my camera mounted in a tree near the male toilets, albeit pointing the other way. The police were called and announcements made along the beach for the owner of the camera to contact officials immediately. The festival organisers had forgotten about my project—we all laughed in the end!

In my own work the ethics of which images may be shown and not shown in research dissemination has frequently arisen. One of my first encounters with the 'dangers' of photographs and videoing was that I documented a 'reality' that could otherwise be dismissed as hearsay if not for the photographic evidence. My photograph captured a media cameraman filming a woman at the beach; a woman who was clearly indicating that she did not want to be filmed (Image 5.8) (lisahunter 2015b).

The question of whether to 'show' this sensational illustration of female sexualisation at a surfing event, created a tension for me: between witnessing the symbolic violence enacted and calling the media to account and the violence of revealing the perpetrator. As part of the narrative of female participation in surfing, this was an illustration that identified the cameraman and the complicit female reporter standing behind him. While they had not agreed to participate in my research, neither had the woman on the beach agreed to participate in their media. The use of this image is an ethical dilemma that has been discussed at conferences and in research classes.

[3] For a good summary see Wiles, R., Prosser, J., Bagnoli, A., Clark, A., Davies, K., Hollands, S., & Renold, E. (2008). *Visual ethics: Ethical issues in visual research* and Waycott, J., Guillemin, M., Warr, D., Cox, S., Drew, S. E., & Howell, C. (2015). Re/formulating ethical issues for visual research methods. *Visual Methodologies: A Postdisciplinary Journal*, *3*(2). doi: http://dx.doi.org/10.7331/vm.v3i2.64

Image 5.8 Female beach goer insists cameraman does not film her—the vision going global via live internet feed and including on the two-story screen at the physical beach location

A second example to illustrate some of the issues associated with visual narratives is that of copyright and permission to reproduce visual evidence. In this fast changing context, questions of permission to reproduce are not always clear. For example, although I had secured permission from Google Image to reproduce an image in a recent chapter, the publisher's criteria for gaining permission differed to the producer of the image—after much to-ing and fro-ing between myself and the publisher, many images had to be removed from the chapter. The images were screen shots from a public forum on the internet, but they did include individuals and potentially put them in a poor light, hence the publishers disallowed the use of the image. So too were commonly available and easily accessible website images of female surfers taking on the 'babe' or 'sexy' image for sponsorship disallowed. So while these images were public and freely available, presumably the publishers concern about litigation or copyright were at the heart of their concern.

Visioning the Future: Some Closing Thoughts

Sztompka (2015) identifies the growing importance of the visual domain; we live in a society of icons, spectacle, display, design, surveillance, and gazing. As I pen these last passages, wishing I had the skills or money and time to create this chapter as a graphic non-fiction, I find myself reflecting on this list. I pause to check my emails for the new day. The screen is framed by stunning visual naturescapes that I meditate on every time I open my emails in order to maintain a positive mental state for my academic work. The now very familiar email title "Billions of views are generated every day on YouTube: make your research part of this" sitting at the top of the list (email from Cogent Education, 18 March, 2016). I would show you the email screen shot with visuals but have run out of the energy to collect the permissions! But I am sure you are familiar with such prompts. Statements such as "Articles with a video attached are ten times more likely to be downloaded than those without" and "Watch the video abstract in which author Timothy Lynch presents his article …"; "Make your work stand out from the crowd"; "Watch this short video and find out how…"; "Having a video alongside your article means readers can find your research more easily and grasp the concept of your work quickly, compelling them to find out more"; or "researchers outside your field, including the general public, are more likely to come across your research…" (email from Cogent Education, 18 March, 2016).

The visual along with the story it conveys or captures, is no doubt increasing in importance as it becomes more (re)producible and communication forms more prevalent. This is changing the way we communicate and narrate our lives. As Jones (2015) notes:

> As technological advances change the way we communicate and view the world through apps and mobile devices, the centrality of the image/text creates a dire need for visual literacy. Reading the world is no longer limited to reading the word: students need to be able to read images as they read text to decode for meaning, intention and effect. Educational policy is moving away from teaching about the visual as arts budgets are cut and focus continues to be on the standardized assessment of reading and math skills. In this globalized world, students need greater instruction in critical textual, media, and visual literacy that engages with representations of difference in race, ethnicity, gender, sexuality, class, and location. (p.199)

Visual literacy, like many 'literacies' captured in the New London Group's call for pedagogies of multiliteracies, are the world we live in and of great importance in making meaning and making sense of this highly mediated world. As Horstkotte and Pedri note, photography "had a significant impact not only on the way reality is perceived, but also on how it is narrated" (2008, p. 9), so too do other visual forms (and other senses) shift how we make sense of our world.

As new subfields emerge, such as the comingling of photography and cartooning in comics (Pedri 2015), visual narrative practices come to play a much bigger role in actually storying our worlds rather than just documenting or accompanying written text (as picture book producers and readers have long known). The flexibility of these narrative forms offers greater possibilities for each of the three research moments, but therefore also requires researchers to develop new skills or new partnerships, to harness the power of visual narrative. For example, as a "more-than-textual", "multi-sensorial" medium (Bates 2015, p. 11), video as methodology is still emerging. It acts as a sensory method that also exceeds the visual realm, exploring sound, movement and evoking emotional responses, warranting development with and beyond visual narrative.

As we step more into the virtual worlds that employ visual and other sensorial modes, I think there is an exciting future for the researching relationship between the visual and narrative at each of the three research moments, and in between and

Image 5.9 Seeing her: keeping abreast of female surfer subject positions…athletic performer, beach babe, or/and…

beyond. Jungnickel's concept of "making there" and "feeling there" (2015, p. 139) is instructive for research dissemination and a caution for claims of 'out there' data or field texts. She reinforces the point that the ethnographer makes knowledge rather than just observes and documents. The epistemological shift of "video methods [being] less useful for 'capturing' reality than they are for evoking distinct, multiple, competing and often contradictory aural and visual impressions" is reinforced by Vannini (2015). Like graphic narratives, video no longer has a "reproductive" role, but also a "poetic" one (Vannini 2015, p. 231) and an opportunity to communicate research to previously inaccessible audiences (for example, the TED talk TED.com). As well, new ethical and methodological challenges arise. Such methodologies also harken to participatory methods, blurring the role of researcher and producer with participant and consumer.

The increasing proliferation of research employing visual narrative, and guides for doing visual research more generally,[4] indicates there a rich and exciting future ahead for research bringing together narrative and the visual. While I continue to ponder what is worth looking at as my research, I know there is a place for keeping abreast of the misogynist culture of surfing to question the image production of what constitutes surfer and who gets to imagine surfing, but perhaps I need to grapple with other visual repertoires to make the points, if you see what I mean (Image 5.9).

All I need is a graphic artist to pair up with. What about you?

[4] Such as Bank's visual methods in social research, 2001; Bates' *Video methods: Social science research in motion*, 2015; Harpers *Visual sociology*, 2012; Rose's *Visual methodologies*, 2012; and Pink's *Advances in visual methodologies*, 2012.

Discussion Questions

1. Consider your research question or topic. Map how visual elements could complement your field texts (or data). Consider analysis of those texts.
2. How might you use visual texts to disseminate your research both to a scholarly audience and beyond the scholarly audience. Be sure to consider the ethical concerns and how you might navigate them.

References

(2015). Special issue: The narrative function of photography in comics. *Image [&] Narrative*, 16(2), 1–145.

Amihay, O. (2015). Red diapers, pink stories. Color photography and self-outing in Jewish women's comics. *Image [&] Narrative, 16*(2), 42–64.

Arthur, P. (2014). Out of frame. *a/b: Auto/Biography Studies, 29*(1), 1–9.

Azzarito, L. (2012). Photography as a pedagogical tool for shedding light on 'bodies-at-risk' in physical culture. *Visual Studies, 27*(3), 295–309.

Bach, H. (1999, April). Breast wishes: A visual narrative. Poster/paper presented at the annual meeting of the American Educational Research Association, Montreal, Quebec, Canada.

Bach, H. (2007). Composing a visual narrative inquiry. In D. J. Clandinin (Ed.), *Handbook of narrative inquiry: Mapping a methodology* (pp. 280–307). Thousand Oaks: Sage.

Bamburg, M. (2006). Stories: Big or small: Why do we care? *Narrative Inquiry, 16*(1), 139–147.

Barkhuizen, G. (2008). A narrative approach to exploring context in language teaching. *ELT Journal, 62*(3), 231–239. doi:10.1093/elt/ccm043.

Barthes, R. (1977). *Image-music-text*. (ed. and trans. S. Heath). London: Fontana.

Barthes, R. (1983). The photographic message. In *Selected writings*. New York: Fontana.

Bates, C. (Ed.). (2015). *Video methods: Social science research in motion*. London: Routledge.

Becker, H. (Ed.). (1981). *Exploring society photographically*. Evanston: Northwestern University Press.

Bekkers, V., & Moody, R. (2014). Accountability and the framing power of visual technologies: How do visualized reconstructions of incidents influence public and political accountability discussions? *The Information Society: An International Journal, 30*(2), 144–158.

Bell, S. E. (1999). Narratives and lives: Women's health politics and the diagnosis of cancer for DES daughters. *Narrative Inquiry, 9*(2), 347–389.

Berger, J. (1972). *Ways of seeing*. London/Harmondsworth: British Broadcasting Corporation/Penguin.

Bourdieu, P. (1977). *Outline of a theory of practice*. Cambridge: Cambridge University Press.

Brown, D. (2006). Surfing: Historic images from Bishop Museum archives. Honolulu: Bishop Museum Press.

Busanich, R., McGannon, K., & Schinke, R. (2016). Exploring disordered eating and embodiment in male distance runners through visual narrative methods. *Qualitative Research in Sport, Exercise and Health, 8*(1), 95–112.

Caine, V. (2010). Visualizing community understanding narrative inquiry as action research. Educational Action Research, 18(4), 481–496.

Calhoun, C. (2012). Foreward. In F. Franz Schultheis & C. Frisinghelli (Eds.), *Picturing Algeria: Pierre Bourdieu* (pp. i–xvi). New York: Columbia University Press.

Cantiello, J. (2014). School pictures: Photographs in the memoirs of White Teachers of Native American Children. *a/b: Auto/Biography Studies, 29*(1), 79–106.

Carrington, S., Allen, K., & Osmolowksi, D. (2007). Visual narrative – A technique to enhance secondary students' contribution to the development of inclusive, socially just school environments – Lessons from a box of crayons. *Journal of Research in Special Educational Needs, 7*(1), 8–15.

Cashmore, A., Green, P., & Scott, J. (2010). An ethnographic approach to studying the student experience: The student perspective through free form video diaries. *The International Journal of the First Year in Higher Education, 1*(1), 106–111.

Chansky, R. (2014). When words are not enough: Narrating power and femininity through the visual language of Judy Chocago's The Dinner Party. *a/b: Auto/biography Studies, 29*(1), 51–77.

Clandinin, D. J., & Connelly, M. (2000). *Narrative inquiry: Experience and story in qualitative research* (1st ed.). San Francisco: Jossey-Bass.

Cohn, N. (2013). Visual narrative structure. *Cognitive Science, 34*, 413–452.

Comer, K. (2010). *Surfer girls in the new world order*. Durham: Duke University Press.

Eisner, W. (1985). *Comics and sequential art*. Tamarac: Poorhouse Press.

Ernst, N. (2015). Authenticity in graphic memoirs. Two nordic examples. *Image [&] Narrative, 16*(2), 65–83.

Everett, M. (2015, online). Fostering first-year students' engagement and well-being through visual narratives. *Studies in Higher Education.*

Evers, C. (2015). Researching action sport with a GoPro™ camera: An embodied and emotional mobile video tale of the sea, masculinity and men-who-surf. In I. Wellard (Ed.), *Researching embodied sport: Exploring movement cultures* (pp. 145–163). Routledge: London.

Ewert, J. (2000). Visual narrative: Art Spiegelman's "Mauss". *Narrative, 8*(1), 87–103.

Frohmann, I. (2005). The framing safety project: Photographs and narratives by battered women. *Violence Against Women, 11*(11), 1396–1419.

Fyfe, G., & Law, J. (1988). Introduction: On the invisibility of the visible. In G. Fyfe & J. Law (Eds.), *Picturing power: Visual depiction and social relations* (pp. 1–14). London: Routledge.

Gillies, V., Harden, A., Johnson, K., Reavey, P., Strange, V., & Willig, C. (2005). Painting pictures of embodied experience: The use of nonverbal data production for the study of embodiment. *Qualitative Research in Psychology, 2*, 199–212.

Goffman, E. (1979). *Gender advertisements*. London: Macmillan.

Greenwood, K., & Jenkins, J. (2015). Visual framing of the Syrian conflict in news and public affairs magazines. *Journalism Studies, 16*(2), 207–227.

Hamburger, J. (1997). *Nuns as artists: The visual culture of a medieval convent*. Berkeley: California University Press.

Harper, D. (1998). An argument for visual sociology. In J. Prosser (Ed.), *Image-based research: A sourcebook for qualitative researchers* (pp. 24–41). London: Falmer Press.

Harper, D. (2002). Talking about pictures: A case for photo-elicitation. *Visual Studies, 17*, 13–26.

Harper, D. (2012). *Visual sociology*. London: Routledge.

Harrison, B. (2002). Photographic visions and narrative inquiry. *Narrative Inquiry, 12*(1), 87–111.

Hoecker, R. (2014). Visual narrative and trauma recovery. *Narrative Inquiry, 24*(2), 259–280.

Horstkotte, S., & Pedri, N. (2008). Introduction: Photographic interventions. Photography in fiction. In S. Horstkotte & N. Pedri. (Eds.), *Special issue of Poetics Today, 29*(1), 1–29.

Hunter, L. (2002). Young people, physical education, and transition: understanding practices in the middle years of schooling. (Doctoral Thesis), The University of Queensland, Brisbane.

Hunter, L. (2004). Bourdieu and the social space of the PE class: Reproduction of Doxa through practice. *Sport, Education and Society, 9*(2), 175–192.

Jacobs, D. (2007). More than words: Comics as a means of teaching multiple literacies. The English Journal, 96(3), 19–25.

Jay, M. (1993). *Downcast eyes: The denigration of vision in twentieth-century French thought*. Berkeley: California University Press.

Jenks, C. (1995). The centrality of the eye in Western culture. In C. Jenks (Ed.), *Visual culture* (pp. 1–12). London: Routledge.

Johnson, G. (2004). Reconceptualising the visual in narrative inquiry into teaching. *Teaching & Teacher Education, 20*, 423–434.

Jones, R. (2015). *(Re)thinking orientalism: Using graphic narratives to teach critical visual literacy*. New York: Peter Lang.

Jungnickel, K. (2015). Jumps, stutters, blurs and other failed images: Using time-lapse video in cycling research. In C. Bates (Ed.), *Video methods: Social science research in motion* (pp. 121–140). London: Routledge.

Kang, J., & Lin, C. (2015). Effects of message framing and visual-fear appeals on smoker responses to antismoking ads. *Journal of Health Communication: International Perspectives, 20*(6), 647–655.

Kress, G., & van Leeuwen, T. (2006). *Reading images: The grammar of visual design* (2nd ed.). New York: Routledge.

lisahunter (2006). *Fueled by desire: Token hotties, celebrities, girls who kick arse and hardcore candy as possible representations in board cultures*. Paper presented at the 13th Commonwealth International Sport Conference, Melbourne.

lisahunter. (2012). "You hurt me Fizz-edd": The socially classed discursive practices of the PE lesson. In F. Dowling, H. Fitzgerald, & A. Flintoff (Eds.), *Equity and difference in physical education, youth sport and health: A narrative approach* (pp. 140–149). London: Routledge.

lisahunter. (2013). What did I do-see-learn at the beach? Surfing festival as a cultural pedagogical sight/site. In L. Azzarito & D. Kirk (Eds.), *Physical culture, pedagogies and visual methods* (pp. 144–161). New York: Routledge.

lisahunter (2014a). *Exploitation and (unqueering) public pedagogy: Gender and sex parody in YouTube surf festival promotion*. Paper presented at the Gender & Education, Melbourne, Australia.

lisahunter (2014b). *She was/is naked on a surfboard: Making sens* of female, surfing, and the Pacific*. Paper presented at the Contemporary Ethnography Across the Disciplines, Waikato, Aotearoa New Zealand.

lisahunter (2015a, Feb, 26). *Positioning female participation in the field of surfing: Illusio, equity and sex*. Paper presented at the Beyond the fields we know: A cross-disciplinary colloquium on Bourdieusian Field methods and theories, Sydney.

lisahunter. (2015a). 'Stop': 'No'. Exploring social suffering in practices of surfing as opportunities for change. In lisahunter, W. Smith, & E. Emerald (Eds.), *Pierre Bourdieu and physical capital* (pp. 47–56). Abingdon: Routledge.

lisahunter (2015c). Digital $%#@ smarts a lot! An autoethnographic account of academic work. In N. Wright & D. Forbes (Eds.), *Digital smarts: Enhancing learning and teaching* (pp. 179–208). The University of Waikato: Wilf Malcolm Institute of Educational Research http://www.waikato.ac.nz/wmier/publications/books/digital-smarts-enhancing-learning-and-teaching

lisahunter. (2016). Spinning wheel very pretty: Cybridity and the cyborg academic. In E. Emerald, R. E. Rinehart, & A. Garcia (Eds.), *Global South ethnographies: Minding the senses* (pp. 147–152). Rotterdam: Sense Publishers.

lisahunter (in press a). Desexing surfing? Pedagogies of possibility. In D. Hough-Snee, & A. Eastman (Eds.), *Radical politics, global culture: A critical surf studies reader.* Durham: Duke University Press.

lisahunter (in press b). Visual narratives of 'female' as a political position: Pedagogies of surfing events and their media. In H. Thorpe & R. Olive (Eds.), *Women in action sport cultures: identity, politics, experience and pedagogy.* Basingstoke: Palgrave Macmillan.

lisahunter, & Austin, H. (2006). Pedagogy of the surfing magazine: Learning to be female. Unpublished paper, Griffith University.

lisahunter, Wubbels, T., Clandinin, D. J., & Hamilton, M. L. (2014). Moving beyond text: Editorial for special issue. *Teaching & Teacher Education, 37*(1), 162–164.

Luttrell, W. (2003). *Pregnant bodies, fertile minds: Gender, race and the schooling of pregnant teens*. New York: Routledge.

MacDougall, D. (2006). The corporeal image film, ethnography, and the senses. *Alexander Street anthropology* (pp. 1 online resource (xiii, 312). Retrieved from http://www.aspresolver.com/aspresolver.asp?ANTH;1666491
McCloud, S. (1993). *Understanding comics: The invisible art.* New York: HarperCollins.
McNutt, J. (2013). Art therapy as a form of visual narrative in oncology care. In C. Malchiodi (Ed.), *Art therapy and health care* (pp. 127–135). New York: Guilford Press.
Mirzoeff, N. (1999). *An introduction to visual culture.* London: Routledge.
Pedri, N. (2015). Thinking about photography in comics. *Image [&] Narrative, 16*(2), 1–13.
Phoenix, C. (2010). Seeing the world of physical culture: The potential of visual methods for qualitative research in sport and exercise. *Qualitative Research in Sport and Exercise, 2*(2), 93–108.
Pink, S. (Ed.). (2012). *Advances in visual methodologies.* London: Sage.
Postema, B. (2013). *Narrative structure in comics: Making sense of fragments.* Rochester: RIT Press.
Prosser, J. (2011). Visual methodology: Toward a more seeing research. In N. K. Denzin & Y. S. Lincoln (Eds.), *The Sage handbook of qualitative research* (4th ed., pp. 479–495). Thousand Oaks: Sage.
Radley, A. (2004). Pity, modernity and the spectacle of suffering. *Journal of Palliative Care, 20*(3), 179–184.
Refaie, E. (2014). Looking on the dark and bright side: Creative metaphors of depression in two graphic memoirs. *a/b: Auto/Biography Studies, 29*(1), 149–174.
Rich, M., Patashnick, J., & Chalfen, R. (2002). Visual illness narratives of asthma: Explanatory models and health-related behavior. *American Journal of Health Behavior, 26*(6), 442–453.
Riessman, C. (2008). *Narrative methods for the human sciences.* Thousand Oaks: Sage.
Rose, G. (2012). *Visual methodologies: An introduction to researching with visual materials* (3rd ed.). London: Sage.
Schultheis, F., & Frisinghelli, C. (Eds.). (2012). *Picturing Algeria: Pierre Bourdieu.* New York: Columbia University Press.
Shohat, E., & Stam, R. (1998). Narrativizing visual culture: Towards a polycentric aesthetic. In N. Mirzoeff (Ed.), *The visual culture reader* (pp. 27–49). London: Routledge.
Smith, B., & Sparkes, A. (2008). Narrative inquiry in sport and exercise psychology: What can it mean, and why might we do it? *Psychology of Sport and Exercise, 10*, 1–11.
Sontag, S. (1977). *On photography.* New York: Picador.
Sontag, S. (2003). *Regarding the pain of others.* New York: Farrar, Strauss and Giroux.
Sztompka, P. (2015). Visual sociology. In J. Wright (Ed.), *International encyclopedia of the social & behavioral sciences* (2nd ed., Vol. 25, pp. 191–196). Amsterdam: Elsevier.
Tamboukou, M. (2014). Narrative personae and visual signs: Reading Leonard's intimate photo memoir. *a/b: Auto/Biography Studies, 29*(1), 27–49.
The New London Group. (1996). A pedagogy of multiliteracies: Designing social futures. *Harvard Educational Review, 66*(1), 60–92.
Vannini, P. (2015). Afterword: Video methods beyond representation: Experimenting with multimodal, sensuous, affective intensities in the 21st century. In C. Bates (Ed.), *Video methods: Social science research in motion* (pp. 230–240). London: Routledge.
Walker, S. (2005). Artmaking in an age of visual culture: Vision and visuality. Visual Arts Research, 59, 23–37.
Walkerdine, V. (1990). Video replay: Families, films and fantasy. In M. Alvarado & J. Thompson (Eds.), *The media reader* (pp. 339–357). London: BFI.
Zelizer, B. (1998). *Remembering to forget: Holocaust memory through the camera's eye.* Chicago: University of Chicago Press.

Chapter 6
Where Words Fail: Storying Audio-Visual Data

Jessica O'Bryan

Abstract Audio-visual video as a data generation tool enables researchers to repeatedly view immensely rich, detailed footage of people in their lived worlds, while the visual and aural veracity of the medium adds valuable fine-grained data to narrative and ethnographic studies. However, there are ethical and methodological challenges in documenting, analysing and storying such data in narrative inquiry approaches. In a collective case study examining the cultural habits of three eminent tertiary classical singing teachers, the teachers videoed several hours of one-to-one lessons with their undergraduate students over the course of a semester. After repeated views of the video footage, several excerpts were transcribed and formed into discrete scenes within larger narratives. Using one such scene as exemplar, participants' conversation, song, gesture, music and the lived space are described and transcribed, shaped into a storied excerpt, and analysed. This chapter discusses the use of video in the study and considers some of the benefits and hazards of storying video data in narrative inquiry methods.

Keywords Classical singing lessons • Tertiary music learning and teaching • Master/apprentice • Narrative inquiry • Audio-visual documentation • Video data • Video • Data generation • Methods

Introduction

The use of audio-visual recording devices to record lived worlds has grown rapidly in recent years, with the advent of smart phones, go-pro cameras and other video tools offering myriad ways of documenting events, incidents and interactions. For researchers, video has become a valuable tool to document these lived worlds. However, the use of video in research is not without ethical challenges, and visual documentation is as yet not fully reconciled by the academy as its own medium in

J. O'Bryan (✉)
Griffith University, Brisbane, QLD, Australia
e-mail: jessica.obryan@gmail.com

© Springer Science+Business Media Singapore 2017

R. Dwyer et al. (eds.), *Narrative Research in Practice*,
DOI 10.1007/978-981-10-1579-3_6

the dissemination of research, which poses methodological issues for narrative inquirers in the creation of research texts. In this chapter I discuss the processes of audio-visual data generation, transcription and analysis, and the transformation of these into a narrative text. The following introductory section reports on a collective case study investigating the values, beliefs and practices of expert tertiary classical singing teachers and their students.

Studying Classical Singers

I am a long-term member of the classical singing community, having both taken classical singing lessons and given them across most of my adult life, and am fascinated by expert classical singing teaching and learning in a tertiary one-to-one lesson setting. I believed a study examining learning and teaching of expert classical singing teachers would inform my own teaching practices and lead to a reflexive positioning of my own learning and teaching ideologies.

The project had two main aims. The first was to identify singing teacher and student values and beliefs, and the second was to examine how these values and beliefs informed the learning and teaching interactions within a semester-long series of one-to-one tertiary classical singing lessons.

A difficulty of investigating this learning and teaching paradigm is that it is a characteristically private transaction between teacher and student (Davidson and Jordan 2007), due to the confidential nature of the dyadic relationship and the ancient cultural traditions of the master/apprentice approach that actively discourage open discourse (O'Bryan 2014; Polanyi 1958; Sennett 2008). It is poorly documented in research on music learning and teaching. There was (and remains) very little empirical research on the values and beliefs of expert singing teachers and how these inform their pedagogical practices in the teaching studio, as personal accounts of singing and teaching experience tend to dominate the singing pedagogy literature (Callaghan 1998; Miller 1996; Welch et al. 2005). Conversely, there is plenty of research on the human voice and its physical processes, mostly through scientific and medical inquiry approaches. The research on music learning and teaching, too, until quite recently, came from classroom teaching, and usually employed quantitative methodologies. Therefore, the warrant for such a project was clear, as was my decision to employ narrative inquiry as the methodological framework.

Narrative inquiry enabled me to write about the situated pedagogical experiences of singing teachers and students in ways I hoped would be meaningful and relevant to other singing teachers, and this approach offered a powerful way of illuminating classical singing learning and teaching that nevertheless mirrored personal accounts of the current singing pedagogy literature. In music education research, however, this approach is as yet uncommon. Bowman (2009) comments on the potential of narrative inquiry to inform music education research:

> Multiplicity, particularity, and personally or individually constructed meaning do not sound to me at all like the things music education has traditionally sought to affirm and honour in its professional discourses. To that extent, narrative inquiry is indeed a distinctive—perhaps even a revolutionary—way of pursuing questions of music's (and education's, and music education's) potential meaning(s) and value(s). (2009, p. 213)

The use of narrative inquiry methods within a case-study framework also offered the opportunity to reflect on how values and beliefs informed teaching and learning practices. I was not interested in how many times the student played with her hair while singing: I was much more interested in the possible significance of why she played with her hair.

Why Use Video to Document Experience?

The location of the study participants helped determine the use of some data generation tools: in particular, audio-visual recordings. The participant teachers were situated hundreds of kilometres apart, across state lines, in three tertiary music institutions. It was impossible to attend every singing lesson of each dyad. Lessons mostly take place weekly, over a semester, in the teacher's singing studio. Sometimes lesson times and days change, and I simply did not have the financial resources to travel to each locale each week. Also, both sound and gesture were being recorded. Both are temporal, and need repeated viewings/ hearings to make sense of the practices taking place. Likewise, as the study attended to cultural habits of singing teachers, the data needed to be repeatedly viewed to unpack these tacit and sometimes easily missed habits. Significantly, the presence of a researcher in what is normally a private learning and teaching transaction between two people may have coloured participant behaviours in the lesson. Therefore, a participatory research framework using video positioned and filmed by the teacher participants was the practical and ethical solution to these obstacles.

Each dyad filmed up to 10 h-long lessons each. After collecting the videos, I repeatedly viewed them, took substantial field notes and time coded each one. I examined dialogic and relational processes between teachers and students in the course of pedagogical singing instruction, including gesture and movement. Various moments and events became "interim starting points" (Clandinin et al. 2010, p. 83) for focused inquiry at that point and a range of musical, vocal and pedagogic elements were examined.

There were four data generation events in the study besides video data. Denzin and Lincoln name this data generation 'Bricolage', in which the researcher is a "maker of quilts", who "uses the aesthetic and material tools of his or her craft, deploying whatever strategies, methods and empirical materials are at hand" (2011, p. 5). These were two semi-structured interviews per participant; field notes and written reflections; collection of university artefacts and emails; and secondary incidental data such as concert events and newspaper reviews.

The final interview for each participant was a video-prompted one. I had spent the previous year recursively exploring and analysing the video footage of each dyad. I isolated several learning incidents from each and used the final individual interviews to seek further discussion about those incidents, which allowed me to check my biases and interpretations (Rowe 2009). These interviews were lively ones and useful both to me and my participants, as meanings were co-constructed through this process. Once all of the data was collated, I spent more than 2 years analysing and creating narratives that were subsequently member checked by the participants, again for accuracy and added verifiability, and also to once again co-construct meanings.

In this chapter I report on one particular dyad: Judy (teacher) and Charlotte (student), and present a storied transcript that was created from about 10 min of video footage. I analyse my approach to storying this video excerpt, and discuss the benefits and hazards of using video data to create narrative accounts of experience.

The following sections position the literature on video data within observational data, and discuss the ethical ramifications of how such a tool might be employed in qualitative inquiry approaches. From there, I discuss how representations of experience from the raw video data to field, interim and research texts might be managed.

Observational Data

Observation is considered one of the cornerstones of social and behavioural sciences. It occurs both in the field through naturalistic observation and field notes, or through recorded phenomena, using moving or still picture, sound and other forms of documentation. However, observation is not just a data-collection tool. It "forms the context in which ethnographic fieldworkers assume membership roles in communities they want to study" (Angrosino and Rosenberg 2011, p. 470). For narrative inquirers, whose work requires attention to ethical and relational dimensions of research, how observational data is positioned and generated in the field, recorded, transcribed, and analysed is as important as the narratives thereafter.

Until relatively recently, visual research was considered all but invisible (Prosser, 2011), but researchers are now using technology such as video to document human experience through filmed interactions in the field, walk-alongs, video diaries, documentaries, art-based creative audio-visual works and other approaches. Video footage enables researchers to capture and re-visit complex data sets that cannot be captured through even comprehensive field notes and recorded interviews. Video allows for remote observation when the phenomenon being studied is a private transaction or in a locale where the researcher cannot stay in the field. For qualitative researchers, video is becoming a useful tool in participatory research, where participants are collaborators in the research process. Even more than field notes and audio-recorded interviews, video footage offers researchers a detailed and nuanced view of study participants in their lived worlds, which Geertz described in

1973 as "thick descriptions" (p. 6). Mondada (2006) sees video partially as a situated practice, where "perspective focuses on researcher's visual perception as a social and situated action" (p. 2). There is potential for such a rich data generation method to become more widely used in qualitative research. Prosser, when writing about the future of visual research, goes so far as to claim "nothing will stop visual methods becoming one of the most important qualitative research methodologies in the twenty-first century" (2011, p. 494).

Yet, using video as research data has the capacity to not only document lived worlds but to "capture and fix 'reality'" (Angrosino and Rosenberg 2011, p. 472) in ways that vary from the lived experience of fieldworkers. The very act of filming a phenomenon binds the data to the very moment captured, and the framing of the phenomenon in the camera can limit the "ebb and flow, …the ambiguities of life as it is lived by people in real circumstances" (Angrosino & Rosenberg, ibid.). The act of filming can also alter how participants act and behave during the time when the video is running, which can result from a culture familiar with visual mediums and technology (Holliday 2007; Mondada 2006) but also because the intrusion of such recording devices into the field can shape human interactions. Mondada (2006) claims that videos "aim at preserving relevant details and phenomenal field features and reflexively contribute to the configuration of the very interactional order they document" (p. 15), suggesting that the very use of the technology aimed at documenting lived experiences can alter the actions of both the researched and the perceptions of the researcher, and create its own limitations of representation.

Sensitive issues around ethics, privacy and confidentiality must also be managed. Angrosino and Rosenberg (2011) observe, "video recording (still or moving) poses definite challenges to the ethical norms of the protection of privacy and the maintenance of confidentiality" (p. 472). What are the provisions in a study using possibly sensitive visual data around the right to participants' privacy and anonymity? How is the video to be filmed and by whom? How is the data to be analysed and presented? From the outset, deciding how recorded observational data in a qualitative research project is to be managed is a fundamental aspect of any project (see lisahunter Chap. 5 this volume).

For researchers with limited available time to spend in the field, and who wish to video-document specific interactions, a participatory research framework is one possible approach. It has the added benefit of giving agency and empowerment to participants, and allows the notion that participants are the experts of their own lives and "able to define or refine the research, the agenda, and process" (Prosser, 2011, p. 484). Participants are given basic parameters of what the researcher wishes to document (such as learning and teaching interactions), but may choose how, where and when the interaction is documented. They may choose who to show in the camera frame, and indeed which interactions to document, and for how long. In short, the participant controls the flow of data, and makes an active contribution to the research.

As to visual data as its own mode of representation, Eisner in 1997 considered ways of framing new meanings for research:

> It is an image that acknowledges the variety of ways through which our experience is coded. It is about the ways in which the transformation of experience from the personal to the public can occur. It is about what we can learn from each of these transformations. It is about the trade-offs that are inevitable in the selection of any option. It is about exploring the edges and re-examining the meaning of research. (1997, p. 7)

These alternative representations of research are only now being accepted by the wider academic community, and arguably have some way to go before enjoying the same pre-eminence as text-based work. In 2006, despite methodological and technical texts on the use of video in research, there was little accompanying research on the analytical processes of video or its use as "a timed accomplishment and as a social practice" (Mondada 2006, p. 1), or indeed, with its own praxial embodiment. lisahunter (Chap. 5 this volume) reports too on the ongoing difficulty of securing permission to display or reproduce audio-visual data, noting that academic publishing is still poorly set up to manage such issues. Nevertheless, Pink reported in 2012,

> The field has since developed in exciting and divergent ways. It is losing none of its momentum and indeed continues to inspire innovative and important studies across a range of disciplines as well as further theoretical and methodological reflection. It is, moreover, an area of academic and applied research that demonstrates particularly powerfully that the relationship between theory, technology and method should not be separated. (Pink 2012, p. 3)

Despite these exciting developments, textual analyses still form the basis for findings to a typical academic audience, and, as Prosser (2011) notes: "missing from major methodological texts are colours, movements, and sounds that are central representational forms in visual research" (p. 486). For narrative inquirers, the potentially rich stories to emerge from video recordings are bound by the limitations of the written word, and there is a danger that in the narrative shaping of the small story the power and immediacy of the interaction, captured so vividly on camera, may be lost in the retelling.

Ethical Dimensions of Narrative Inquiry and Video Data

In narrative inquiry, research is often seen as "relational inquiry" (Clandinin et al. 2010), or "the study of people in relation studying the experience of people in relation" (2010, p. 82). As previously noted, visual data must be managed in light of various ethical dimensions of research, particularly around participant rights to agency, empowerment, privacy and anonymity. In choosing to use video data in a narrative inquiry study, attention must be paid to the ethical underpinnings of such a data generation tool, how it is employed and by whom, the storying of video data into narrative accounts, and how the accounts are negotiated with the participants. While qualitative research recognises the centrality of storytelling in human existence, narrative inquirers acknowledge the "interactive quality of the researcher-researched relationship" (Pinnegar and Daynes, 2007, p. 7). As the ethical underpinning of qualitative research requires attention be paid to these relationships and to how researchers negotiate "entry, exit and representations of experience" (Clandinin and Caine 2008, p. 543), so the tools used to document the experience must also be subject to the same considerations. For more on the ethical use of visual images, see lisahunter's chapter on visual methods. Goldman-Segall points out that due to researcher positioning, there is a danger the interpreter might bias the intentions of the participant, writing that "a major problem in making sense of video data is that video data are especially subject to the infusion of at least one person's point of view" (1993, p. 2). For qualitative researchers, a collaborative, participatory research approach—where the participant is invited to film various events, view the completed footage and discuss their version of events as part of the member checking process—can partly resolve this issue, as it allows for interpretive corroboration and discussion of how the participant wishes to be represented, including use of anonymising features and other considerations. A clear ethical framework around how the participants' rights are being met with regards to video data thus needs to be implemented as part of the research plan.

Likewise, the choice of data generation approaches is bound partly by these ethical issues, but also financial, geographical and time constraints. If fieldwork is required, what is the capacity of the researcher to be available in the field for the duration of the study? While fieldwork offers narrative researchers the opportunity to "live alongside, to become part of lives, theirs and ours, in motion" (Clandinin et al. 2010, p. 83), more often than not limitations of time, financial resources and geography preclude extended forays in the field.

For qualitative researchers, a multiplicity of data generation events is the norm (Denzin and Lincoln 2011). Video data can be generated through researcher-led video of incidents, or through participatory visual methods including video-diary, walk-alongs, video-elicitation, and other visual mediums (Prosser, 2011; lisahunter Chap. 5 this volume; Mondada 2006; Pink 2012). Video can be a static frame (on a tripod), or moving (point of view), or dual frame. Each of these approaches has their benefits and limitations. Mondada (2006) claims that the very act of filming situates it within a praxial act as a configuring device, and that, therefore it is of "fundamental importance to integrate into the analysis the practical ways in which recordings are produced" (p. 2). These practical ways can include ethical dimensions of who produces the video, through whose eyes, and to what end, bearing in mind the epistemological, ontological and methodological foundations of the research.

As is often the case in qualitative studies, data generation can occur alongside analysis, through an inductive, recursive approach, and each can inform the other (Ratcliff 2003). Thus, the process of meaning-making will often occur from the beginning of the filming. Meaning-making of video data occurs when the researcher takes the observed interactions and creates rich, thick description of the events through a particular epistemological lens or methodological and theoretical framework. However, video data is immensely complex. Ratcliff (2003) admits "video contains an incredible amount of information; one can spend hours describing a 10-min segment of video if the goal is to include as much detail as possible" (p. 116). Thus, video data are usually recursively viewed, as repeated viewings provide the researcher with added interpretive elements that may have been missed on the first viewing. Goldmann-Segall (1993) explains how a fellow visual researcher re-views and re-interprets video data:

> Each viewing becomes a new reading as the layers of her seeing add to her interpretation. In other words, in this situation, layering means repeated viewing and layers of interpretations added with each viewing… with video data, we are drawn back to the original data more than to the analyses… interpretations are not only a product of the particular circumstances under which we *observe* our data, but they are also a product of the circumstances under which we *view* our data. (1993, p. 7–8) (emphasis added).

The term *view* is used by Goldmann-Segall as a way of seeing and interpreting video through a particular research lens.

The next stage is to select the sections of video for analysis. Erickson describes five steps to video analysis (in Ratcliff 2003), in which the first step involves repeated viewing of the raw data, taking copious field notes of the whole of the filmed event. The second step involves selecting the event to be analysed, using "boundaries between events" (Ratcliff 2003, p. 121) to determine the precise frame. The third stage involves linking events with others, creating a type of skeletal structure that determines the mutual influences between participants. The fourth stage involves transcription and stage five uses a comparative analysis with the remaining video data "to determine their degree of representativeness" (ibid.).

To a certain extent, these steps are intuitive. The stories may only emerge after repeated reflexive viewing and analysis of the footage, as Pinnegar and Daynes note: "narrative inquirers recognize the tentative and variable nature of knowledge. They accept and value the way in which narrative inquiry allows wondering, tentativeness, and alternative views to exist as part of the research account" (2007 p. 33). Stories may only emerge after repeated analytical turns.

Representation of Experience

One way of representing experience is through transcription. Ratcliff describes two alternatives for transcribing events, which take into account the time-consuming nature of transcribing video. The first is a "partial, focussed transcription" (2003, p. 117), where portions of the video are transcribed. The second is to create no transcription at all, and instead use a codified analysis system, on computer programs created for such a purpose. For the purposes of this chapter, only the former is discussed.

Once field notes are taken of the longer video and discrete events selected, what then should the transcription include? Depictions of place? People? Conversations and dialogue? Gesture? Sound? For narrative inquirers inspired by the work of Clandinin and colleagues, attention to time, people and place are central to the storying process, so all of the elements deemed central to the theoretical framework may be considered. What then should the researcher eliminate? This process takes a little longer and may change with each viewing and pass of analysis. Attention should be paid to the research questions and whether the events within are serving the purpose of the research, or indeed providing previously unforeseen layers of richness to the study. Viewing and reviewing video data can add many layers to interpretation, and in the writing of the interim texts these interpretations also become richer and more complex. Observations become sharper, and the opportunity for reflexive analysis also becomes more frequent.

The analysis of video data varies with each methodological approach, and for narrative inquiry researchers, *storying* video data within a text-based medium adds another layer of complication to an already complex analytical process. The negotiation of understanding through recursive reframing of the data becomes apparent in the composition of the research text, as Clandinin explains, there is great "fluidity and recursiveness as inquirers compose research texts, negotiate them with participants, compose further field texts and recompose research texts. These transitions from field and field texts to authoring research texts are tension-filled" (Clandinin 2006, p. 48). These transitions are no less difficult in the transcription and storying of video data. Narrative inquirers use words, amongst other texts, as data. Bruner (1996) writes that despite the importance of logical-scientific thinking "it is only in narrative mode that one can construct an identity and find a place in one's culture" (1996, p. 42), while Gergen and Gergen remind us of "the pivotal function of language in creating intelligible worlds" (2008, p. 818). However, the use of text creates a problem for those using recorded audio-visual data. Words get in the way. Video is immediate: the data is visible and audible (most of the time). This immediacy is seductive and offers an astute modern audience an immediate shortcut to understanding rather than explanation through the written word. Why, then, add an intermediary of written narrative to events we could just watch?

The answers are manifold. In many studies, the privacy and anonymity of the participants is paramount. Words must be used in place of video where research participants have requested anonymity and where ethical regulations require it. Often the publication does not have multi-media delivery modes, such as in most academic publishing, which therefore limits aspects of representation to little more than text-based form. Interpretation of events can be vague due to the speed of the interaction—consider how many times in a game of football a moment of tricky play might be replayed and (re)interpreted by the TV commentators. Also, visual documentaries are invariably created through the epistemological lens of the documentary maker, and the finished product has already gone through a remarkable transformation before being seen by the viewer. There's a story board, image capture, and detailed editing, mixing, and finishing off that arguably distorts the original product as much as words might. Composing a written narrative, by this reckoning, then, is no better or worse than viewing edited video footage. Through words, actions can be analysed, contracted, expanded, and interpreted in different ways, according to the parameters of the research approach.

In composing research texts Clandinin and Caine (2008) claim researchers must be attentive to both participants and public audiences, but also to the scholarly community, in which questions of relevance and worthiness will be asked of the research text. They note that, ultimately, "research texts develop out of the repeated asking of questions regarding the significance of the research" (2008, p. 543). Narrative analysis is more than telling a story: Hollingsworth and Dybdahl (2007) claim that narrative analysis requires close attention to conversation, structure and dialogic processes within the interview transcripts themselves, through employment of a "bricolage" (Denzin and Lincoln 2000, 2005) of critical epistemologies and theories.

To this end, how the transcription is then storied becomes in itself another recursive analytical act, where the relevance and significance of the events are attended to alongside descriptions of place, people, conversation, and structural processes of the event. And, as in the choices made of how the video is filmed and by whom, subsequent analysis will depend on the epistemological, ontological and methodological foundations of the research project.

The next section introduces Judy and Charlotte, explains the processes of filming the singing lessons, the selection of video data and presents a storied transcript of a short video excerpt.

Judy and Charlotte

In this chapter we visit Judy, a tertiary classical singing teacher and Charlotte, a second year undergraduate student.

The filming portion of the study took place in Judy's work studio, using a static camera on a tripod. Given the participatory research framework, Judy was given carte blanche to film the singing lessons as she and the student desired. The strategy was selected as an "unobtrusive means by which the interactions between the teacher and student can be observed without the possible contamination of behaviours through reaction to the researchers' presence" (Barrett and Gromko 2007, p. 216). The use of video impacted on how the participants managed their interactions within the time frame of the filmed sequence, and how they perceived their place and role in the interaction. Mondada (2006) explains: "What these recordings try to reconstruct are the details to which participants orient when they produce and interpret their own and the others' conducts" (p. 5). Somewhat frustratingly, Judy chose to remain off camera for the majority of the lessons, reflecting the limited level to which she was prepared to be present in the study. Judy was shaping the study to her own interpretation, and ensuring her conduct could not be easily seen; rather, she chose to make the student the focus of the lessons.

Each video was of an hour-long singing lesson over the course of a semester, about ten lessons in all. After repeatedly observing the video footage, a larger story was revealed in the way that Charlotte developed her understanding of Mozart song over a semester. Therefore, the excerpt in this chapter is one of five in which Charlotte was learning a Mozart song, which provided a means to track Charlotte's vocal development and Judy's approach to the same material. Employing a recursive, iterative analysis approach, the five partial, focussed transcription excerpts explored a range of pedagogical strategies and learning and teaching interactions.

In the storied transcript in this chapter I employed a simple dialogic analysis of the participants' verbal cues, gesture, aural mimicry, and musical cues. Importantly, as singing was a primary focus, the video excerpt showed Charlotte engaged in the act of singing, and how her teacher enabled a Knowledge of Results loop (Welch et al. 2005) for improved learning outcomes. Storying aural concepts was a vital feature of the narrative. Following the story is an analysis of just some of the learning and teaching elements observed, with a subsequent analysis of the approach to the transcription and narrative account.

The Ears Have to Be Ahead!

Torna di Tito a lato (Return to Titus's side) is an aria from an opera seria (serious, or noble opera) by W. A. Mozart called La clemenza di Tito (The Clemency of Titus), K.621. It is a Da Capo aria, in that it has an A section, a B section, then a return to the A section. It is sung in Italian by a mezzo-soprano, and was first performed in 1791, during what has become known as the Classical Period in Western Art music. It is one requiring much consideration of text and has numerous technical vocal demands, with which Charlotte has been struggling. This week the song "Torna" is sung at the end of the lesson. The excerpt is about 10 minutes long and the pace of the interaction is very quick.

*****

Singing teacher Judy is giving undergraduate singing student Charlotte a singing lesson in her music studio. Judy is off-camera, sitting at the grand piano on which the camera tripod is resting. The video is trained on Charlotte, who stands in the piano's black curve behind three neat piles of music scores. Charlotte's long, dark hair is loose and she wears a form-fitting maroon jersey dress. A small pendant on a delicate chain hangs around her slender neck. Gentle sunlight from an unseen window shines on her face and body, brighter and more focused than the fluorescent lights that bathe the room in a bleak glow. On the tired beige wall behind and to the left of Charlotte is a picture of a garden scene framed in bright blue, and beneath it, lined up near the studio door, are some old white plastic tub chairs. In the far right corner of the studio rests Judy's work desk and chair, and some well-stocked bookshelves.

"Ok." Judy prepares to play, then mutters almost unintelligibly about not having the music.

Charlotte starts. "Oh, I just gave you the music for that!" She lifts the display folder with the study score from the piano and hands it to Judy.

"Oh, you did," replies Judy. "God, it's heavy! Oh!"

Charlotte chuckles.

Judy plays the first bar of the piece and Charlotte enters, her large mezzo-soprano voice warm and rich, if yet a little immature. She is unprepared, still sweeping her hair behind her ears and moving into position. She sings the first phrase securely, but the second phrase catches her out. She sings the wrong notes, stops and grimaces. "Oh!" she exclaims. Charlotte glances at the music, and doubles over in mock pain.

Judy sings the miss-sung phrase, modelling the correct notes. "Never mind!" she says, chuckling.

"You know what I did?" says Charlotte, crossly, "I sat out here [in the corridor] in the 5 min before and I went through that bit so I wouldn't do that!"

Judy laughs.

"And you know what I did?" wails Charlotte, laughing. "I did something else! I didn't even do the bit that comes in at the end—I just made up a NEW bit!" She puts on her reading glasses and glares at her music, hands on hips.

Judy agrees. "You did, that's true!"

They start again. Judy sings along with her warm, light-lyric soprano, then makes an error in the second bar of the piano part, harmonising the wrong note. "Oh dear!" she exclaims, but continues. As with previous lessons, Judy repeats her directive of "repeat, and" during the rests. She calls out "diaphragm" as the next phrase begins. Charlotte's singing becomes noticeably less controlled once she reaches the rising phrase and her jaw shakes slightly on the top note.

Charlotte sings the next phrase, but misses the starting note, and is a semitone flat.

"Oh!" She stops singing and looks quizzically at Judy.

Judy sings the correct notes, saying "but you get—you have to sing the D against this in the piano" as she repeatedly hits the C note. "There's a C in the piano—in the orchestra—"

"It doesn't like me!" whines Charlotte, raising her arms in mock tantrum. She grimaces at the music.

Judy sings the phrase again and says, "because that's what an appoggiatura does!"

Charlotte joins in at 'appoggiatura does', smiling ruefully. "Sorry!" She realises she has forgotten about the 'lean' of the appoggiatura in which the melody clashes deliberately with the notes of the accompanying chord. It's a particular compositional device used throughout Western art music.

Judy explains: "It's a clash followed by a resolution." She repeats the phrase as Charlotte joins in, and they immediately continue. Prior to the B section, Judy calls out "diaphragm". Charlotte begins the phrase strongly and with a clean attack, accompanied by Judy playing forte. "Lovely!" calls out Judy as Charlotte enters the second phrase of section B.

Again, in the two bars before the repeat of the A section, Charlotte sings the first '*Torna*' too high. She frowns, runs her hands through her hair and throws her head back as she mutters quickly, "I'm [*inaudible*] doing this".

Judy soothes, "that's fine, don't worry about it!"

They backtrack a few bars and continue. At the return of the A section Charlotte sings the opening phrase and Judy calls, "that's nice! Very nice line!" Charlotte and Judy continue the song, but once again at '*con replicate emenda*' Charlotte's voice cracks a little, and she once again frowns, flicking her hair about as she shakes her head.

They finish the aria. Immediately, Judy says: "Exit! Um, what's his name? A—a—a"

"Annius", answers Charlotte promptly, as she pulls her hair into a ponytail.

"Annius!" Judy echoes. "Good. Beautiful work. It's coming. I'm glad we're doing this properly, before we look at *Deh Per Questo*, because it's really a WHOLE style of its own, isn't it? And it needs to be physicalized a bit. Which is what we're doing now. And I suspect you're probably not happy with yourself, doing this, are you?"

"Not with what I just did then, no", Charlotte confesses. She appears palpably frustrated, and fidgets with her hair as Judy talks.

"No. But it's coming on, and I can hear that it is, and I can hear you remember what we've spoken about. The one generalized comment that I can make about this is: now, I know that you're thinking about your diaphragm and that's great. By the way, the part that was fantastic was '*lacerbo tuo dolore*'. That was great! Did you feel that, in your body?"

Charlotte smiles, agreeing, "Yeah."

Judy continues. "Um, it's just now not to get too messed up by things." She plays a phrase on the piano with wide melodic leaps. "That's a lot of jumping around—"

Charlotte fidgets with her hair some more and nods.

Judy continues "—but just to go 'I'm open' and go straight forward." As she says 'I'm open', her voice becomes audibly more resonant and open sounding.

The mention of 'open' prompts Charlotte to yawn and she apologises: "I think it's still—sorry, as you said 'open' my throat started to open. I think it's still those same sections: *con replicate*"—she sings the last syllable down the octave and indicates with her hand to show the height of the pitch.

Judy agrees: "of course, because that's a tenth", as she plays the interval on the piano. "That's a big distance. Literally, if you were looking at your vocal folds on a video, they would be going 'nyer', quite a bit longer as you go up." Out of view, Judy seems to be demonstrating vocal fold length with her hands, which Charlotte copies in camera view. Judy exclaims, "that's it!"

Judy sings the Italian word '*con*', and explains, "knowing that *ker, ker, ker*, closes you, so you have to open up and then make the body—and I say that sort of advisedly—make the body make a *ker*. In passing, and without over physicalizing the *ker*, so that it doesn't close you, just when you've already got ready to go up."

"Yeah." Charlotte agrees and pushes her hair behind her ears. She yawns a bit and covers her mouth quickly with her hands.

Judy sings 'con *koh koh koh*', and clarifies, [it's] "just a little touch of the back of your tongue on your top teeth."

Charlotte attempts the same, her mouth shaping the consonant. Her hands move in sympathetic shape with her voice as she sings the '*con replicate*' phrase. She struggles again with the top note and Judy immediately models the phrase '*emenda*' several different ways, playing with vowel shape. Judy's impressive vocal mastery is evident as her warm, honey-toned instrument changes with each repetition of the phrase, from a rich and full tone to a light and brilliant one.

Charlotte tries again, mimicking Judy's aural model. This time her full, rich voice is free and easy on the high top note, and the sound spins in the room. It is a thrilling, beautiful sound.

Judy stops and murmurs in wonderment: "oh lord."

Charlotte looks surprised and pleased as she says excitedly, "that worked!"

Judy responds animatedly, "That would be the one. That would be the one."

She models the interval again twice. Charlotte mimics the interval again but doesn't look happy with the result. She frowns and asks, "is that right?" Her vocal quality is slightly harsh-sounding and tight, unlike her previous lush, free sound.

Judy replies, circumspectly, "pretty close, love, yah, mmm, yah." She pauses momentarily. Then she advises, "Don't over-work on that and certainly don't stress about it—"

Charlotte speaks over the top of Judy, exclaiming: "I think that's what it is! I think, when it worked just before—so the one just before the one I did, I just went '*ok fine, I'm not going to think of anything*', and it just went *wah*, not like *blah*, but just like, it's open and prepared and I'm not gonna—anything!"

Charlotte gesticulates wildly. On '*wah*' she takes one hand down below her waist and the other very high, indicating a vertical tube of air, and at the *wah* sound she sticks her tongue out, jaw low and mouth open. When she says "not like *blah*", she makes a long face with the jaw very slack, slumping her body, suggesting loss of bodily engagement in her sound production.

Judy affirms, "yeah, that's right, don't do extra when you get there. Oddly enough sometimes that can get in your way too."

Charlotte agrees, "yeah, I think that's the instinct is, to go '*I'm going up, keep it up there!'* No, no, it will GO up there". Her hands shape the internal movement of low larynx position and high soft palate.

Judy remarks simultaneously, "it is, it is! Yeah, you already did the work, you already did the work, that's why I say to send it straight out, and in that I'm talking about the air of course". She points to somewhere beyond Charlotte's head, her hand just visible in the video frame.

"And I think that, it's just my body wants to do something else." Charlotte rubs her belly as she speaks, flustered by the opposing commands of her body.

"Yeah, yeah, yeah, yeah," Judy agrees.

Charlotte continues, "and I think it should be continuous I guess…" she tapers off.

Judy adds, "but I think, you know, don't ever forget there's a process of learning the stuff where—"

Charlotte interjects loudly, "stupid process of learning!", stamps her foot and swings her arms, mimicking a tantrum but grinning broadly all the while.

Judy bursts into laughter and they laugh together merrily as she finishes, "—the ears have to be ahead!"

*****

Analysis of Learning and Teaching Elements

Instruction does much, but encouragement everything. (Letter to A.F. Oeser, Nov. 9, 1768) — Johann Wolfgang von Goethe, Early and Miscellaneous Letters of J. W. Goethe: Including Letters to His Mother. With Notes and a Short Biography

In this excerpt, Charlotte is wrangling with a Mozart song. She struggles to sing it with accuracy, and the one short moment of success is so brief as to be impossible to replicate with accuracy. Her frustration is palpable and readily articulated throughout the excerpt. Nevertheless, Judy is consistently positive in her approach with Charlotte. Her directions use positive reinforcing language, and even her criticism is couched in positive language and an encouraging demeanour.

I looked at how the language used shaped the conversational interactions. There was a constant interplay of positive explanation by the teacher and an affirming statement by the student. For example, towards the end of the excerpt Judy explains, *"yeah, that's right, don't do extra when you get there. Oddly enough sometimes that can get in your way too."* Charlotte agrees, *"yeah, I think that's the instinct is, to go 'I'm going up, keep it up there!' No, no, it will GO up there"*. For both Judy and Charlotte there is notable difficulty in explaining embodied, hidden physical concepts, so when Judy explains a physical movement that shapes an aural result, Charlotte then reinterprets this using her own analysis, in her own words. Judy also praises the successful sections, ensuring Charlotte has a sense of success at the end of the lesson. Judy expertly steers Charlotte to greater understanding through positive direction and affirmation of Charlotte's observations mostly *after* the singing takes place: *"Good. Beautiful work. It's coming"*. Judy makes a comment about one particular aspect of breath management that seems to be working well: *"I know that you're thinking about your diaphragm and that's great. By the way, the part that was fantastic was 'lacerbo tuo dolore'. That was great!"* Judy models a positive affirmation of success, and refrains from trying to completely fix the entire rendition. Many of the verbal interactions use this explanation and affirmation approach, and for a linguist or conversation analyst these interactions may be the focal point of the analysis.

For the things we have to learn before we can do them, we learn by doing them. — Aristotle, The Nicomachean Ethics

Nevertheless, for me, perhaps what I am most interested in is the "doingness" of the lesson interactions. Much of the lesson is about the singing itself, more than the dialogic processes that occur during and after Charlotte sings. In terms of learning and teaching, one-to-one singing lessons characteristically falls under the master-apprentice mode of learning. In the above excerpt we read how Charlotte relies on Judy's input for assistance, particularly in making sense of aural and body concepts. Alongside Charlotte and Judy co-constructing understandings through language and discussion, Judy *models* many aural concepts:

Judy sings the Italian word 'con', and explains, "knowing that ker, ker, ker, closes you, so you have to open up and then make the body—and I say that sort of advisedly—make the

body make a ker. In passing, and without over physicalizing the ker, so that it doesn't close you, just when you've already got ready to go up."

"Yeah." Charlotte agrees and pushes her hair behind her ears. She yawns a bit and covers her mouth quickly with her hands.

Judy sings 'con koh koh koh', and clarifies, [it's] "just a little touch of the back of your tongue on your top teeth."

Judy is explaining how the use of "*ker*" in singing a consonant can close up the vocal tract and prevent free flow of air for the remainder of the phrase. Judy is using three modes of explanation: she explains *why*, sings an aural model, then explains *how* to achieve the physical act. Charlotte is then encouraged to try the process for herself, separate from the act of singing the whole song.

This quick-step model/copy process allows Charlotte to make aural judgements about her singing, which are then corrected or affirmed by Judy:

Judy sings 'con koh koh koh', and clarifies, [it's] "just a little touch of the back of your tongue on your top teeth."

Charlotte attempts the same, her mouth shaping the consonant. Her hands move in sympathetic shape with her voice as she sings the 'con replicate' phrase. She struggles again with the top note and Judy immediately models the phrase 'emenda' several different ways, playing with vowel shape. Judy's impressive vocal mastery is evident as her warm, honey-toned instrument changes with each repetition of the phrase, from a rich and full tone to a light and brilliant one.

Charlotte tries again, mimicking Judy's aural model. This time her full, rich voice is free and easy on the high top note, and the sound spins in the room. It is a thrilling, beautiful sound.

Judy stops and murmurs in wonderment: "oh lord."

Charlotte looks surprised and pleased as she says excitedly, "that worked!"

Judy responds animatedly, "That would be the one. That would be the one."

This mimicry provides a shortcut for Charlotte's development of aural expertise. In the typical singing teacher/student interaction a cyclic, reiterative approach is usually evident, where a student will sing, the teacher will provide feedback, then the student will attempt to effect change according to what they perceive is the intended outcome. This is a simultaneous feedback loop, also known as Knowledge of Results (Welch et al. 2005) (see Fig. 6.1). They note that "feedback in singing is both intrapersonal and interpersonal" (p. 229), and that an internal feedback system needs to be mediated from without by an external source (such as a teacher), as without this even minor idiosyncratic behaviours can be rehearsed into habit .

Recent research into motor learning processes indicates that feedback that directs attention to the *effect* of the action rather than the action itself will be most useful when delivered post-performance—after the singing has finished—as cognitive overload can result in failure of the student to effect positive change (Nisbet 2010; Welch et al. 2005; Roth and Verdolini-Abbott 2014).

Judy also models internal vocal tract shape through the use of gesture and encourages Charlotte to do the same, as the following excerpt indicates:

Judy agrees: "of course, because that's a tenth", as she plays the interval on the piano. "That's a big distance. Literally, if you were looking at your vocal folds on a video, they would be going 'nyer', quite a bit longer as you go up." Out of view, Judy seems to be

Fig. 6.1 Knowledge of results feedback loop (Welch et al. 2005)

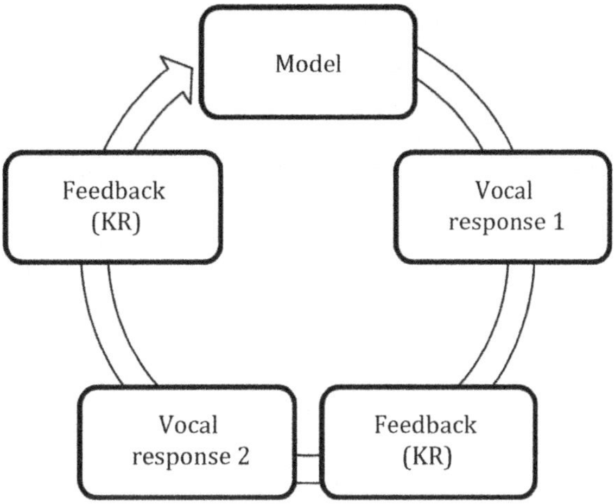

demonstrating vocal fold length with her hands, which Charlotte copies in camera view. Judy exclaims, "that's it!"

Also evident is Charlotte's attempts to externalise the internal vocal tract shape through gesture and movement: *Charlotte attempts the same, her mouth shaping the consonant. Her hands move in sympathetic shape with her voice as she sings the 'con replicate' phrase.* These gestures enable Charlotte and Judy to co-construct a common language of embodied actions that spoken language cannot fully explain. Nevertheless, even as gesture replaces language as a tool of understanding, Judy reminds Charlotte of the need for the "ears to be ahead" of the internal and embodied aspects of singing, which Charlotte recognises is a slow and laborious process of learning. There are no shortcuts.

Judy adds, "but I think, you know, don't ever forget there's a process of learning the stuff where—"

Charlotte interjects loudly, "stupid process of learning!", stamps her foot and swings her arms, mimicking a tantrum but grinning broadly all the while.

Judy bursts into laughter and they laugh together merrily as she finishes, "—the ears have to be ahead!"

Through this short excerpt, ostensibly little more than Charlotte singing through the song, several vocal technical elements are touched on, including airflow and support, articulation, vowel shape, laryngeal and soft palate movement and tracheal resonance, as well as musical elements such as musicianship. Judy targets specific learning areas, making expert decisions on how best to approach Charlotte's learning at this point in the lesson and in her vocal education journey. And both Judy and Charlotte are engaged in creating a common language encompassing aspects of "bodymind" and voice (Thurman and Welch 2001), which attend to Charlotte's voice in its corporeal and ethereal states.

Creating Judy and Charlotte's Story

As indicated earlier, the transcription segment is an excerpt of a longer lesson. It was viewed perhaps twenty times throughout the transcription and analysis process. Segments like this were placed in a larger narrative account that included detail provided through other data generation events.

It became clear early on I would need to "story" the transcript from the outset, using 1-min time markers as reference on the transcript. At first, however, I just reported the human conversations and actions. In the first draft of the transcript, I did not comment on the quality of the voice as I was more interested in the interactions between participants, rather than the results of the actions. However, this became limiting. The details of sound and voice were of fundamental importance to both the transcription and the understanding of the learning and teaching taking place. I hadn't previously considered what I was hearing. Conversely, the sheer amount of visual detail I had included was probably unnecessary, and I looked for tautological statements, depictions and visual images that did nothing to enhance the story. These were removed. Over time the transcription of events became clearer, yet dense with nuances of observed data.

Narratives and stories usually want a beginning, a middle section and an end. They also want a climax and possibly a denouement. With research stories, the difficulty is in reporting an incident that may not at first glance have any such shape, particularly in applied music, where learning can take place over years and in private. Nevertheless, according to Barrett and Stauffer "narrative work provides a means to re-conceptualise the ways in which we think about music engagement, music education, and inquiry in music education" (2009, p. 2). In this learning incident of a classical singing teacher with her student the story shape was of small-step learning, of gentle, encouraging direction by the teacher and of a student allowed to make mistakes and articulate both her frustration and her learning approach. The literal climax of the story is when Charlotte succeeds in singing the high note, which evokes a remarkable reaction from her teacher and which Charlotte then tries to replicate. The boundaries of the story were the incident itself: the beginning of the song to the end of its discussion. There was a natural rhythm to the interaction that enabled it to be written up in its entirety. One of the ongoing dilemmas I faced was whether to break up the story with explanatory or analytical text. I decided that, as I had not been a participant in the room during the filming sessions, I wanted the story to unfold without my researcher voice impinging on the action. The acts of transcription and storying were already a partial and implicit analysis. The overt analysis and explanation, both of the learning and teaching elements and the text, could come later.

One of the ethical considerations in storying this excerpt was that the participants requested anonymity, which was written into the informed consent packages. Consequently, the physical space was anonymised. The names of the participants were also changed, although the song was not as the transcription would have lost too much in the telling. Charlotte's appearance was generic, and I kept some identifying features such as eye and skin colour hidden. Judy's appearance and vocal tone were not mentioned, as any mention of physical or aural features aside from her sung voice might render her recognisable to her peers.

One of the great difficulties I had of transcribing the video excerpt was transmitting aural concepts without creating overly-interpretive prose. It is impossible to accurately depict a beautiful voice singing, or a voice in development. Commonly used descriptors such as "harsh", or "bright", "warm", "honey" or "rich" give some indication of a timbral quality, but the only good way to depict an unheard voice is to compare it to a well-known singer's instrument. As voices are unique, this proposition is almost moot. One of the ways in which vocal quality was indicated was through the use of the words "thrilling" and "spinning". These terms indicate a vocal shape, which for voice experts at least, show evidence of acoustic space in the vocal tract that allows the air to resonate at full efficiency, helping create what most experts agree is a beautiful vocal tone (Mitchell 2014).

Another difficulty was to articulate Charlotte's state of mind without presuming to speak for her. One of the ways to manage this was to examine and re-examine the footage, to ensure that if she was "mimicking a tantrum", or "grimacing at the music" that it was as described. This was a recursive process with considerable deliberation on the use of descriptive language for Charlotte's emotional state. As a researcher with "insider knowledge" of classical singing, I empathised with her frustration and sensed her difficulty in articulating physical technical concepts, however, this empathy may have created a biased and sympathetic portrayal, and presumption of knowledge of her inner life. Therefore, descriptive language mostly indicated instead the *appearance* of emotion.

Conversation and the spoken voice were relatively easy to transcribe. The spoken words were accurate, although again it is difficult to imply accent, colour, intent or tone through words alone. Use of descriptors such as "chuckles", "wails", "laughs", "mutters" helped to articulate tone and response, alongside more prosaic words such as "says", "replies" and "answers". These words were the most likely to impose bias on the interaction as they could shape a response or retort not intended by the speaker, yet my original unvarying use of "says" became repetitious and lacked nuance. Storying the video footage at this point became about shaping the narrative to ensure reader interest without forfeiting visual and aural veracity.

Physical gestures were perhaps the easiest to describe. Movement can be tracked, and laughter can be reported. Nevertheless, making repeated movement interesting was a challenge. Was Charlotte's hair play a habituation or a deliberate focussing strategy? Why did Charlotte yawn? Was she bored, was it a physical singing strategy to improve airflow, or was she mentally tired from concentrating? I questioned the need to include these details, wondering whether they furthered the story. Were they just small snippets of useless information or were they the tacit actions of Charlotte's state of mind? The actions, after considerable deliberation, I determined were unique to Charlotte's learning style, given that they were observable across all five video excerpts. I perceived them to be an aspect of Charlotte's approach to learning. They seemed to be a coping mechanism. By moving or fidgeting, she seemed to be managing her frustration at learning complex embodied vocal techniques. This brings to mind what Erickson refers to as step five in video analysis: looking for "comparative analysis with the remaining video data" (Ratcliff 2003, p. 121). These actions were included in the final narrative account.

Finally, I considered how I wanted the excerpt to read. I used full words and transcribed very few ums and ahs, as there were surprisingly very few in the original recording. I ensured that each speaker was readily identifiable, and I used typical written English language conventions to ensure the events in the scene were clear. I used present tense to indicate immediacy of time, and tried to make the interrupted speech patterns easy to understand. Many lay readers wouldn't understand the musical conventions referred to, and the expectation was that classical singers, singing teachers, musicians and music education experts would be the main audience, hence the use of some technical language they would presumably comprehend.

I was, and am, ongoingly frustrated by my rather prosaic attempts to describe this incident. To my critical gaze there is little poetry or colour in my writing style. Compared with the writing of others, particularly my favourite fiction authors, this account seems distressingly bereft of life. Nevertheless, in writing it I was concerned with veracity. I wanted to document the incident, rather than colourfully embellish it. Problematically, I couldn't SEE Judy in the video. Even though I knew her well, I could not report on her gently ironic demeanour, or her fiercely intelligent countenance. I was bound by the constraints placed on me by the participant and of the limitations of the documentation process itself.

Conclusion

There are benefits and hazards to the use of video data in narrative inquiry methods. The hazards are many. Video data provides such rich and diverse detail that managing the sheer quantity of data is an extremely slow, frustratingly recursive process of viewing, analysis, and reviewing, often occurring over years. The substantial ethical concerns around participant agency, empowerment, privacy and confidentiality mean that the video footage needs to be ethically managed throughout the filming, analysis and storying processes, to ensure participants are satisfied with their representation. When a participatory research framework is utilised, the participants may choose—as mine did—to be partially hidden from camera, limiting both their participation in the footage and their representation in the story. For the narrative inquirer, remote observation is a barrier to researchers "living alongside" their study participants in the field, attendant to the small bumps and tensions of the participants' stories lived and told in place and time.

Nevertheless, the use of video data in a study such as mine allowed for repeated forays into the raw data. Despite geographical and financial limitations I was able to conduct a richly detailed study investigating a private learning and teaching paradigm characteristically resistant to open discourse. Importantly, remote observation through video enabled participants to be co-constructors of the study from data generation through to their representation in the narrative accounts.

Storying video footage seems to add a layer of frustrating complexity to what is already a medium rich in visual and aural detail, and for which there are already viable audio-visual methodological approaches available. I struggled with many restricting elements. I was not at any time able to accurately or meaningfully describe sound. I could only describe what the sound of the voices *resembled*, metaphors such as honey, or descriptors such as "warm" or "bright". I was frustrated by Judy's decision to be off-camera, as I could only report what I could hear, not see. There was so much data that I had to limit my written observations, potentially reducing useful findings. The story needed to show narrative shape, pace and movement, which is difficult to convey in a research text. And the story needed to meaningfully engage the reader without distorting or misrepresenting the original footage.

Storytelling is an immensely powerful way of illuminating human interactions. For narrative inquirers, attention to the stories lived in time and place by their study participants is a central feature of the approach. Yet, for me, words are not enough. The limitations of the written word simply cannot adequately convey nuances in sound or movement. From my perspective, in storying my video excerpt, words failed. They failed to evoke the soaring quality of the singers' voices, to pick out the subtle differences between them, or to convey the joy demonstrated by the student when she managed to successfully replicate a vocal phrase. Words failed to convey the subtleties of the relationship between learner and teacher, or to adequately describe movement that is vital to understanding the human voice as an embodied instrument.

Video is a vital tool for capturing complex data required by researchers who are concerned with documenting nuances in sound, gesture and vision. And, as Prosser (2011) writes, "increasingly, we live in a visual world and currently no topic, field of study, or discipline is immune to the influences of researchers adopting a visual perspective" (p. 479). Audio-visual data, despite the ethical issues around participant agency, empowerment, privacy and confidentiality, will continue to build prominence as a vital data source, as the academy realises the benefit of such a medium to easily and directly convey movement, gesture, sound, visual texture, and meaning in the social sciences. Video succeeds where words fail.

Discussion Questions

1. In choosing audio-visual tools to gather data, first think about your theoretical framework. What are your epistemological and ontological positions? How will these apply to your methodology?
2. Once you have gathered your data, how do you intend to analyse its contents? Data analysis will depend on your theoretical and methodological framework, and as narrative inquiry is a broad church, consider which approach you may want to use. There are many good texts regarding video analysis: a recent one is Sarah Pink's 2012 edited volume: Advances in Visual Methodology, through Sage publications.

References

Angrosino, M., & Rosenberg, J. (2011). Observations on observation: Continuities and challenges. In N. K. Denzin & Y. S. Lincoln (Eds.), *The Sage handbook of qualitative research* (4th ed., pp. 467–478). Thousand Oaks: Sage.

Barrett, M., & Gromko, J. (2007). Provoking the muse: A case study of teaching and learning in music composition. *Psychology of Music, 35*(2), 213–230.

Barrett, M., & Stauffer, S. (2009). Narrative inquiry: From story to method. In M. S. Barrett & S. L. Stauffer (Eds.), *Narrative inquiry in music education* (pp. 7–17). Dordrecht: Springer. doi:10.1007/978-1-4020-9862-820.

Bowman, W. (2009). Charting narrative territory. In M. S. Barrett & S. L. Stauffer (Eds.), *Narrative inquiry in music education* (pp. 211–222). Dordrecht: Springer. doi:10.1007/978-1-4020-9862-820.

Bruner, J. (1996). *The culture of education*. Cambridge, MA: Harvard University Press.

Callaghan, J. (1998). Singing teachers and voice science–an evaluation of voice teaching in Australian tertiary institutions. *Research Studies in Music Education, 10*(25), 25–41. doi:10.1177/1321103X9801000103.

Clandinin, J. (2006). Narrative inquiry: A methodology for studying lived experience. *Research Studies in Music Education, 27*(1), 44–54.

Clandinin, J., & Caine, V. (2008). Narrative inquiry. In L. M. Given (Ed.), *The Sage encyclopedia of qualitative research methods* (Vol. 2, pp. 514–544). Thousand Oaks: Sage.

Clandinin, J., Murphy, S., Huber, J., & Orr, A. M. (2010). Negotiating narrative inquiries: Living in a tension-filled midst. *The Journal of Educational Research, 103*, 81–90. doi:10.1080/00220670903323404.

Davidson, J., & Jordan, N. (2007). "Private Teaching, Private Learning": An exploration of music instrument learning in the private studio, junior and senior conservatories. In L. Bresler (Ed.), *International handbook of research in arts education* (pp. 729–744). Dordrecht: Springer.

Denzin, N., & Lincoln, Y. (Eds.). (2000). *The Sage handbook of qualitative research* (2nd ed.). Thousand Oaks: Sage.

Denzin, N., & Lincoln, Y. (2005). *The Sage handbook of qualitative research* (3rd ed.). Thousand Oaks: Sage.

Denzin, N., & Lincoln, Y. (2011). *The Sage handbook of qualitative research* (4th ed.). Thousand Oaks: Sage.

Eisner, E. (1997). The promise and perils of alternative forms of data representation. *Educational Researcher, 26*(6), 4–10.

Geertz C. (1973 [2000 edition]). *The interpretation of cultures*. New York: Basic Books— Perseus Books Group.

Gergen, K. J., & Gergen, M. M. (2008). Social constructionism. In L. M. Given (Ed.), *The SAGE encyclopedia of qualitative research methods* (Vol. 2, pp. 816–820). Thousand Oaks: Sage.

Goldmann-Segall, R. (1993). Interpreting video data. *Journal for Educational Multimedia and Hypermedia, 2*(3), 261–282.

Holliday, R. (2007). Performances, confessions, and identities: Using video diaries to research sexualities. In G. Stanczak (Ed.), *Visual research methods: Image society and representation* (pp. 255–280). Thousand Oaks: Sage.

Hollingsworth, S., & Dybdahl, M. (2007). Talking to learn: The critical role of conversation in narrative inquiry. In D. J. Clandinin (Ed.), *Handbook of narrative inquiry: Mapping a methodology* (pp. 146–176). Thousand Oaks: Sage.

Miller, R. (1996). *On the art of singing*. New York: Oxford University Press.

Mitchell, H. (2014). Perception, evaluation and communication of singing voices. In S. D. Harrison & J. O'Bryan (Eds.), *Teaching singing in the 21st century* (pp. 187–200). Dordrecht: Springer. doi:10.1007/978-94-017-8851-9.

Mondada, L. (2006). Video recording as the reflexive preservation and configuration of phenomenal features for analysis. In H. Knoblauch, J. Raab, H. G. Soeffner, & B. Schnettler (Eds.), *Video analysis* (pp. 51–67). Bern: Lang.

Nisbet, A. (2010). You want me to think about what?! A discussion about motor skills and the role of attentional focus in studio voice teaching. In S. Harrison (Ed.), *Perspectives on singing teaching: Australian vocal pedagogues sing their stories* (pp. 101–121). Bowen Hills: Australian Academic Press.

O'Bryan, J. (2014). Habits of the mind, hand and heart: Approaches to classical singing training. In S. D. Harrison & J. O'Bryan (Eds.), *Teaching singing in the 21st century* (pp. 21–34). Dordrecht: Springer. doi:10.1007/978-94-017-8851-9.

Pink, S. (Ed.). (2012). *Advances in visual methodology*. London: Sage.

Pinnegar, S. J., & Daynes, G. (2007). Locating narrative inquiry historically: Thematics in the turn to narrative. In D. J. Clandinin (Ed.), *Handbook of narrative inquiry* (pp. 3–34). Thousand Oaks: Sage.

Polanyi, M. (1958). *Personal knowledge: Towards a post-critical philosophy*. Chicago: University of Chicago Press.

Prosser, J. (2011). Visual methodology: Toward a more seeing research. In N. K. Denzin & Y. S. Lincoln (Eds.), *The Sage handbook of qualitative research* (4th ed., pp. 479–495). Thousand Oaks: Sage.

Ratcliff, D. (2003). Video methods in qualitative research. In P. M. Camic, J. E. Rhodes, & L. Yardley (Eds.), *Qualitative research in psychology: Expanding perspectives in methodology and design* (pp. 113–129). Washington, DC: American Psychological Association. http://dx.doi.org/10.1037/10595-000

Roth, D., & Verdolini-Abbott, K. (2014). Vocal health and singing pedagogy: Considerations from biology and motor learning. In S. Harrison & J. O'Bryan (Eds.), *Teaching singing in the twenty-first century* (pp. 69–90). Dordrecht: Springer.

Rowe, V. C. (2009). Using video-stimulated recall as a basis for interviews: Some experiences from the field. *Music Education Research, 11*(4), 425–437. doi:10.1080/14613800903390766.

Sennett, R. (2008). *The craftsman*. London: Penguin Books.

Thurman, L., & Welch, G. (2001). *Bodymind & voice: Foundations of voice education*. Minneapolis: The VoiceCare Network.

Welch, G. F., Howard, D., Himonides, E., & Brereton, J. (2005). Real time feedback in the singing studio: An innovatory action-research project using new voice technology. *Music Education Research, 7*(2), 225–249.

Chapter 7
Sensual, Sensory and Sensational Narratives

lisahunter and elke emerald

Abstract Sensory and sensual methodologies are becoming more commonplace, although feminists, indigenous, performance and artistic scholars have been using such methodologies for some time. It is through our senses that narratives become possible in their construction and in their communication. This chapter summarises the current state of sensory methodologies and discusses the sensory shifts within qualitative research, from largely ocular-centric hegemony to a myriad of senses now being explored. As a way in to sensory narratives, we suggest a framework that intersect the three research 'moments' field, interim and research texts, with four sense epistemes – senses, sensual experience, sensory geographies, and sensational learning/turning points.

Keywords Sensory narrative • Narrative • Senses • Sensual • Sensational • Embodiment • Emplacement

Researching the Surfing Festival

Being there was a sensory feast: I *felt* the intense heat of an unforgiving sun that parched whatever of my skin was not covered by the shade of tents and umbrellas; or the maximum covering of clothing that was hot to touch, sticking in uncomfortable bunches at joints. In another moment, cyclonic winds and rain belting everything; I *felt* the soft white sand tickle the soles of my feet, dropping from my skin as it dried around my imprints which turned to concrete after hours of standing in order to see over the heads of the thousands around me; yet yielding to every move and allowing for moulding a comfortable seat in the moments I could sit and rest; I *smelled* the salt, wafting from onshore breezes that danced across the ocean, sometimes barely disturbing the water's surface or so strong that they created monster waves over three metres; I *tasted* salt, licked from my drying lips, mixed with the

---

This chapter is a development of lisahunter and elke emerald (2016) Sensory narratives: capturing embodiment in narratives of movement, sport, leisure and health, *Sport, Education and Society*, 21:1, 28–46. Some text is reproduced here with permission of Taylor and Francis www.tandfonline.com.

lisahunter (✉)
Freelance Academic, Independent Scholar, Hamilton, New Zealand
e-mail: lisahunteracademic@gmail.com

e. emerald
School of Education and Professional Studies, Griffith University, Brisbane, Australia

© Springer Science+Business Media Singapore 2017
R. Dwyer et al. (eds.), *Narrative Research in Practice*,
DOI 10.1007/978-981-10-1579-3_7

> sharp taste of sunscreen and relieved by the litres of water I buried in 2 litre PET bottles in the sand beside me; I *heard* the early morning swish of small waves lapping at the sand, and the crash of waves against the rocks or sea-on-sea on days of foul weather, accompanied by the ceaseless chatter from the multitude of speakers spread along the beach, announcing the activities of the day, advertising sponsors and sharing music designed to get spectators vibrating to the sounds or that of bygone golden and iconic eras of surfing. (Field notes summary, lisahunter 2013)

> … an incredible atmosphere of calm and peace would radiate out … it felt a bit like chamois leather. A very soft, leathery, yellow, warm quality would engulf me as I watched them, ruminating. I became totally captivated by this. …They taught me about a soft, gentle approach to the world, a total quiet relaxation, a regurgitation of thought, of the day's events, the events of a chewing over and a reswallowing, down into the unconscious. I sat there, engulfed in this atmosphere …it was totally real. (Stephan Harding talking about his study of deer) https://www.youtube.com/watch?v=Jbfrl9lIaj4 (1:16:30)

The work of capturing our experiences, as embodied, emplaced and multisensorial, has captured the imagination of qualitative research. Here we ponder how sensual and sensory methods and methodologies can help us to capture our storied worlds in ways that reveal complex embodied, emplaced, multisensorial social phenomena. Narrative inquirers face two particular challenges (at least) when considering questions of the sense-body and that body in place: How to capture, analyse and represent storied worlds in embodied ways and how to capture sensed and embodied experiences in narrative. For example, how might we capture the essentially embodied experience of researching a surfing festival or an encounter with a deer (above), riding a pushbike or eating a peach (with allusion to the poetry of T.S. Eliot, The Love Song of J. Alfred Prufrock), how might we analyse that, and how might we represent that in a way our reader/viewer/listener can engage—and even engage as a body-experience.

As Dwyer and emerald (Chap. 1, this volume) note, there are many possible pathways for a narrative inquiry. The question of which moments in the research will focus on narrative itself is one of the early ones for the inquirer and is driven by epistemological, theoretical and methodological concerns. In a recent paper (lisahunter and emerald 2016), and here, we explore *sensory narratives* as forms that captures embodiment in rich ways, ways that recognise that our 'experience of life is inevitably mediated through our bodies' (Shilling 1993, p. 22), providing multimodal possibilities, new timespace possibilities, and new insights. To seriously engage embodiment and emplacement, we present a framework that considers the three research moments that Jean Clandinin and Michael Connolly propose (2000): field; interim, and, research texts—in terms of four 'sense' epistemes: senses, sensual experience, sensory geographies, and sensational learning/turning points. We do this to explore the possibilities for moving beyond telling stories of us *having* bodies to those that address us *as* bodies (Ellsworth 2005), that is, embodied, emplaced and multisensorial—seeing/feeling/hearing/tasting/smelling/moving… and more.

Sensoriality, Embodiment, and Emplacement

Our storied worlds are, by their very nature, embodied, emplaced and multisensorial. However, to make sense of participants' experiences of their lived worlds, we are often forced to reduce these stories to words on paper; as interview transcriptions, field observations, coded and remodelled summaries, or fragments of narrative written by the participants or researchers. As such, although Dewey's (1938) classic work on experience has progressively been taken up by the social sciences, it is yet to be fully operationalised.

'The body' is not new—scholars such as Pierre Bourdieu worked with the concept of 'habitus' (1977) to break the mind-body duality and consider embodiment, and feminist scholars alerted us to the body, for example Elizabeth Grosz using the concept of 'embodied subjectivities' (1994), and its absence (see for example Birke 1999; Butler 1999; Davies 2000; Gatens 1995, and for a good overview see Brook 2014; Davis 1997; Price and Shildrick 1999). The 'corporeal turn' in sociology recognized that the body had an 'absent presence in sociology' (Shilling 1993, p. 9) and sought to make changes. The concept of 'embodiment' works to recognise that knowledge is not something that resides only in the mind, rather, that knowing is embedded in embodied practices (Pink 2011a). Sensory ethnographers have explored research methods that acknowledge 'that all human experience is mediated via the body and thus the senses' (Sunderland et al. 2012, p. 1057).

More recently, there have been moves to recognise the body as situated in time and place: 'emplacement' recognises the situated/placed/spaced/temporal nature of experience. Emplacement understands place as an 'event', an 'entanglement' of all components of the environment such as 'geological forms, the weather, human socialities, material objects, buildings, animals and more' (Pink 2011a, p. 349). Sarah Pink recognises 'place' as a 'complex ecology of social, material, affective and sensory environmental processes' (Pink 2011a, p. 353). She says "'things' in movement combine to constitute place and the perception of place" (p. 349); so, in her investigation of bullfights,

> the bullfight as place-event is each time reconstituted through the convergence of an intensity of things in process, emotions, sensations, persons and narratives. They are sufficiently similar to previous bullfights to be recognizable as the same event, but they actually constitute a new place-event. The performance of the bullfight is thus much more than embodied. It is better interpreted as part of a complex ecology of things (p. 350).

The bullfight, emplaced, is both in the ring with sand and heat and noise, and embedded in a long history, a national identity and a political milieu. lisahunter's research at surfing festivals (2013), her 'place', the festival, includes the beach, the ocean, the sun, wind and rain, the topology of the ocean floor, the tide, the surfers, locals and visitors, social interactions and positioning, surf boards and wetsuits, sunblock, cars, carparks, dogs, tents, food vendors, coffee vendors, wax and leg ropes, surf lifesaving clubs, practices of standing and looking, and the time of day as well as longitudinal time—as each festival is placed in time in relation to a history (and a future) of such festivals.

Embodiment and emplacement call on us to consider the constraints of written and spoken language in expressing specifically sensed experiences. We might for example, use visual, audio-visual, mobile and arts-based methods to pay attention to sight, sound and spatial knowings. These methods have explored the boundaries of language itself as a mediator of meaning and increasing attention has been given to understanding narratives of specifically sensed experiences. For example, Karen Barbour explores place and performance in her dance scholarship (2014). Andrew Irving (2013) explored peoples' experience of crossing bridges in New York. His field texts were recordings of people's 'think aloud' as they crossed the bridge, his film and photographs of them crossing as they recorded the think aloud, and then his reflections as he retraced their steps whilst listening to their recording. He then (re) presented this research as a fairly usual and formal journal article which included some photographs, but the article also included links to audio and video recordings. We as readers could retrace the journey with the participant and researcher.

Sensory Studies and Sensory Ethnography

Sensory studies are not new. However, we offer that as narrative research, in its many forms, aims to understand *experience*, there is much to learn from both sensory studies and sensory ethnography in particular. Sensory studies set out to explore the senses; especially those beyond the Westernized lenses of touch, taste, sound, smell, vision (Howes 2005, 2009). David Howes, a seminal scholar in sensory studies, has traced a detailed history of sensory studies (http://www.sensorystudies.org/sensorial-investigations/the-expanding-field-of-sensory-studies), citing work throughout the twentieth century such as Margaret Mead and Rhoda Métraux's (1957) cultural study, John Huizinga ([1919] 1996) and Lucien Febvre's ([1942] 1982) transmission of 'historical sensation', and Claude Lévi-Strauss' deciphering of 'sensory codes' in *The Raw and the Cooked* ([1964] 1970). Lévi-Strauss locates a more recent 'sensory turn' in history and anthropology in the 1980s (2003). Since, we have examples such as: Loïc Wacquant's experience of boxing (1995); Elizabeth Probyn's exploration of food (2000); Kirby et al. (2015) who explored the sensory experiences of children with autism spectrum disorder; Filipa Wunderlich (2008) examining the sensing of urban space through walking and rhythmicity; Valtonen et al. (2010) investigating the role of the senses in consumer research; Greg Downey's exploration of learning (2005); lisahunter's research of the surf festival (2013); Jayne Caudwell's bodily sensations of rowing (2011; 2015) and Sarah Pink's exploration of gender and domestic objects (2004).

Sensory ethnographers, like narrative inquirers, draw upon broader sociological perspectives to capture experiences that may precede interpretation, communication, sense-making, or even active awareness and render them recognizable (Sunderland et al. 2012). Sarah Pink (e.g., 2006, 2007, 2009, 2011a, b, c, d, 2013, 2014) has emphasised the participatory nature of sensory research and has developed her sensory ethnography where 'researchers … do not seek to "read", unveil, or decipher a pre-existing, static, or objective cultural "text" but, rather, engage as co-learners and co-creators in the world, sharing and empathising with other people's experiences and actions' (2011d, p. 270).

Acknowledging the work of narrative inquirers such as Cathy Reissman (2012), Greer Johnson (2004) and Hedy Bach (2007), we play with sensory ethnography to offer **sensory narratives**—focusing particularly on creating field, interim and research texts that capture and account for our bodily experiences as multisensorial, embodied and emplaced.

The Sensory Narratives at the Three Research Moments

There are many pathways to and through narrative inquiry and, by definition, many forms of narrative inquiry avoid prescription, rather, allowing and even encouraging back-and-forth and iterative processes. Drawing on Jean Clandinin and Michael Connolly's work (2000) we frame our thoughts around the three moments of research; the construction of *field texts*, the analysis of such texts to create *interim texts*, and, the *research texts* that function to communicate the findings of the research exercise to others. In research processes, these three moments are not necessarily separate or clearly defined, and there are many variations possible at each moment. The overtly 'narrative' element may be most evident at any or all of these three moments.

Sensory Field Texts

The **field texts** that inform a Sensory Narrative, as we pose it here, will have an aim of capturing the sense experiences of participants and of researchers. Considerations arise for what we sense epistemologically, and therefore what we story in field texts. For example, the visuality of surfing is prominent and has therefore been a significant source of field texts in lisahunter's research, among others. These field texts are in the form of photographs, films, magazines, websites, museums and collections, and the social spaces at beaches and alternate surfing sites, competitions, and surf festivals. But there are also many other senses operating in the experiences of surfing, spectating surfing, and even researching surfing (lisahunter 2013, 2014a, b, 2015).

When we have tried as researchers to access senses through interviews *in situ* (e.g., at the beach) we have found there is a sensorium order of the visual, then aural, with little attention to senses such as touch, smell and taste. In surfing research, kinaesthetic, temporal and affective senses are sometimes referred to, albeit in rather coded ways, with a shorthand of 'stoke', 'flow' or something 'sublime' (see for example Ford and Brown 2006; Stranger 2011). So, to extend the sensorial tapestry, researchers might probe the tastes, smells, pleasures, temporality, spatiality, pressures, temperatures and discomforts. For example, Jacquelyn Allen-Collinson and John Hockey explore the haptic sense in distance running and scuba diving (2010); Åsa Bäckström investigates kinaesthetic experiences in skateboarding (2012). In the introduction to this chapter, we saw how Stephan Harding talked about his felt sense of the quality of his experiences researching deer in the forest.

In doing sensory narrative research, the question of *which* senses and *how* to capture them is alive. Multimodal methods under debate and in experimentation in the field of Sensory Ethnography give us some guidance, including, for example, interviews, written texts, photos, videos, sound recordings, performances, and art-works. Sensory ethnographers remind us that, as demonstrated in Stephan Harding's efforts to capture his experience, 'sensory engagement with places and people involves diverse and complex interactions between senses (i.e. 'multisensoriality') and encompasses senses that are not commonly recognised in western cultures; such as movement, progression of time, and insight' (Sunderland et al. 2012, p. 1057). It is no simple thing to create field texts that capture this complexity. Anna Harris and Marilys Guillemin (2012) use sensory questions as access points during interviews with patients to ask patients about their experiences of being a hospital inpatient. Noreen Orr and Cassandra Phoenix (2015) explored using photographs to capture sensual experiences of ageing bodies during physical activity. Vera Caine gave 2nd and 3rd grade students cameras to record their understanding of 'community' (2010). Arts based and performance scholars have long explored senses, such as Karen Barbour's explorations of movement in dance (2014).

When we start out, we might try to capture this complexity by first 'sensitizing' ourselves, through searching the literature and other sources (e.g., film, poetry and so forth), to explore what senses are already articulated in the contexts we are about to research, and how. Then we need to account for our own sensorial subjectivity and intersubjectivity through our own autoethnography in order to situate ourselves reflexively (see Pink 2009 for example) and guide text construction methods. In turning to others, we might ask participants to tell us their story, and focus on the five assumed Western senses: what did you see, feel (touch), hear, taste, and smell? Our own experience as researchers at surfing festivals is that participants quite easily recounted what they saw and heard, then slowed down at feel (hot, cold, sandy, the rise and fall of the swell as a surfer waits out the back for their turn to catch a wave), but stalled, or nearly so, at taste and smell (although in surfing research, the potent context of the ocean offers 'salt' as both a taste and smell—allowing interviewees some entre into a potentially unfamiliar recount). However, recognising multisensoriality, Sunderland et al. (2012, p. 1057) notes:

> data collection techniques and technologies in sensory ethnography are not expected to directly capture a specific "sense" such as sight, sound, touch, taste, or smell… any one recording can represent numerous sensorial experiences including the five western senses as well as sensorial experiences that are less commonly acknowledged.

So, taking lisahunter's text as an example—while that text cycles through the Western sensorium, feel, touch, smell, taste, hear, see,—as a Sensory Narrative we can hope that through evocative writing the 'whole is greater than the sum of the parts'. For example, Jayne Caudwell (2015) explores the possibilities for pleasure through monotonous and slow bodily movement. Jayne evokes the senses of sight and smell and sound, but also evokes the kinaesthetic senses and connects the kinaesthetic to affect:

> This is my favourite place to sit…Ignoring the grunts from the hefty young man on the rowing machine next to hers, she settles in to her own flows of legs-stomach-arms. Repeatedly, her heels and bum, knees and shoulders press together, for the shortest time, before her body uncoils, again, and again. After the leg-drive, when her upper body rocks backwards, she feels the long, luxurious stretch in the deepest tissues of her gut. Each time, at the end of every drive and pull, she opens up, like a big cat exposing its underbelly. She loves this cycle of coiling and recoiling, in and out; the slippages of the powerful and the vulnerable; the churning of the strong and the weak. (p. 310)

And

> Someone sits next to her. She senses their presence, smells their being and she catches their form in the corner of her eye. But she doesn't stop; she doesn't turn and look. On few occasions she rows alongside friends. Most of the time she rows with strangers. When this stranger gets going she slots into their rhythm. She doesn't do this with the fast, only with the slow. She adapts the length and pressure of her strokes to make them fit. She can row with a stranger for a long time. She loves these unisons without eye contact, without words; the gentle console of silent, human, physical synergy. (p. 316)

In 'powerful', 'vulnerable', 'churning', 'strong', 'weak', 'sensing presence' and 'the gentle console of silent, human, physical synergy' Jayne invites us in to some of the qualities of that sensual and sensory 'whole'.

Sensory Interim Texts

Different field texts suggest and enable different forms of analysis, and the two research points may often be inseparable, data being produced through the researcher's sensorium. As always, the creation of **interim** texts will be informed/driven by the questions of methodology, epistemology and theory that underpin the research, and by questions of the purpose of the research. Two questions arise for us; firstly, how might we analyse the texts (in whatever form they are), and secondly, how might we employ our own senses in or as analysis?

In working to push beyond words on a page, visual analysis is certainly a well developed sensory form of analysis with established roots in a variety of disciplines from discourse analysis, film analysis and art (see lisahunter, Chap. 5, this volume). One of our first visual analyses was a qualitative and quantitative content analysis of visual representations of females in surfing magazines (lisahunter and Austin 2008). Moving beyond the visual, our preliminary analysis of the soundscape of a surf festival placed the recorded soundscape alongside interview and survey responses from spectators and competitors. This analysis highlighted the importance of sound speakers for competitors on the waves—to know their scores and also to 'get pumped' or 'in the zone' during competition. Spectators reported varying responses to the festival soundscape, from annoyance at the 'inane and constant drivel' of the commentators, to pleasure in the music creating a 'festival vibe' and appreciation of the informative commentary (lisahunter and emerald 2013; lisahunter 2014a). Competitors reported the use of earphones and specific music prior to competition as a significant feature of competition preparation in both blocking the public soundscape and creating a private one. Jacquelyn Allen-Collinson and Helen Owton (2014) also approach soundscape in their analysis of the auditory work associated with asthma and sporting embodiment. Bernie Krause (2013) records wild soundscapes; the wind in the trees, the chirping of birds, the subtle sounds of insect larvae. He uses the soundscape to plot the health of habitats, especially in environments that have been radically altered by humans.

In analysis, Kathleen Riach and Samantha Warren (2015), tried to understand how participants used senses in their storying of something. As a way in to analysis, their work asked—can we analyse the participants' narrative as a documentation of their sensory experience? They studied the everyday smells in offices and analysed the field texts as three elements of bodily integrity: 'sensual signifiers', 'cultural permeability' and 'locating smell in between' (p. 1).

As researchers, interim texts raise questions of theory, for example Gordon Waitt explores the changing relationships between space, gender and surfing bodies, examining how gender and surf space are mutually constituted. His analysis is explicitly 'framed within theoretical works relating to Elspeth Probyn's spatial imperative of subjectivities and the performance of corporeal femininities and masculinities' (Waitt 2008, p. 75).

Employing our own senses in analysis might entail listening to recordings of interviews rather than reading transcripts, or smelling/tasting/watching/feeling field texts. Such sensory analysis is frequently used in consumer marketing to test products by using human senses to understand why some products are preferred over others. emerald and Carpenter (2015) ask whether their own physical (e.g., pain) and emotional (e.g., sadness, overwhelm) responses can be understood as a field text, that is, a form of 'data' or 'evidence'. They examine the possibilities and pitfalls of 'reading' their own sensory experience for 'analysis'.

Sensory Research Texts

The third research moment speaks to sensory **research** texts or representations of the research. Questions of how, when and in what form to present the research are informed by questions of audience, context, theory, methodology and epistemology. Having gathered and created a rich variety of field and interim texts, it is in the question of (re)presentation or research texts that we may feel most frustrated by the limitations of the printed word even though options abound for (re)presentation, both within print genres and beyond; for example, print genres include narrative, autoethnography, poetry, and the historically more usual manuscripts (books, chapters, articles). Moving beyond print, we ask how we can we challenge the linear written word and employ multisensory and multimodal means to open up the possibility to 'read' the research through other senses for example, performance, art, music, drama, film, audio. Our own narrative research has been (re)presented in many ways as we explore this relationship between sensory and narrative—as reports, newspaper articles, journal articles, book chapters, participant play performances, researcher performances, film, websites, installations and paintings. Conferences such as the International Congress for Qualitative Inquiry (QI) and Contemporary Ethnography Across the Disciplines Hui (CEAD) include many performance modes for research texts. For example, lisahunter's installation at CEAD 2014 employed sound, vision, and space to create an experience of tension (2014b); elke produced and facilitated a communal painting ethnography (2014a) and presented a completed painting installation (2014b); John Dahlsen exhibited a range of photographic works that used found objects on the beach to explore human relationship with the environment (2014, 2016). Other presentations included dance, videos, performance and poetry.

Alternate forms of representation may produce tension for us as researchers; so schooled are we in didactically presenting 'research findings'. To what extent can we submit to the uncertainty of interpretation that alternate forms might evoke? 'Indeed, if it were possible to characterise sensations and feelings precisely, would poetry continue to exist? Would language not work more like math? Would all of the arts not feel like positive sciences?' (Vannini et al. 2012, p. 6). While multimodal forms are now more common in qualitative fields, they are yet to find true legitimation within the academy alongside the written text you are engaged with right now, this was the subject of a recent journal's special issue (lisahunter et al. 2014).

Intersections for Making Sense

Here, from our interest in sensory narratives across three moments of research we suggest a systematic approach to sensory narrative through a framework of the senses/sensory. In the spirit of inquiry this framework is experimental. It is systematic, but not intended as prescriptive or exhaustive. In Fig. 7.1 we intersect the research moments with four epistemes of sensory inquiry: the senses; the sensual; sensory geographies of emplacement, and, sensational learning points and turning points. Each of the intersections raises considerations for research, summarized (Fig. 7.1) and then discussed.

	Senses	Sensual	Sensory geographies of emplacement	Sensational – learning points and turning points
Field texts considerations of 'evidence' or 'data'	Collecting sights, sounds (and silences) tastes, touches and smells. How to we 'gather' or 'record' movement for example? How do we gather what these senses evoke in participants?	Recording the quality of senses within a narrative-how does touch, for example, play out as pleasure, pain or nostalgia. How do we record affect – how do we record stories in ways that evoke happiness, anger, disgust and so on as the storyteller experienced it.	Capturing and documenting the entanglements of place/space/time/materiality/biology	The question of 'what captures your attention'. Capturing the sense experiences that change us or turn us. The critical incident.
Interim texts considerations of analysis	How to analyse sights, sounds (and silences) tastes, touches and smells. Is there a grammar? A code?	What do pleasure, pain and so on mean to participants and to the research. How do we 'analyse' these qualities?	How to analyse and organize complex entanglements of place/space/time/materiality/biology	The reflective and reflexive turn - Why did that capture my attention, how has is turned me, how/what did I learn. Noticing patterns in my own and my participants attention.
Research texts issues of representation	Problems of using language to represent the senses: what are the languages of taste, touch, smell, sound and so on. Challenges in representing movement and temperature for example. Writing evocatively Issues of representation arts, words, visuals, etc Trusting the reader and trusting the text Using the senses to create a text and creating a text that can be engaged sensorially: can it be touched, smelt, tasted, can a research text evoke pleasure or pain, where/when is it in place/space/time, how can a text capture me in a way that 'turns' me?			

Fig. 7.1 Considerations in sensory narrative intersections: 3 moments and 4 epistemes

The Four Intersections

Senses

A focus on the senses themselves raises issues. Across all three research moments we can ask *which* senses are being attended to by the research, which are overlooked, which may be alive to participants but not recognized by the researcher's sensorial subjectivity, and what are the complex interactions of multisensoriality

(Sunderland et al. 2012, p. 1057)? However, to be awake to senses beyond one's own or the dominant 'Western' sensorium may be quite challenging to those of us colonised by the western academy (see Classen 1993).

Each research moment presents challenges of experiencing, describing and languaging the senses (if we choose to use words, that is). New technologies give new ways to gather, create, document and record researchers' own sense/s and those of participants. These technologies, like any, have their own practical requirements (data storage for example) and present us with the familiar method questions of the relationship between experience and data, in this case, the relationship between the sensation, the recording and transcription/translating for analysis. Given, as Rhys-Taylor (2013, p. 363) reminds us, '...the precise meanings of specific sensations are presented as being, ultimately, in the eyes, ear, fingers and nostrils of the beholder', the sensory researcher, like many qualitative researchers, might grapple with capturing human experience that is 'true' to that experience, in some way that represents experience in a recognisable and communicable form.

One of the challenges of research in sense perception is that both participants and researchers may find it difficult to draw on precise terms to language what we are sensing—be it to communicate something of the experience to the researcher at the field text moment or to disseminate research at the research text moment. Each sense-field is itself a developed area of study, yet as researchers we are not expert in them all, nor will our participants be. For example, while the science of smell is well developed in fields such as perfume making, wine tasting and certain food development industries, many of us have quite limited language of smell, often describing a thing rather than a smell ('it smells lemony') and few have the language to describe even the seven classes of odour: musky, putrid, pungent, camphoraceous, ethereal, floral and pepperminty. Likewise, experience and language of taste encompasses sweet, sour, salty, bitter and umami. When experiencing, describing and articulating touch, we might consider both the tactile (texture and temperature for example) and the haptic (kinaesthetic information or a sense of position, motion and force). When considering sound, we might experiment with soundscapes and learn to represent silence in our sensory narratives. Visual research is extensive. So, a question for us as narrative researchers is how we enter the edges of these fields in fruitful ways. And again, as always, are questions of representation, the extent to which we are able to 'show not tell' and the extent to which we are able to use written language (still the prime means of communicating in academia) to real effect (certainly a preoccupation of narrative inquirers) or move beyond the grasp of written language.

Sensual

Taking into account affect, mood and emotion,[1] this second episteme asks us to consider the *experience* of senses at each of the three research moments; what are the *qualities* of experience; pleasure, pain, nostalgia, melancholy, joy and so on.

[1] These are often conflated terms. We consider feelings to be personal and biographical, emotions are social, and affects are prepersonal, although we do not unpack these in this chapter.

How might we access these qualities, as an experience (for ourselves and participants) and how might we language these in effective and evocative ways, for example 'showing' not 'telling'? How might we evoke sensual qualities in research texts when so much is unsaid and unsayable? And conversely, how might we avoid the well-worn tropes (and, even, clichés) of those who have languaged sensual experience before us? How might we pay attention to our own sensuality when participating with others as subjects and how do we analyse texts that are rich in emotion and affect? Recall Stephan Harding describing the sensual quality of his observations:

> … an incredible atmosphere of calm and peace would radiate out … it felt a bit like chamois leather. A very soft, leathery, yellow, warm quality would engulf me as I watched them, ruminating. https://www.youtube.com/watch?v=Jbfrl9lIaj4 (1:16:30)

Stephan uses metaphors of touch, colour and temperature to capture affect.

Sensory Geographies of Emplacement

Given the 'complex ecology of things' Pink (2011a, p. 353), the entanglements of time, space, and 'things'—be they material, living, non-living or symbolic 'things' —we have to acknowledge that narratives are embedded in relationships with people, objects, space, place and time. But drawing out what might be tacit knowledge makes for a difficult process in creating, articulating, or translating narratives sensescapes. At each of the research moments we face the familiar qualitative challenge of knowing which of the 'things' entangled in this space/place/time are 'relevant' (whatever relevant may mean), which are recordable, and how to record, reframe (analyse) and (re)present in a sensory narrative. Consider for example, Eileen Honan's exploration of the interview (2014). She works to disrupt what have become usual and routine habits of interviewing in qualitative inquiry and presents an assemblage that enables reader access to many facets of the entanglement of space/place/time/history/politics that could have easily been glossed as 'an interview' in her research. Using photographs, pieces of transcript, her own critical commentary alongside the text, retelling of events from history, and, screen shots, Eileen enables 'thinking of different ways of writing/speaking/representing the interactions between researcher and researched that will breathe new life into qualitative inquiries' (2014, p. 1).

Sensational—Learning Points and Turning Points

This episteme draws attention to the questions of 'what has captured my (participant or researcher) attention', 'turned' me in some way (which could even be physically turning to look). It is 'critical' or 'sensational' not necessarily because it is sensational in a conventional sense of shocking or surprising, indeed it may be a mundane, routine or common thing, but because it moves my senses so that I am turned toward it to give my attention. In describing sensational pedagogies Elizabeth Ellsworth (2005) explored a variety of public sites, such as museums, that stimulated the senses, took participants' attention or acted as learning points. David Tripp (1993) talks of 'critical incidents' that act as turning points in practice. For example, a graduate student, herself a primary school teacher, once described to elke how she suddenly 'got' the concept of heteronormativity when asking her students at school to line up in two lines; girls and boys. This mundane practice was sensational to her—it alerted her not only to what heteronormativity is, but to the myriad ways that our society works to wrap a million thin threads of normativity around taken-for-granted concepts. This sensational moment was a path in to critical scholarship for this student. Our sensory narratives can capture these sensational moments of particular learning as another entry to expressing and understanding our topic of enquiry. A sensational moment might be state of flow, intense lighting, a soothing soundscape, cold air, or the presence of particular smells and these can evoke moments of learning, or enhance ones' learning. Although for different reasons, both advertisers and pedagogues are invested in what makes a difference to a consumers/learners engagement. Sensory narratives may capture these sensational phenomena. In the following extract from a research text, Ian Davis (2015) describes sensational moments of learning and turning in his life with his grandfather, in mundane activities like watching his grandfather shave, go to work or read the newspaper, moments where the author explores learning to be masculine in his early childhood. As we read, we can ask what might have been his field texts, his analysis, his interim texts, his intersections, and what might be additional research texts in the future?

Bedminster, Bristol 1969

I used to practice shaving, using my finger as a razor, scraping the recently brushed on soap away while making the right faces in the mirror; feeling the bitter soap on my lips, the steam on my face and the cold tiles under my tiny feet. In a modest terrace house in Bristol my Granddad and I bookended the generations of women that we lived with. My Granddad had fathered three daughters; as his first grandson I was dubbed his 'one and only' a title that made me as uncomfortable as it did proud. Leaving for work in the morning he would often say, 'right me one and only—you're the man of the house now', passing an invisible baton; an instruction that, for a three year old, left me perplexed and anxious. But I observed him in earnest and followed his lead. I played at polishing shoes, laying them out on sheets of newspaper in the back kitchen. I claimed my own exclusive spot within the living room and began standing outside on the driveway, practicing a posture that appeared purposeful. I tried weeing standing up, struggling to reach the rim, and I always, always, was very grateful for any food and the care of the women that surrounded me. Was this what he meant?

Being at work all day and in the garden or shed most evenings, my Granddad hardly inhabited the house at all, yet our home smelt primarily of him, smells of manliness; shoe

> polish, diesel fuel from his work coat, shaving soap, a musky minty sweaty tang. As a scent, manliness pervaded the household; yet none of us, including my Granddad, was clear who owned this smell, where it came from or how it could be claimed. Once he left for work I would gaze at the women of the house, my mother, my aunts and Grandmother, getting ready for their day. This activity involved covering up, putting on of tights and girdles, nail varnish, talcum powder, make up, hairspray and rollers. The women I knew had an armory of tools and disguises, and as this was the sixties, sometimes included wigs, big eyelashes or extra-long nails. We had no such disguises, my Granddad and me. (Davis 2015, p. 12)

What Now?

As narrative researchers and inquirers generally—we imagine that you will resonate easily with the assertion that our experience of the world is, by its very nature, embodied, emplaced and multisensorial, and, as such, our stories, counter-stories, meta stories and cultural stories have their roots well in the senses. The narrative, body, spatial and sensory turns in qualitative inquiry have provided us with new perspectives, new questions, new methodologies and new epistemologies. We see that bringing such turns into deliberate and closer alignment will create significant intersections between research moments; using the narrative form in a way that can further inform us epistemologically (sensorially) and methodologically (intersections). Giving attention to the multisensorial and translating that to multimodal possibilities for research heralds exciting times for narrative researchers attempting to move beyond ocularcentric research and written-text based representations. We face ongoing challenges of creating/capturing, analysing, and representing storied worlds in embodied and emplaced ways. Performance, arts based and sensory ethnographers have opened the way for us and we believe that further experimentation and dialogue about the methodological and epistemological affordances of sensory narratives lays the ground for more extensive and sophisticated research that will not only inform the narrative and sensory fields but may also provide the disruption needed to pay attention to the embodied and emplaced consciousness of the subjects in our research. We propose that considering the senses in the form of these four epistemes—senses, sensual experience, sensory geographies, and sensational learning/turning points—will push theoretical boundaries by acting as means to examine in some detail the (im)material experiences and meaning making associated with embodiment. This may facilitate interruptions to Cartesian duality, dissolve distinctions between body, mind and representation, and postulate new possibilities for discussion beyond other dualities such as reality-representation, inside-outside and so forth. Consideration of the senses must include considerations of the timespace possibilities that open up new senses and new methodologies to engage with these possibilities; ultimately providing new insights, forging new directions and research possibilities to explain complex social relations embedded in enduring narratives and those we have not yet sensed.

Discussion Questions

1. Consider your research question or topic. Map how sensory or sensual elements could complement your field texts (or data). Consider analysis of those texts.
2. How might you use sensory devices within your research texts? How might this enhance the reader's experience?

References

Allen-Collinson, J., & Hockey, J. (2010). Feeling the way: Notes toward a haptic phenomenology of distance running and scuba diving. *International Review for the Sociology of Sport, 46*(3), 330–345.

Allen-Collinson, J., & Owton, H. (2014). Take a deep breath: Asthma, sporting embodiment, the senses and 'auditory work'. *International Review for the Sociology of Sport, 49*(5), 592–608.

Bach, H. (2007). Composing a visual narrative inquiry. In D. J. Clandinin (Ed.), *Handbook of narrative inquiry: Mapping a methodology* (pp. 280–307). Thousand Oaks: Sage.

Bäckström, Å. (2012, August). Knowing and teaching explosiveness in skateboarding: Remembrance and expression of kinaesthetic experience. *Sport, Education & Society, 19*(6): 1–21, 752–772.

Barbour, K. (2014). Place-responsive choreography and contemplative pedagogies: A sensual experience. In Contemporary Ethnographies Across the Disciplines (CEAD) Hui. Hamilton: The University of Waikato.

Birke, L. (1999). *Feminism and the biological body*. Edinburgh: Edinburgh University Press.

Bourdieu, P. (1977). *Outline of a theory of practice*. Cambridge: Cambridge University Press.

Brook, B. (2014). *Feminist perspectives on the body*. Abingdon: Routledge.

Butler, J. (1999). Bodies that matter. In M. Shildrick & J. Price (Eds.), *Feminist theory and the body* (pp. 235–245). Edinburgh: Edinburgh University Press.

Caine, V. (2010, December). Visualizing community: Understanding narrative inquiry as action research. *Educational Action Research, 18*(4), 481–496.

Caudwell, J. (2011). 'Easy, Oar!': Rowing reflections. *Qualitative Research in Sport, Exercise and Health, 3*(2), 117–129. doi:10.1080/2159676X.2011.572179.

Caudwell, J. (2015). 'Feeling blue': The ordinary pleasures of mundane motion. *Qualitative Research in Sport, Exercise and Health, 7*(3), 309–320. doi:10.1080/2159676X.2014.935462.

Clandinin, D. J., & Connelly, F. M. (2000). *Narrative inquiry: Experience and story in qualitative research*. San Francisco: Jossey-Bass.

Classen, C. (1993). *Worlds of sense: Exploring the senses in history and across cultures*. New York: Routledge.

Dahlsen, J. (2014). *Communicating an emergent vision through environmental art. Discussing economic viability for artists creating environmental transformation*. Presentation at Sensual Landscapes of Ethnography the Contemporary Ethnography Across the Disciplines Conference, 25–28 November, Hamilton, New Zealand.

Dahlsen, J. (2016). Communicating an emergent vision through environmental art: Discussing economic viability for artists creating environmental transformation. In e. emerald, R. Rinehart, & A. Garcia (Eds.), *Global South ethnographies: Minding the senses*. Amsterdam: Sense.

Davies, B. (2000). *A body of writing, 1990–1999*. Walnut Creek: Alta Mira Press.

Davis, K. (Ed.). (1997). *Embodied practices: Feminist perspectives on the body*. London: Sage.

Davis, I. (2015). *Stories of men and teaching: A new narrative approach to understanding masculinity and education*. London: Springer.

Dewey, J. (1938). *Experience and education*. New York: Macmillan.

Downey, G. (2005). *Learning capoeira*. Oxford: Oxford University Press.

Ellsworth, E. (2005). *Places of learning: Media, architecture, pedagogy.* New York: Routledge Falmer.
emerald, e. (2014a). *Painting ethnography.* Presentation at Sensual Landscapes of Ethnography the Contemporary Ethnography Across the Disciplines Conference, 25–28 November 2014, Hamilton, New Zealand.
emerald, e. (2014b). *So I have my ducks in a row: Performativity in the academy.* Art piece and exegesis at Sensual Landscapes of Ethnography the Contemporary Ethnography Across the Disciplines Conference, 25–28 November 2014, Hamilton, New Zealand.
emerald, e., & Carpenter, L. (2015, October). Vulnerability and emotions in research: risks, dilemmas and doubts. *Qualitative Inquiry, 21*(8), 741–750.
Febvre, L. ([1942] 1982). *The problem of unbelief in the sixteenth century: The religion of Rabelais* (B. Gottlieb, Trans.). Cambridge, MA: Harvard University Press.
Ford, N., & Brown, D. (2006). *Surfing and social theory: Experience, embodiment, and narrative of the dream glide.* London: Routledge.
Gatens, M. (1995). *Imaginary bodies: Ethics, power, and corporeality.* New York: Routledge.
Grosz, E. (1994). *Volatile bodies: Toward a corporeal feminism.* St. Leonards: Allen and Unwin.
Harris, A., & Guillemin, M. (2012). Developing sensory awareness in qualitative interviewing: A portal into the otherwise unexplored. *Qualitative Health Research, 22*(5), 689–699. doi:10.1177/1049732311431899.
Honan, E. (2014). Disrupting the habit of interviewing. *Reconceptualizing Educational Research Methodology, 5*(1). https://journals.hioa.no/index.php/rerm/article/view/929
Howes, D. (Ed.). (2005). *Empire of the senses: The sensual culture reader.* Oxford: Berg.
Howes, D. (Ed.). (2009). *The sixth sense reader.* Oxford: Berg.
Huizinga, J. ([1919] 1996). *The autumn of the Middle Ages* (R. Payton & U. Mammitzsch, Trans.). Chicago: University of Chicago Press.
Irving, A. (2013). Bridges: A new sense of scale. *Senses and Society, 8*, 290–313.
Johnson, G. (2004). Reconceptualising the visual in narrative inquiry into teaching. *Teaching & Teacher Education, 20*, 423–434.
Kirby, A., Dickie, V., & Baranek, G. (2015, April). Sensory experiences of children with autism spectrum disorder: In their own words. *Autism, 19*(3), 316–326.
Krause, B. (2013). The voice of the natural world. *Ted Talk* http://www.ted.com/talks/bernie_krause_the_voice_of_the_natural_world?language=en
Lévi-Strauss, C. ([1964] 1970). *The raw and the cooked: Introduction to a science of mythology* (Vol. 1, J. Weightman & D. Weightman, Trans.). New York: Harper and Row.
lisahunter. (2013). What did I do-see-learn at the beach? Surfing festival as a cultural pedagogical sight/site. In L. Azzarito & D. Kirk (Eds.), *Physical culture, pedagogies and visual methods* (pp. 144–161). New York: Routledge.
lisahunter. (2014a). *Shifting tides: The NZ Surf Festival 2014* (pp. 1–22). Kirikiriroa/Hamilton: The University of Waikato.
lisahunter. (2014b). Spinning wheel very pretty and the cyborg academic, Installation at *Sensual Landscapes of Ethnography* the Contemporary Ethnography Across the Disciplines Conference, 25–28 November 2014, Hamilton, New Zealand.
lisahunter. (2015). Seaspaces: Surfing the sea as pedagogy of self. In B. Humberstone & M. Brown (Eds.), *Seascapes: Shaped by the sea* (Embodied narratives and fluid geographies, pp. 41–54). Surrey: Ashgate.
lisahunter, & Austin, H. (2008, May 28–31). *Pedagogy of the surfing magazine: Learning to be female.* Paper presented at the Hawaii International Conference on Social Sciences, Waikiki.
lisahunter, & emerald, e. (2013). *A little-big event: The NZ Surf festival 2013.* Kirikiriroa: The University of Waikato.
lisahunter, & emerald, e. (2016). Sensory narratives: Capturing embodiment in narratives of movement, sport, leisure and health. *Sport, Education and Society, 21*(1), 28–46.
lisahunter, Wubbels, T., Clandinin, D. J., & Hamilton, M. (2014). Moving beyond text: Editorial for special issue. *Teaching & Teacher Education, 37*(1), 162–164.

Mead, M., & Métraux, R. (Eds.). (1957). *The study of culture at a distance*. Chicago: University of Chicago Press.
Orr, N., & Phoenix, C. (2015, August). Photographing physical activity: Using visual methods to 'grasp at' the sensual experiences of the ageing body. *Qualitative Research, 15*(4), 454–472.
Pink, S. (2004). *Home truths: Gender, domestic objects and everyday life*. Oxford: Berg.
Pink, S. (2006). *The future of visual anthropology: Engaging the senses*. Abingdon: Routledge.
Pink, S. (2007). *Doing visual ethnography: Images, media, and representation in research* (2nd ed.). London: Sage.
Pink, S. (2009). *Doing sensory ethnography*. London: Sage.
Pink, S. (2011a). From embodiment to emplacement: Re-thinking competing bodies, senses and spatialities. *Sport, Education & Society, 16*(3), 345–355.
Pink, S. (2011b). Images, senses and applications- Engaging visual anthropology. *Visual Anthropology, 24*(5), 437–454. doi: http://dx.doi.org/10.1080/08949468.2011.604611
Pink, S. (2011c). Sensory digital photography: Re-thinking 'moving' and the image. Visual Studies, 26(1), 4–13.
Pink, S. (2011d). Multimodality, multisensoriality and ethnographic knowing: Social semiotics and phenomenology of perception. Qualitative Research, 11(3), 261–276.
Pink, S. (2013). Engaging the senses in ethnographic practice. *The Senses and Society, 8*(3), 261–267.
Pink, S. (2014). Digital–visual–sensory design anthropology: Ethnography, imagination and intervention. *Arts & Humanities in Higher Education, 13*(4), 412–427. doi:10.1177/1474022214542353.
Price, J., & Shildrick, M. (Eds.). (1999). *Feminist theory and the body: A reader*. Edinburgh: Edinburgh University Press.
Probyn, E. (2000). *Carnal appetites: Foodsexidentities*. New York: Routledge.
Reissman, C. (2012). Sensual and seductive aspects of narrative inquiry. *Rassegna Italiana Di Sociologia, 53*(4), 553–572.
Rhys-Taylor, A. (2013). The senses in self, society, and culture: A Sociology of the senses. *The Senses & Society, 8*(3), 362–364.
Riach, K., & Warren, S. (2015, May). Smell organization: Bodies and corporeal porosity in office work. *Human Relations, 68*(5), 789–809.
Shilling, C. (1993). *The body and social theory*. London: Sage.
Stranger, M. (2011). *Surfing life: Surface, substructure and the commodification of the sublime*. Farnham: Ashgate.
Sunderland, N., Bristed, H., Gudes, O., Boddy, J., & Da Silva, M. (2012). What does it feel like to live here? Exploring sensory ethnography as a collaborative methodology for investigating social determinants of health in place. *Health and Place, 18*, 1056–1067.
Tripp, D. (1993). *Critical incidents in teaching: Developing professional judgement*. New York: Routledge.
Valtonen, A., Markuksela, V., & Moisander, J. (2010 June). Doing sensory ethnography in consumer research. *International Journal of Consumer Studies, 34*(4), 375–380. doi:10.1111/j.1470-6431.2010.00876.x.
Vannini, P., Waskul, D., & Gottschalk, S. (2012). *Contemporary sociological perspectives: Senses in self, culture, and society*. Florence: Routledge.
Wacquant, L. (1995). Pugs at work: Bodily capital and bodily labour among professional boxers. *Body & Society, 1*(1), 65–93.
Waitt, G. R. (2008). 'Killing waves': Surfing, space and gender. *Social and Cultural Geography, 9*(1), 75–94.
Wunderlich, F. M. (2008). Walking and rhythmicity: Sensing urban space. *Journal of Urban Design, 13*(1), 125–139.

Chapter 8
Who Is Asking the Questions?

Using Co-constructed Interviews in the Study of Perceived Discrimination from a Discourse Analytical Perspective

Sol Rojas-Lizana

Abstract In co-constructed interviews interviewers act as facilitators engaging with the participant in a dialogical situation but foregrounding the role of the interviewee in the construction and negotiation of meaning. In this chapter I show how the nature of co-constructed interviews is discursively present in the Perceived Discrimination discourse of two stigmatised groups in Australia through key linguistic devices and strategies. The analysis shows the discursive elements that make co-constructed interactions different from other forms of interviews, the type of discourse that emerges when the facilitator is an in-group member, and how it can affect positively the way talk develops. I first present the discursive strategies used by the interviewers where the strategies of offering their own experiences as examples would trigger further participation on the part of the interviewee. Other strategies such as the use of colloquialisms and in-group nomenclature help to produce a relaxed and informal environment during the interaction. The respondents on their part resorted to discursive strategies that included colloquialism, swearing, translanguaging, and in-group terminology. These all reflect the respondents' positive dispositions to retell and discuss their experiences with someone who would understand them, therefore helping to produce data that allow a deeper understanding of the phenomenon studied and of the discourses produced.

Introduction

The 'co-constructed interview' (CI) approach proposes that the roles of both interviewer and interviewee need to be considered in the process of building qualitative data (Miller 2011). In keeping with the genre 'interview', however, the CI

S. Rojas-Lizana (✉)
The University of Queensland, Brisbane, Australia
e-mail: i.rojaslizana@uq.edu.au

© Springer Science+Business Media Singapore 2017

R. Dwyer et al. (eds.), *Narrative Research in Practice*,
DOI 10.1007/978-981-10-1579-3_8

foregrounds the role of the interviewee in the construction and negotiation of meaning. Co-constructed interviews are different from co-constructed narratives, that is, in CI, interviewers act as facilitators who intentionally activate the narrative production of the other by engaging with the participant in a dialogical situation (Holstein and Gubrium 1995), while participants in narratives jointly build the discourses produced (Ellis 2008).

Working with interviews in the field of Discourse Analysis means that special attention is paid not only to what is said in the interview but also to how it is said, as researchers are looking for patterns in language that characterize the topics they are studying. This chapter claims the ideal condition for carrying out an effective CI that includes a sensitive topic is that the interviewer is an insider of the community with which the participant self-identifies. This is desirable for several reasons. Firstly, people produce a social version of themselves, or positioning (Davies and Harré 1990), as a result of the influence of their interlocutor(s) and the situation (genre) in which they are conversing. Studies have shown that participants feel more comfortable with and therefore disclose more to members of their own group given the common ground of understanding that is implicitly shared (Allen 2004; Couture et al. 2012; Dwyer and Buckle 2009; Silverman 2004). Secondly, as facilitators have an emic perspective, they would be aware of their bridging role (in-group to out-group or insider to outsider), and intentionally use a series of linguistic strategies to promote symmetrical communication (Rhee 2008), go into sensitive issues, and provide clarifications for outsiders when carrying out their interview.

The (Applied Linguistics) literature that uses co-constructed interviews has scarcely explained how this type of interview informs their data, analysis and results, although the "language in which the interview is conducted is integrally related to the nature of the co-construction" (Mann 2011, p. 15). In this chapter I address this methodological problem by providing a microanalysis of co-construction that proves that relationship. I point readers to issues of co-construction that show how the interviewers' participation is influential in the final respondents' discourse.

In terms of organisation, after establishing my research assumptions, I give an overview of the interview genre, followed by a presentation of the type of approach I use in connection with co-constructed interviews and a description of my data and the aims of the Perceived Discrimination project. Finally, I analyse the interactive discursive richness that emerges in the co-constructed interview, paying particular attention to the recurring patterns of the exchange. I show how the nature of co-constructed interviews is discursively present in the Perceived Discrimination discourse of two stigmatised groups in Australia through key linguistic devices and strategies. In terms of the interviewees' responses, some of these devices are expressed in the use of in-group jargon and informal language. On their part, the interviewers adopt strategies aimed at creating rapport, expressing empathy and support, as well as making in-group knowledge available to outsiders. It is important to state here that I am not claiming that this modality is superior to other forms of interview, as there may also be disadvantages involved in using in-group interviewers (Rhodes 1994). However, this modality seems to be the most appropriate in the context of doing discourse analysis of Perceived Discrimination, as it accounts for the respondents' experiences, the interviewers would not be identified with perpetrators of discriminatory acts, and would also be seen as fellow discrimination-experiencers.

Research Assumptions

Discourse Analysis (or Discourse Studies) is a multidisciplinary field under the umbrella of Applied Linguistics that adopts a social constructionist approach (Wodak and Meyer 2009). That is, it embraces a paradigm which assumes that reality is constructed and worldview is relational (Burr 2003; Maturana and Dávila 2015). Adopting a constructionist view has several implications in relation to research. First, that phenomena are analysed holistically given that they are interconnected and multidirectional; second, that the context is very important to understand the reality of the phenomenon. Third, that, epistemologically, meaning is situated and constructed in relation to the perspective of the actors (Shkedi 2005).

Discourse Analysis collects data from several sources such as the press, textbooks, social media, discussion fora, billboards, interviews and storytelling. In each case, the researcher will not only look at 'what' is said but also 'how' it is being said. In other words, attention is paid to content in terms of topics and ideas as well as to its linguistic construction, following the cognitive linguistics principle that meaning and form are interconnected (Lee 2001; Taylor 2002). For all these reasons, when discourse analysts work with interviews, they work with a discursive approach as explained in the following section.

The Co-constructed Interview

Qualitative data can be collected in a variety of ways depending on the aims and scope of the research. In Linguistics, narrative was among the first discourse genres analysed (de Fina and Johnstone 2015); now narrative inquiry has become popular as research approach in the past few years (Benson 2014). Interviews have been used for many years in Linguistics, especially in research that looks at identities, experiences and ideology (Mann 2011).

Interviews are established practices which are often encountered in everyday life interactions. People have a general notion of what an interview is, what it conveys and therefore, what to do in the case of being the subject of one. The participants then consciously or unconsciously accommodate this knowledge to their discourse production as they interact within the boundaries of this genre. The interaction itself is somewhat restricted in that each turn is shaped by the previous turn. Interviewees also have an audience in mind apart from the interviewer and thus their discourse may present limitations and different degrees of explicitness, to name a few features.

There are several types of interviews, e.g. standardised interviews, structured and semi-structured interviews, narrative interviews, anecdotal, focused, ethnographic, and co-constructed interviews (Flick 2009). In general, the co-constructed interview is distinguishable by how interviewers act as facilitators who intentionally activate the narrative production of the interviewee, by engaging with the participant in a dialogical situation. Interviewers follow a set of questions, and in that sense these are semi-structured interviews, but are more flexible in that interviewers can facilitate the production of narratives within the interview.

It is important to bear in mind when analysing interviews that it is not so much the type of interview but the approach the researcher adopts that influences the analysis (Mann 2011; Talmy 2010). In this sense, I support Holsten and Gubrium (2004), who consider all types of interviews to be social interactions (naming them 'active interviews'), in the sense that they construct meaning in the collaboration between interviewer and interviewee.

Since I work in the field of Discourse Analysis, my approach to interviews is discursive. This means that "the interview is conceptualised explicitly as a socially-situated 'speech event' (Mishler 1986) in which interviewer(s) and interviewee(s) make meaning, co-construct knowledge, and participate in social practices (Holstein and Gubrium 1995, inter alia)." (Talmy and Richards 2011, p. 2). Therefore, when using interviews as data, I not only consider both participants in the process of meaning construction, but the interviews themselves are used both as research instruments and analysed as a social practice; i.e., as a topic of investigation (Talmy 2010). In this view, interviews are defined as social encounters co-constructed by interviewer and interviewees, in which the influence of each upon the other constructs the specific discourse that is produced in language.

Talmy's (2010) table below (Table 8.1) synthetises clearly what it means to work with interviews as research instruments or as social practice.

Given that the interviewer has an impact on the way that participants respond and may intentionally 'activate narrative production' (Holsten and Gubrium 1995, p. 39) by engaging with the participants, I see that the role of the interviewer in the co-constructed interview is not only to ask, but to encourage, prompt, facilitate, connect and suggest, in order to uncover the richness and complexities of the participants' experiences.

Table 8.1 Contrasting conceptualizations of the research interview (Talmy, 2010, p. 132)

	Interview as research instrument	Research interview as social practice
Status of interview	A tool or resource for "collecting" or "gathering" information	A site or topic for investigation itself
Status of interview data	Data are "reports," which reveal truths and facts, and/or the attitudes, beliefs, and interior, mental states of self-disclosing respondents	Data are "accounts" of truths, facts, attitudes, beliefs, interior, mental states, etc., coconstructed between interviewer and interviewee
Voice	Interviews "give voice" to interviewees	"Voice" is situationally contingent and discursively coconstructed between interviewer and interviewee
Bias	Interviewers must strive to obviate data contamination	Reflexive recognition that data are collaboratively produced (and analysis of how they are); data cannot therefore be contaminated
Analytic approaches	Content or thematic analysis, summaries of data, and/or straightforward quotation, either abridged or verbatim, i.e., the data "speak for themselves."	Data do not speak for themselves; analysis centers on how meaning is negotiated, knowledge is coconstructed, and interview is locally accomplished
Analytic	Product-oriented	Process-oriented
Focus	"What"	"What" and "how"

Data and Methodology

The Perceived Discrimination (PD) Project and the Participants

Until recently, most studies on discrimination and prejudice have centred on the attitudes and behaviours of the perpetrators; however, to better understand discrimination, we also need to examine the perspective of their victims (e.g. Essed 1991, 1992; Lalonde and Cameron 1993; Mellor 2003, 2004; Merino et al. 2009; Rojas-Lizana 2014). PD is the study of discrimination that centres on the victim's experience through the analysis of their accounts. The first studies of PD were of a quantitative nature in the field of social psychology. They would resort to surveys and report their results in terms of numbers. Qualitative studies increased in the 1990s offering another view of the phenomenon of discrimination and its effect on the victims.

Perceived Discrimination and Discourse Analysis

Discourse analysis is a method of carrying out linguistic and social research that has its basis in the ancient study of rhetoric (van Dijk 1996). Generally speaking, it studies language in use in the form of written or spoken text, and within a context, to help understand human systems. Critical discourse analysis (CDA) has traditionally studied elite discourse in order to expose unequal power relations and manipulation (Fairclough 1995, 2002; van Dijk 1997; Wodak and Meyer 2009). It centres on those who have the power to impose their views and how their discourse is used to perpetuate and 'normalize' dominant ideologies. My research, however, belongs to a small number of studies that have focused on the perspectives of the victims of discrimination to develop a greater understanding of the phenomenon and their discourses by classifying their accounts and examining how people who have experienced discrimination convey these stories (Mellor 2003, 2004; Merino 2006; Merino et al. 2009). PD in the field of Discourse Analysis emphasises the discursive aspects of PD by looking at the data in terms of what is said and how it is said. It has been defined as a "cognitive phenomenon embedded within a sociocultural and historical context, which is mostly mediated by discourse." (Merino and Mellor 2009, p. 216).

The data used in this chapter are part of a larger project on Perceived Discrimination that aims to contribute to the investigation of the phenomenon of discrimination, stigma and exclusion by documenting and analysing the discourse of PD reported by people with stigmatized identities during semi-structured, open-ended interviews conducted in Brisbane, Australia (Rojas-Lizana 2014). Studying the discourse of PD offers ways to explore discrimination and social identities from multiple and complex angles, and allows the experiencer to represent themselves to readers in their reflective and active dimensions. These findings help to establish the state of discrimination in specific settings in terms of awareness, disposition and priorities, as well as to show how widespread, settled or rejected certain views about the 'other' are located in the community. The outcome of this research can also inform applied disciplines such as social psychology, human resources management and mental health, and have an impact on policy making. In terms of field contribution, this study aims to advance the knowledge base of Discourse Analysis by increasing the scarce literature that centres on Perceived Discrimination.

The participants constituted two groups: non-heterosexual people in Brisbane (group 1–G1, see Table 8.2); and Spanish speaking immigrants to Australia (group 2–G2, see Table 8.2). In the first group, 18 people self-identifying as LGBTIQ members of the community were interviewed individually. The sample included an age range of 18–65 years; however, 15 of the participants were young adults between the ages of 18 and 30. Sixteen of the participants had tertiary qualifications and two

Table 8.2 Demographics of two participant groups in the Perceived Discrimination project

	LGBTIQ Group (G1) 18 participants	Spanish Speakers Group (G2) 11 participants
Age range	18–65	30–55
Education	16 tertiary, 2 secondary	11 tertiary
Nationality	15 Australia, 1 Singapore, 1 UK, 1 US	2 Argentina, 7 Chile, 1 Ecuador, 1 Spain
LGBTIQ identity	9 Gay or Lesbian, 3 Bisexual, 6 Transgender, 7 Queer	Not asked
Cultural identity	Not asked	2 Argentinean, 1 Australian, 7 Chilean, 1 Ecuadorean, 1 Iberian, 2 Latino/a

had secondary education. They were all interviewed in the Brisbane Metropolitan Area. Fifteen of the participants were Australians, one was a US citizen, one was a UK citizen, and one was a Singaporean. In terms of gender and sexuality, some participants used more than one term to refer to their self-identification. Hence, nine people identified as gay or lesbian, three as bisexual, six as transgender, seven as queer, and five used other terms not included in the acronym. These participants were recruited using a snowball sampling technique, the starting point being the Queer Collective organisation at The University of Queensland.

The second group constituted 11 Spanish-speaking immigrants in Australia. The sample included eight females and three males with an age range of 30–55 years; however, nine of the participants were between the ages of 30–40. All of the participants had tertiary qualifications. They were all interviewed individually in the Brisbane Metropolitan Area using a snowball sampling technique. Seven of them were Chileans, two were Argentineans, one was a Spanish citizen, and one was Ecuadorian. Their residential status comprised five Australian citizens, one permanent resident, two with working visas, and three international students.

Procedure

Ethical clearance from The University of Queensland was obtained before initiating this research. Open-ended interviews were conducted at a preferred location for the participants (e.g. their home, the researcher's office, and university spaces). Individuals in both groups were interviewed by three trained researchers who are members, or self-identified as members, of the LGBTIQ community (Group 1) as well as the Spanish speaking community (Group 2). Participants were recruited using a snowball sampling technique (Lindlof and Taylor 2011), with the data collection phase ending when data saturation occurred. Saturation is present when "a critical threshold of interpretive competence has been reached—when for example, we cease to be surprised by what we observe or we notice that our concepts and propositions are not disconfirmed as we continue to add data" (Lindlof and Taylor 2011, p. 129).

The participants received an information sheet and a consent form which explained the aims and nature of this research, and that they would expect to be asked about experiences of discrimination. They were told that their participation would be anonymous and data would remain confidential. Data were later analysed using Discourse Analysis tools from the fields of Discursive Psychology and Cognitive Linguistics, with the software Leximancer used to validate the recurrence of topics and themes. The examples from Group 2 (G2) were translated into English from Spanish, which was the medium of interview preferred by all participants. When it was found to be linguistically necessary, Spanish was retained in the transcript. In each case, codes G1 or G2 are followed by 'I' ('interview') and a number that chronologically locates each interview.

Results

In this section I show how the discourse of a co-constructed interview in which the interviewer is an in-group member is evidenced in the data. Quoting from the interviews, I first present the discursive strategies that the interviewer uses to co-construct their interview, and then illustrate how the participants' discourses revealed their interaction with the in-group facilitator.

Interviewers' Discursive Strategies in a Co-constructed Interview with In-Group Members

This section centres on the interviewers' linguistic strategies used to co-construct their interaction with the respondents.

Using Colloquial and In-Group Language

In-groups tend to adopt sociolinguistic codes to express their group membership in the form of linguistic and paralinguistic cues. The use and frequency of these expressions in speech depend on the pragmatic situation; hence, this register switching can occur when interacting with either insiders or outsiders. In-group expressions or jargon, as it has been called by some authors, is important as it "plays a major role in the recognition and concealment of identity, as well as in the development of in-group solidarity, and for protection against out-group hostility" (Lumby 1976, p. 385). In interviews with non-group members, language is generally formal and neutral, and the interviewer tends to use formal register and orthophemisms, which are more formal and direct than the correspondent euphemism (Allan and Burridge 2006).

However, in these co-constructed interviews, colloquialisms are frequently used by both interviewer and interviewee, thus marking in-group membership and informality. In-group expressions are also used to less extent. Colloquialisms such as the basic slang 'cool' (Moore 2004; see Sample 6), 'yeah', and 'like' (see Sample 8) in the case of the Facilitator in Group 1; and 'o sea' ('that is', see Sample 5), 'ya' ('sure'), and 'fíjate' ('you see', see Sample 7) in the case of the Facilitator in Group 2 are used frequently in most interviews.

Sample 1

G2I6 Facilitator: <u>Cuéntame</u> un <u>poquito</u> las razones por las que <u>te vienes</u> a Australia (Tell me a little bit about the reasons why you came to Australia)

Sample 2

G2I9 Facilitator: Buena onda ….No hay que ser súper técnico (Cool….you don't have to be very technical [to give me a definition]).
G2I6 Facilitator: Sí poh (sure, of course)

Sample 3

G1I17 Facilitator: Wow. That's very sneaky.
Interviewee: Yeah. Actually, that was the sneakiest period of my time, I think.

Sample 1 is the first (indirect) question in the interview and it shows right from the start that the facilitator is using colloquial forms to address a recipient. First, Spanish is a T-V language, which means it has both a formal and informal way to address its second person. This is reflected not only in the personal pronouns, when present,[1] but also in the verbal conjugation 'Cuéntame' (tell me), and other pronouns (the reflexive 'te' in this case). The use of the formal 'usted' (formal 'you') has several pragmatic functions such as respect and politeness (Zambrano-Paff 2009), but it may also create distance and emphasise unequal relations (such as age and social status) in an interaction. Hence, the facilitators chose not to use the formal 'usted' in any of the interviews (age proximity may have been a factor too). In this example, the facilitator also uses the diminutive of 'poco': 'poquito' (a little bit), which is a colloquialism. One of the functions of diminutives in Spanish is to express good feelings towards others (Travis 2004); however, they are not used in formal language in Standard Spanish.

Sample 2 contains examples of slang emphasised in the underlined words and expressions. The phrase 'sí poh' is a dialectal expression as well as slang, as it is typical of Chilean Spanish. In this particular case, both the facilitator and the participant are from Chile. In Sample 3, the facilitator uses a colloquial and emotional interjection to demonstrate surprise and appreciation, followed by the colloquial adjective 'sneaky', which involves a personal judgement and may be ambiguous in its positive or negative value. Notice that the participant of Sample 3 agrees with the facilitator in this appreciation and confirms it by saying 'Yeah. Actually, that was the sneakiest period of my time.'

Humour

Humour has several functions depending on the situation and the side of the interview that interactants are on. For example, in the case of the interviewer, it can be used as a strategic tool to test the disposition of others (Pogrebin and Poole 1988), to create solidarity if there is a perceived hierarchical difference between people, to share similarities within the same group, or to cope in difficult situations (Ervin-Tripp and Lampert 1992). However, using humour and laughter may not be

[1] Spanish is a partially pro-drop language which means that it allows the deletion of the subject pronoun when not pragmatically necessary.

appropriate in unequal interview situations such as a job interview where the interviewer is perceived as having power over the interviewee (Glenn 2010). In those cases, it has been observed for instance that interviewees would only laugh after the interviewer invited laughter, and not only would their laughter not escalate but they would attempt to return to the 'business at hand' (Glenn 2010, p. 1486). In the interviews under discussion, laughter is common in both groups and it is initiated by both facilitators and participants (see, Samples 4, 6, and 12).

Humour on the part of the facilitator is present in most interviews (15/18 in group 1, 8/11 in group 2). Samples 4 and 5 below illustrate humour in the form of jokes.

Sample 4

G1I3 Interviewee: [...] people just look at me and they see a girl in guy's clothing and they're like, well, lesbians are everywhere, it's not really a big deal.
Facilitator: Especially ones that look like Justin Bieber.
Interviewee: [Laughs] You're so funny. Yeah, it's fairly common; it's not really an issue. If I walked with that but said my name tag is XX and I prefer you to say 'he', I guarantee you I'd get a lot more shit, but obviously people don't pick up on that.

Sample 5

G2I6 Facilitator: Ah peruanos, o sea comes ceviche...qué bien (Ah Peruvians, so you eat ceviche...that is good)
G2I3 Facilitator: La pregunta del millón ([Here comes] the question of the million dollars)
Interviewee: [Laughs]

Making jokes that involve physical appearance can be especially problematic, even among members of an in-group. Here, the participant in Sample 4 acknowledges the joke and continues their narration in the same informal tone that they had been using earlier, which means they had not been disconcerted by it. This is marked in the use of the colloquialism 'it's not really a big deal', the colloquial agreement backchannel 'Yeah', and the expletives 'a lot more shit', all highlighted. In this case, making a joke is not a strategic move by the facilitator to put the participant at ease; rather, it is a natural reaction in a comfortable interaction. In Sample 5, the facilitator makes light jokes during the interview to which the participant responds with laughter. Notice that the first example in Sample 5 (interview 6) involves a shared cultural knowledge of Peruvian cuisine, which in this instance is another marker of membership in the in-group.

Offering Own Experience as Example

Personal experiences in co-constructed interviews are offered for several reasons, such as to support, orientate, prompt more information and create rapport. This is a feature that is not found in formal interviews. Further, as the facilitator has the status of an in-group member, this helps them to communicate to the participant that they had been in similar situations and positions. In all instances when this happens, the contribution triggers a verbal reaction on the part of the participant that enriches the data.

In Sample 6 below, the participant responds in a dismissive way to questions of coming out (as LGBTIQ) and of discrimination. After the question on what would influence the participant's decision to come out to some and not to other people, the participant makes it appear that it is not really an issue for them, and that they had come out to people as result of getting drunk. To this the facilitator says:

Sample 6

G1I12 Facilitator: Cool [laughs]. That's definitely cool. Oh, yes, I was so nervous [when I came out].

Interviewee: Didn't come out to my brothers till this Easter…

By revealing their own experience and showing the vulnerability they felt when coming out ('I was so nervous'), the facilitator puts the participant at ease with the question. This cue is taken up by the participant as we see in their comment immediately after, implying that it is not that easy after all as they came out to their family just recently. In this Sample the facilitator is also using laughter and emphasis ('That's definitely cool.') as a strategy to reinforce their approval of the participant's statement.

Sample 7

G2I6: Facilitator: Fíjate que a todas las personas que nos ha pasado algo así es una reacción muy típica pensar que uno está hacienda algo mal. (You see, it is common for all people, me included, who have experienced something like this to think that it may be our fault).

Sample 7 is the result of a dialogue in which the participant manifests their distress at not being sure whether the instance of discrimination they describe was 'real' discrimination, whether it is their own fault, or whether they are exaggerating the experience. The facilitator tries to comfort the participant by showing solidarity with them and understanding of the situation, and expressing clearly that the facilitator had been in a similar situation. After this comment the participant 'confesses' that the experience: 'me ha afectado un montón' ('[the experience] has affected me a great deal'). They then proceed to describe how it affects them in their social functioning.

Sample 8

G1I2 Facilitator: No. I get so worried about like—thinking about if I should tell my grandma or not…

Interviewee: Oh yeah.

Facilitator: Because she's from that generation.

Interviewee: Yeah, I—when I came out as being gay—like a lesbian—I asked my mum to tell my grandparents, and they just said that they wished that they never knew.

Sample 8 is another ‘confession’ made by the facilitator about coming out to family. Before that, the participant had not talked about instances of discriminatory behaviour in their own family. The facilitator’s input triggers the participants’ reflection about their own family and their rejection by their grandparents.

Sample 9

G2I9 Facilitator: In my case, my son’s teacher at his school…would speak to me veeeery sloooowly…[laughs].

The facilitator offers this example to indicate their understanding that there are degrees of discrimination and that they, like the participant, had also experienced discrimination involving language use, which is common among immigrants for whom English is not their first language. After this example, the participant remembers another related instance of discrimination. In Sample 10 below, the facilitator uses their own experience to ask about the participant’s feelings on joining the Queer Space for students at their university.

Sample 10

G1I7 Facilitator: Do you think—I don’t know, can you elaborate on that because I had that feeling as well once I found the Queer Space, suddenly the world was a bit okay. Can you describe perhaps why that suddenly felt so much better for you?

Finally, Sample 11 below shows an instance of interaction that would never be present in a formal interview:

Sample 11

G1I2 Facilitator: You haven’t come across that? [People calling you ‘it’]
Interviewee: No.
Facilitator: That’s cool.
Interviewee: Yeah, Have you?
Facilitator: Yeah, I don’t know. It was just on kind of Facebook chat walls and you know through computers it’s so much easier just to be mean…

In this interaction, the facilitator asks participant 2 about having experienced discrimination related to the use of pronouns (Rojas-Lizana 2014).[2] The negative answer prompts a colloquial solidarity marker (‘That’s cool’), cool here meaning ‘I am glad’. After that, the participant asks a direct question to the facilitator (‘Have you?’). The facilitator is not taken aback by this and does answer the question (‘Yeah, I don’t know. It was…’). It is not only unusual in an interview to have an interviewee asking a question, it is even more unusual for an interviewer to answer it. In other cases of professional interactions with therapists, police officers and lawyers, for example, when they are asked a direct question, it is left unanswered.

[2] Using the pronoun ‘it’ is a well-known form of verbal abuse “to refer to and address trans people. This is considered a strong insult not because people do not distinguish between male and female, which may be welcomed in cases, but because the addressee is dehumanized.” (Rojas-Lizana 2014, p. 13)

This is a good indicator of how a co-constructed interview creates co-constructed discourse, as we see both participants producing verbal responses to direct questions.

Marking In-Group Membership by Contrast

Although the previous examples are also markers of in-group membership through revealing the facilitators' own experiences, there are specific discourse instances in which the contrast us/them is more openly revealed.

Sample 12

G2I6 Facilitator: nosotros los latinos ('we, Latino people')
G2I6 Facilitator: Yo me hubiera sentido discriminada, absolutamente (Yes, I [in your situation] would have felt discriminated against, definitely)

Sample 13

G1I17 Facilitator: I hate this kind of separation of saying straight people think this and we think that. But I think a lot of straight people think…

The facilitator in Sample 12 categorizes themselves and uses the 'we' pronoun inclusively to include the interviewee as part of the 'Latino' category that excludes the 'non-Latino' (in this context 'Anglo') from their discourse. The facilitator in Sample 13 uses the classical disclaimer 'I am not X but…' (Hewitt and Stokes 1975), as they clearly know they are stereotyping straight people. By saying that straight people behave in some way, they are placing themselves together with the interviewee in a contrastive situation.

Definitions of In-Group Terminology

Samples 14 and 15 below illustrate the facilitator performing their bridging role as they consciously provide and facilitate definitions for the benefit of the out-group. In Sample 14, the facilitator asks the participant to define the term 'queer', while in Sample 15, the facilitator themselves provides the definition of 'the pronoun game' for the benefit of the out-group, as the participant clearly understands it.

Sample 14

G1I2 Facilitator: Sorry you mentioned queer a lot. What do you define that as a…
Interviewee: Yep, I use the word queer for anyone who feels queer.
[Laughter]
Interviewee: Like I know some people who are more heterosexual but still consider themselves queer because they're a bit bent or a bit—like more fluid in their gender or sexuality, less [boxed]. So I guess sometimes people who I know identify as gay but don't identify as queer. So—and some lesbians don't identify as

queer that I know. But a lot of the people that I guess I hang out with are just more fluid with their sexuality and feel that queer is a label that is less [boxing] but still nice to attach yourself to. Yeah.

Sample 15

G1I17 Facilitator: Did you play the pronoun game? Instead of saying, she or my girlfriend or my ex-girlfriend, you'd say, they or my partner?
Interviewee: Yeah. I never really used 'she'. I'd be like so my date, my ex, my that person or if it's an ex, I'll be like, oh, that idiot who broke my heart kind of thing. So there's never a gender.
Facilitator: Just hope that the other person will assume that you're talking about a guy?
Interviewee: Yeah. That usually works, actually.

Requesting and offering definitions and examples of in-group terminology from in-group perspectives and in the participants' own words enrich the quality of the data as unforeseen angles may be foregrounded and backgrounded in their categorisation.

Minimal and Short Responses

In the interviews, there is an abundance of minimal responses (or backchanneling) used by the facilitator to express acknowledgement and agreement (Tolins and Fox Tree 2014), such as 'right', 'I get it', 'agreed', as well as other short responses used to express praise, approval and solidarity. These responses help to create an atmosphere of understanding and to maintain the flow in the interactions. Of the minimal responses, only acknowledgement back-channelling is commonly used by interviewers in formal interviews, since they are considered more 'objective' and unobtrusive. Consider the examples of the facilitators' short responses emphasised in Samples 16, 17 and 18:

Sample 16

G2I9 Interviewee: …and you do it pro bono [tutoring at the university where they studied], a bit because it is a public university and we love it, we love it, you see?
Facilitator: How nice of you!
Interviewee: yep, and my dad too. He was almost professor but he did it too.

Sample 17

G1I2 Facilitator: Is that the same as people who will yell at you in the street? That it will be the same kind of age group?
Interviewee: Yeah, yep that same 20s to 30s I reckon.
Facilitator: I hope they all grow out of it.
Interviewee: Hopefully.

Sample 18

G1I7 Interviewee: Then a few years ago I just had to get away from her [grandmother] so that time away from her we had a bit of time to reflect. Now I live with her with my girlfriend and she's super cool.
Facilitator: Wow, that's amazing.
Interviewee: Yeah, and doesn't judge me…

All these Samples express the facilitator's solidarity with and approval of the participants' statements. These short responses on their part received comments from the participants.

Respondents' Discourse in Co-constructed Interviews with an In-Group Facilitator

In this section I illustrate how the interviewees negotiate and co-construct their interviews in their discourse.

Using Colloquial and In-Group Language

This use is registered in the discourse of both the facilitators (as seen above in the subsection "Using colloquial and in-group language") and the interviewees, with respondents using in-group terms, colloquialisms and slang (Moore 2004). Only group 1 registers the use of swearing, while the participants in group 2, frequently perform linguistic hybridity as evidence of translanguaging or "hybrid practices of languaging bilingually." (García 2011, p. 34) manifested in key English lexical items and expressions.

The use of colloquialism and slang among the participants seems to respond to three of its most typical functions: informality, group membership and opposition to authority (Eble 1996). Samples 19–21 below evidence common in-group terminology and colloquialisms.

Sample 19

G1I4 Interviewee: Basically, it's the simplest way of describing my sexuality to people who may not understand. It's like the other box, because I used to identify as lesbian but I'm dating a boy now and he's not a cis and I don't usually like cis boys.

Sample 20

G2I6 Interviewee: They think that everyone in Latin America, included Brazil, speaks Spanish […]. Those interested are hippie gringos, those who want to travel.

Sample 21

G1I17 Interviewee: Yeah. There's this girl who I like now but I think she's—well I know she used to date other girls but she's actually dating a guy now so I'm like, shit, so she has a working gaydar alright, so I shouldn't talk that much to her even though she might know and I don't want her to know.

In Sample 19 the respondent provides their meaning of the term 'queer'. This definition includes the use of the term 'cis' twice, unexplained. This is a common in-group term referring to identities that manifest the same birth-assigned and current gender identity (Tate et al. 2013). The facilitator chooses not to ask for a definition of 'cis' as they had already asked for the definition of 'queer' and it would have interrupted the flow of the conversation by threatening their cooperation relationship with the respondent (Schaeffer and Maynard 2005).

The use of 'gringo' in Sample 20 denotes that the respondent knows that due to their shared cultural background with the facilitator they can use the word without restrictions. Even though gringo is considered by Anglo people to be an insulting term, most Spanish speakers do not consider it to be offensive (Quintanilla 1945). From an Anglo perspective, the term is considered diminishing because it marks those so named not only as outsiders, but also connotes imperialism, stealing, silliness and even naivety. Anthropologists and archaeologist who work in the Americas have written about the word gringo being used as a sign of objectification or 'reverse essentialism' (Weiss 1993; McGuire 1994). Other examples of slang words and expressions registered in the Spanish speaking group are 'te pega buena onda' ('it gives you a good feeling' I9), 'chevere' ('great' I5), 'como que me empezó a afectar' ('like it started to affect me' I6).

Sample 21 includes the colloquialism 'gaydar', also used by participants in two other interviews. 'Gaydar' can be defined as the ability to identify sexual orientation using indirect or minimal cues. Unlike 'cis', this is a term that out-group members do understand; however, there may be restriction on its use given the debate on visual cues being able to indicate sexuality (Woolery 2007). The respondent in this Sample also uses swearing ('shit') and discloses personal feelings, which indicate that they have established a relationship of equity and trust with the facilitator.

Sample 22

G1I4 Interviewee: [O]ne of my mates travelled up there recently for work as a pharmaceutical representative to talk to doctors. Went to one of the biggest clinics in XX dressed as a dude that day. Because their voice is not that low, kind of high-pitched, as soon as they spoke, this person who had been reading them as male then read them as female, but in dude's clothing, and was like, 'can you please leave? We don't like your sort in here.' In a doctor's surgery. There for official business.

Sample 22 is a good example of the combination of in-group and colloquial language. In terms of in-group language, the use of the gender-neutral pronoun 'they' (Garnham et al. 2012) is consistently used by about half of the participants (especially the young adults). Although its use is registered in the academic literature (as in this chapter), in speech it seems to be restricted to LGBTIQ members and their allies. In fact, this language modality does not come naturally but it is mastered through time, as reflected in the following comment by participant 17 who had only recently joined the LGBTIQ community: "That's a really hard thing to do, to constantly remember not to use the she, don't use the she, don't use the she, that person, that person." (G1I17).

Spanglish

Code-switching is part of translanguaging (García and Wei 2014; García 2011), which is an analytical concept developed to understand linguistic social practices common in bilingual people. The use of Spanish-English code switching is not part of formal speech (Stavans 2000), as traditional understandings of language and bilingualism do not facilitate hybridity and are still strong in official education (García and Wei 2014).

Code-switching has been defined as "alternating continuous and systematic stretches of Spanish and English in the same discourse" (Hidalgo 1988, p. 1). In the US, it is considered a marker of Latino and border identity. In the context of our interviews in Brisbane, its use can be associated with informality and a relaxed ambiance, as code switching is not used in professional settings or in the conversation of people who have just met. People who go back to their native Spanish speaking country consciously avoid mixing languages as they are aware that this may produce a negative reaction on the part of (monolingual) interlocutors who would categorise the use of code-switching as pretentious and annoying. Studies have shown that code-switching within Spanish speaking country is rejected for reasons that include language loyalty, aesthetics and correctness (Hidalgo 1988).

Sample 23

G2I4 Interviewee: Argentina es mucho más community orientated junto con todos los países latinoamericanos [...] tiene que ver con la educación si querés anglosajona de keep to yourself, de ser tan reservados. (Argentina is much more community orientated together with all the other Latin American countries [...] It has to do with the Anglo education of keeping to yourself, of being reserved people).

G2I3 Interviewee: [es una] sociedad tranquila, hay menos undercurrents [...] el mundo científico es sinceramente male dominated. ([Australia] is a calm society, there are few undercurrents'[...] the scientific world is definitely male dominated).

Intersentential switching (changing to English between sentences) and intrasentential switching (changing within sentences) are registered in the interviews. Intrasentential switching has been especially perceived by monolingual Spanish speakers as inexplicable and annoying (Hidalgo 1988). There is therefore a general awareness that translanguaging, as the semiotic use of linguistic hybridity, is something that can be done more freely among multilingual individuals in informal situations.

Swearing

The use and meaning of expletives has different functions depending more on the pragmatics than on the semantics of the expression (Hedger 2013; Christie 2013; Jay and Janschewitz 2008). These functions include creating distance from social norms, as well as expressing anger, insulting, or promoting solidarity for members of a group, among others. As part of our communicative competence, people can judge the situation in which it is appropriate to swear. These situational variables are connected to the pragmatics of the interaction, that is, topic, social-physical place, and with whom the speaker is interacting (Jay and Janschewitz 2008). In the case of these interviews, swearing in direct speech is conversational, denoting an equal relationship between the participants and a relaxed environment. It is never intended to be confrontational, rude or aggressive as it could be interpreted in other contexts.

Sample 24

G1I7 Interviewee: Yeah, I mean walking down the street there's been plenty of times where—I remember once that I just said 'g'day' to some guy who was walking down the road with his kid in a pram and he just says like, 'ah you fucking dyke'.

G2I2 Interviewee: Or just harassed a lot or being just called names like, 'hey trannie', like 'hey, what the fuck's between your legs', like in your workplace.

G2I11 Interviewee: But we walked down the street holding hands one day, she was just being very supportive. A car went by and they yelled out, 'fucking dykes'.

Sample 25

G1I1 Interviewee: So I felt quite upset and taken aback by this person associating somebody who's been considered a paedophile with somebody who's been queer. I thought that was a really shit thing to do.

As shown in Sample 24, strong swearing (Christie 2013) is used in reported speech, that is, as examples of verbal discrimination in which the participants paraphrase the perpetrator's words. In these reported cases, swearing is perceived by participants to be used to cause offence (see Rojas-Lizana 2014). There are other instances in which light expletives are used by participants in their direct speech, as can be seen in Sample 25 (see also the use of 'shit' in Samples 4 and 20 above). Swearing is only registered in Group 1.

Humour

As mentioned in section "Humour" above, regarding the interviewers, humour has different functions depending on the side of the interview people are on. In the case of these interviewees, humour is present in limited occasions and only in the form of self-directed humour. This type of humour may have different social functions, such as creating solidarity in different groups (equalising), protecting the self by identifying a weakness before others (defending), sharing similarities (sharing), and coping with weakness by making light of them (coping) (Ervin-Tripp and Lampert 1992). In many cases, humour makes threatening situations more tolerable; it normalises them and promotes a sense of confidence that problems can be handled (Pogrebin and Poole 1988).

Sample 26

G1I2 Interviewee: …sometimes I think that the more I put it on [a 'manly act'], the more it's coming off as fake [laughs]. Or the more I look like a butch lesbian [laughs]. Yeah, I do put it on. Or like when I meet my girlfriend's parents or something, totally try to butch-up, yep.

Sample 27

G1I12 Interviewee: …like with those particular guys it just meant I always had an easy way to get back at them, by just start acting gay and they'd get the hell out of my room—and I was like, yes. It's useful.

In my data, the use of humour is restricted to strategies of defending and coping. This seems to directly relate to the topic of the interviews (discrimination) in which the respondents identify themselves as victim. Since victimisation has been identified as an aversive phenomenon that has negative consequences, people resort to ways to de-victimise their status and avoid labelling themselves as victims. Victimhood represents loss—loss of value, status, resources, control and self-esteem (Taylor et al. 1983). A victim is therefore seen as someone who does not have control and presents a passive status. Sample 25 shows the respondent laughing at their own attempts to look 'manly', and Sample 27 shows the participant joking about acting the male gay stereotype to make people leave them alone.

Conclusion

Using examples from two sets of data, I have shown in this chapter the discursive elements that make co-constructed interactions different from other forms of interviews. I have also shown the type of discourse that emerges when the facilitator is an in-group member conducting a co-constructed interview, and how it can affect positively the way talk develops. I first presented the discursive strategies used by the interviewers where the strategies of offering their own experiences as examples triggered further participation on the part of the interviewee. Other strategies such as the use of colloquialisms and in-group nomenclature helped to produce a relaxed and informal environment during the interaction. The respondents on their part resorted to discursive strategies that included colloquialism, swearing (in group 1), translanguaging (in group 2), and in-group terminology. These all reflect the respondents' positive dispositions to retell and discuss their experiences with someone who understood them, therefore helping to produce data that allow a deeper understanding of the phenomenon studied and of the discourse produced.

Conducting co-constructed interviews with in-group facilitators produces a type of discourse that, in total, reveals a deep incursion into the delicate topic that is being explored, as it makes emergent the richness and complexities of the participants' experiences. This is especially desirable when doing qualitative research on topics that may be difficult to address due to their sensitive nature, such as the study of Perceived Discrimination, as co-constructed interviews help to explore several forms of discrimination (obvert and covert, intended and unintended) their effects and the coping strategies used by the experiencers.

Furthermore, if the research framework is found within the area of Discourse Analysis where exhaustive semantic analysis takes place, this methodology can prove to be especially useful as people are more likely to express these linguistic behaviours in relaxed environments than in formal environments.

Discussion Questions

1. How might use of an 'in-group' interviewer affect interviews in your field? Speculate on how an insider might respond differently to an outsider interviewer?
2. Compare the benefits and challenges of each of the types of interviews mentioned on page 162. Make a decision about which might be best suited to your own research project and explain your choice.

References

Allan, K., & Burridge, K. (2006). *Forbidden words: Taboo and the censoring of language*. Cambridge: Cambridge University Press.

Allen, D. (2004). Ethnomethodological insights into insider-outsider relationships in nursing ethnographies of healthcare settings. *Nursing Inquiry, 11*(1), 14–24.

Benson, P. (2014). Narrative inquiry in applied linguistic research. *Annual Review of Applied Linguistics, 34*, 154–170.

Burr, V. (2003). *Social constructionism*. London: Routledge.

Christie, C. (2013). The relevance of taboo language: An analysis of the indexical values of swearwords. *Journal of Pragmatics, 58*, 152–169.

Couture, A. L., Zaidi, A. U., & Maticka-Tyndale, E. (2012). Reflexive accounts: An intersectional approach to exploring the fluidity of insider/outsider status and the researcher's impact on culturally sensitive post-positivist qualitative research. *Qualitative Sociology Review, 8*(1), 86–105.

Davies, B., & Harré, R. (1990). Positioning: The discursive production of selves. *Journal for the Theory of Social Behaviour, 20*(1), 43–63.

de Fina, A., & Johnstone, B. (2015). Discourse analysis and narrative. In H. E. Hamilton, D. Tannen, & D. Schiffrin (Eds.), *The handbook of discourse analysis* (pp. 152–167). Malden: Wiley.

Dwyer, S. C., & Buckle, J. L. (2009). The space between: On being an insider-outsider in qualitative research. *International Journal of Qualitative Methods, 8*(1), 54–63.

Eble, C. C. (1996). *Slang and sociability: In-group language among college students*. Chapel Hill: University of North Carolina Press.

Ellis, C. S. (2008). Co-constructed narratives. In L. M. Given (Ed.), *The SAGE encyclopaedia of qualitative research methods* (pp. 85–90). Thousand Oaks: Sage.

Ervin-Tripp, S., & Lampert, M. D. (1992). Gender differences in the construction of humorous talk. In K. Hall, M. Buchholtz, & B. Moonwoman (Eds.), *Locating power: Proceedings of the second Berkeley women and language conference* (pp. 108–117). Berkeley: Berkeley Women and Language Group, Linguistics Department, University of California.

Essed, P. (1991). *Understanding everyday racism: An interdisciplinary theory*. Newbury Park: Sage.

Essed, P. (1992). Alternative knowledge sources in explanations of racist events. In M. L. McLaughlin, M. J. Cody, & S. J. Read (Eds.), *Explaining one's self to others: Reason-giving in a social context* (pp. 199–224). Hillsdale: Lawrence Erlbaum Associates, Publishers.

Fairclough, N. (1995). *Critical discourse analysis: Papers in the critical study of language*. Harlow: Longman.

Fairclough, N. (2002). Discourse and text: Linguistic and intertextual analysis within discourse analysis. In M. Toolan (Ed.), *Critical discourse analysis: Critical concepts in linguistics* (pp. 23–49). London/New York: Routledge.

Flick, U. (2009). *An introduction to qualitative research* (4th ed.). London: Sage.

Garcia, O. (2011). The translanguaging of Latino kindergarteners. In K. Potowski & J. Rothman (Eds.), *Bilingual youth: Spanish in English-speaking societies* (Vol. 42, pp. 33–55). Amsterdam/Philadelphia: John Benjamins Publishing Company.

Garcia, O., & Wei, L. (2014). Translanguaging: Language, bilingualism and education. Houndmills: Palgrave Macmillan.

Garnham, A., Gabriel, U., Sarrasin, O., Gygax, P., & Oakhill, J. (2012). Gender representation in different languages and grammatical marking on pronouns: When beauticians, musicians, and mechanics remain men. *Discourse Processes, 49*, 481–500.

Glenn, P. (2010). Interviewer laughs: Shared laughter and asymmetries in employment interviews. *Journal of Pragmatics, 42*, 1485–1498.

Hedger, J. A. (2013). Meaning and racial slurs: Derogatory epithets and the semantics/pragmatics interface. *Language & Communication, 33*, 205–213.

Hewitt, J. P., & Stokes, R. (1975). Disclaimers. *American Sociological Review, 40*(1), 1–11.

Hidalgo, M. (1988). Perceptions of Spanish-English code-switching in Juarez, Mexico. *Research Paper Series 20 Latin American Institute University of New Mexico.*

Holstein, J. A., & Gubrium, J. F. (1995). *The active interview*. Thousand Oaks: Sage.

Holstein, J. A., & Gubrium, J. F. (2004). The active interview. In D. Silverman (Ed.), *Qualitative research: Theory, method and practice* (2nd ed., pp. 140–161). London/Thousand Oaks: Sage.

Jay, T., & Janschewitz, K. (2008). The pragmatics of swearing. *Journal of Politeness Research, 4*, 267–288.

Lalonde, R. N., & Cameron, J. E. (1993). An intergroup perspective on immigrant acculturation with a focus on collective strategies. *International Journal of Psychology/Journal International de Psychologie, 28*(1), 57–74.

Lee, D. A. (2001). Cognitive linguistics: An introduction. Melbourne: Oxford University Press.

Lindlof, T. R., & Taylor, B. C. (2011). *Qualitative communication research methods* (3rd ed.). Thousand Oaks: Sage.

Lumby, M. E. (1976). Code switching and sexual orientation: A test of Bernstein's sociolinguistic theory. *Journal of Homosexuality, 1*(4), 383–99.
Mann, S. (2011). A critical review of qualitative interviews in applied linguistics. *Applied Linguistics, 32*(1), 6–24.
Maturana, H., & Dávila, X. (2015). *El árbol del vivir*. Santiago: escuelamatriztica, MVP editores.
McGuire, R. H. (1994). The gringo stigma. *Archaeology, 47*(4), 72.
Mellor, D. J. (2003). Contemporary racism in Australia: The experience of Aborigines. *Personality and Social Psychology Bulleting, 29*(4), 474–486.
Mellor, D. J. (2004). Experiences of racism by Vietnamese. *Journal of Ethnic and Migration Studies, 30*(4), 631–658.
Merino, M. E. (2006). Propuesta metodológica de análisis crítico del discurso de la discriminación percibida [A methodological proposal for the critical discourse analysis of perceived discrimination]. *Revista Signos: Estudios de Lingüística, 62*, 453–469.
Merino, M. E., & Mellor, D. J. (2009). Perceived discrimination in Mapuche discourse: Contemporary racism in Chilean society. *Critical Discourse Studies, 6*(3), 215–226.
Merino, M. E., Mellor, D. J., Saiz, J. L., & Quilaqueo, D. (2009). Perceived discrimination amongst the indigenous Mapuche people in Chile: Some comparisons with Australia. *Ethnic and Racial Studies, 32*(5), 802–822.
Mishler, E. G. (1986). Research interviewing: Context and narrative. Cambridge, MA: Harvard University Press.
Miller, E. R. (2011). Indeterminacy and interview research: Co-constructing ambiguity and clarity in interviews with an adult immigrant learner of English. *Applied Linguistics, 32*(1), 43–59.
Moore, R. L. (2004). We're cool, mom and dad are swell: Basic slang and generational shifts in values. *American Speech, 79*(1), 59–86.
Pogrebin, M. R., & Poole, E. D. (1988). Humor in the briefing room: A study of the strategic use of humor among police. *Journal of Contemporary Ethnography, 17*(2), 183–210.
Quintanilla, L. (1945). Gringo not an insulting term (Book review). *Books Abroad, 19*(1), 27.
Rhee, Y. (2008). Risk communication management: A case study on Brookhaven National Laboratory. *Journal of Communication Management, 12*(3), 224–242.
Rhodes, P. J. (1994). Race-of-interviewer effects: A brief comment. *Sociology, 28*(2), 547–558.
Rojas-Lizana, I. (2014). Perceived discrimination in LGBTIQ discourse from Australia: A typology of verbal discrimination. *PORTAL Journal of Multidisciplinary International Studies* 11(1). doi: http://dx.doi.org/10.5130/portal.v11i1.3303
Schaeffer, N. C., & Maynard, D. W. (2005). From paradigm to prototype and back again: Interactive aspects of 'cognitive processing' in standardized survey interviews. In H. T. Molder & J. Potter (Eds.), *Conversation and cognition* (pp. 114–134). Cambridge: Cambridge University Press.
Shkedi, A. (2005). *Multiple case narrative: A qualitative approach to studying multiple populations* (Vol. 7). Amsterdam/Philadelphia: John Benjamins Publishing Company.
Silverman, D. (2004). *Qualitative research: Theory, method and practice*. Thousand Oaks: Sage.
Stavans, I. (2000). Spanglish: Tickling the tongue. *World Literature Today, 74*(3), 556–558.
Talmy, S. (2010). Qualitative interviews in applied linguistics: From research instrument to social practice. *Annual Review of Applied Linguistics, 30*, 128–48.
Talmy, S., & Richards, K. (2011). Theorizing qualitative research interviews in applied linguistics. *Applied Linguistics, 32*(1), 1–5.
Tate, C. C., Ledbetter, J. N., & Youssef, C. P. (2013). A two-question method for assessing gender categories in the social and medical sciences. *The Journal of Sex Research, 50*(8), 767–776.
Taylor, J. R. (2002). *Cognitive grammar*. Oxford/New York: Oxford University Press.
Taylor, S. E., Wood, J. V., & Lichtman, R. R. (1983). It could be worse: Selective evaluation as a response to victimization. *Journal of Social Issues, 39*(2), 19–40.
Tolins, J., & Fox Tree, J. E. (2014). Addressee backchannels steer narrative development. *Journal of Pragmatics, 70*, 152–64.
Travis, C. E. (2004). The ethnopragmatics of the diminutive in conversational Colombian Spanish. *Intercultural Pragmatics, 1*(2), 249–74.

van Dijk, T. A. (1996). Discourse, power and access. In C. R. Caldas-Coulthard & M. Coulthard (Eds.), *Texts and practices: Readings in critical discourse analysis* (pp. 84–104). London/New York: Routledge.

van Dijk, T. A. (1997). *Discourse studies: A multidisciplinary introduction*. London: Sage.

Weiss, W. A. (1993). Gringo… Gringuita. *Anthropological Quarterly, 66*(4), 187–196.

Wodak, R., & Meyer, M. (2009). Critical discourse analysis: History, agenda, theory and methodology. In R. Wodak & M. Meyer (Eds.), *Methods of critical discourse analysis* (2nd ed., pp. 1–33). London: Sage.

Woolery, L. M. (2007). Gaydar: A social-cognitive analysis. *Journal of Homosexuality, 53*(3), 9–17.

Zambrano-Paff, M. (2009). El uso de marcadores de cortesía para controlar las relaciones sociales en los tribunales de inmigración. In D. Bravo, N. Hernández Flores, & A. Cordisco (Eds.), *Aportes pragmáticos, sociopragmáticos y socioculturales a los estudios de la cortesía en español* (pp. 135–160). Stockholm: Dunken.

Chapter 9
Insights into Disability and Giftedness: Narrative Methodologies in Interviewing Young People Identified as Twice Exceptional

Michelle Ronksley-Pavia and Peter Grootenboer

Abstract This chapter describes the fluid methodologies used in a narrative research study involving interviewing children identified as gifted and also having a disability—twice exceptional children. Within the qualitative literature encompassing young people identified as twice exceptional, there is limited discussion of interview techniques and protocols used by interviewers in obtaining their narrative data or field texts. The researchers often skim over this section with phrases like "semi-structured interviews were used to obtain data", with little detail surrounding the actual interview process, the creation of the field texts, and subsequent analysis. In order to guide ongoing research in the area of twice exceptionality, it is important to develop and explain the steps and processes used to obtain qualitative interview data with these young people, and further detail how this might be analysed through narrative methods. In this chapter we discuss the development of an interview protocol which was flexible and dynamic, and able to respond to the needs of both researcher and participant in conducting field research with one twice exceptional child. The focus of this chapter is on how we conducted the interviews, with some insights presented into our process of narrative analysis through description of one participant's narrative presented as a story constellation. The interview protocol involved an inclusive approach where the child's needs were addressed to ensure they were able to participate in the project, regardless of their disability and any communication needs. Conducting the interviews in the child's home, a place of security, whilst spending time getting to know the child to build rapport, increased comfort during the interviews. This chapter concludes with reflecting on our flexible and dynamic interview approach which facilitated Ashley's sharing of her lived experiences of twice exceptionality.

Keywords Interviewing • Disability • Gifted • Twice exceptional • Story constellations

M. Ronksley-Pavia (✉) • P. Grootenboer
Griffith University, Brisbane, Australia
e-mail: m.ronksley-pavia@griffith.edu.au

© Springer Science+Business Media Singapore 2017

R. Dwyer et al. (eds.), *Narrative Research in Practice*,
DOI 10.1007/978-981-10-1579-3_9

Introduction

Twice exceptional children are young people who have been identified as gifted and also have a disability (Foley-Nicpon et al. 2011). There has been limited research with these children and in particular, we know little about their lived experiences. This is perhaps partly due to the issues with collecting qualitative data with twice exceptional children. In this chapter we outline the theoretical perspectives of our qualitative research, and explore the development and use of our dynamic interview protocol in this narrative inquiry. First we describe the phenomenon under study, being the lived experiences of twice exceptional children. We then provide an example of one of the narrative-informed case studies, discussing our narrative analysis through a story constellations' approach. This is undertaken by presenting examples of field texts (data) and the analysis of the story constellation which relates specifically to the lived experiences of one twice exceptional child, Ashley.

Background

Within the qualitative research literature encompassing young people identified as twice exceptional, there is limited discussion of interview techniques and protocols used by researchers in generating their data, or field texts. The researchers frequently skim over these details with phrases like "semi-structured interviews were used to obtain data", with little information about the actual interview process, the collecting and compiling of the field texts, and subsequent analysis. In order to guide ongoing research in the area of twice exceptionality, it is important to develop and explain the steps and processes used to obtain qualitative interview data with these young people, and to further detail how this might be analysed through the use of narrative methodologies. Through a narrative approach to the study the "social reality" that is shaped through social interaction in the children's contexts can be explored, identified and described (Polkinghorne 1995).

The research project described in this chapter is part of a larger study relating to the first author's doctoral research which explored the lived experiences of twice exceptional children aged 9–16 years, in Queensland and New South Wales, Australia. The study explored discursive practices which twice exceptional children encountered in their lives and education. A fundamental issue confronting society and education systems is the exclusion and marginalisation of children with disability and those identified as gifted.

Defining Giftedness, Disability and Twice Exceptionality

Twice exceptionality covers a combination of both disability and giftedness, where disability may refer to any disability—sensory, physical, mental, and intellectual (Foley-Nicpon et al. 2011; Foley-Nicpon et al. 2013; World Health Organisation

2011), and where giftedness refers to "high cognitive abilities" (Gagné 2009, p. 1). Yet defining these two terms is not this clear-cut and there are no universally accepted definitions of giftedness or disability. This lack of consensus leads to compounded problems in identifying children who are twice exceptional (Baum and Olenchak 2002). In 2014, a definition for twice exceptionality was proposed by meetings of the American National Commission on Twice Exceptional Students and other interested parties, which sought to create an operational definition to guide research, planning and provision (Reis, Baum, and Burke 2014). This definition stated that:

> Twice exceptional learners are students who demonstrate the potential for high achievement or creative productivity in one or more domains such as math, science, technology, the social arts, the visual, spatial, or performing arts or other areas of human productivity AND [original capitalisation] who manifest one or more disabilities as defined by federal or state eligibility criteria. These disabilities include specific learning disabilities; speech and language disorders; emotional/behavioral [sic] disorders; physical disabilities; Autism Spectrum Disorders (ASD); or other health impairments, such as Attention Deficit/Hyperactivity Disorder (ADHD). These disabilities and high abilities combine to produce a unique population of students who may fail to demonstrate either high academic performance or specific disabilities. Their gifts may mask their disabilities and their disabilities may mask their gifts. (p. 222)

In essence, twice exceptionality affects the whole child, including their life inside and outside school. They are first a child experiencing childhood and endeavouring to understand themselves and the world around them, with the added facets of trying to comprehend their disability and giftedness. To understand the lifeworlds of these students, the most obvious way to elicit children's experiences appears to be to talk with them, and so interviews seem to be the best research method to employ.

The Participants

Despite the definitional issues outlined above, we had to identify and select participants for the study. To this end, research participants were sought by an expression of interest request sent through support groups for children and parents/carers, asking for children with identified disability and identified giftedness to participate. The participants consisted of eight children—five males and three females. In this chapter we concentrate on Ashley's story. Ashley is described towards the end of this chapter.

Although expressive language was advanced for chronological age among the participants, particularly Ashley, we needed to remain aware throughout the interview process, that due to their disabilities, some of the participants' receptive language skills may not be as well developed. Five of the eight participants had processing disorders that affected their receptive language skills and auditory processing abilities.

Research Methodology and Methods

A narrative informed case study approach offered the opportunity to interpret twice exceptional children's "reality" through their eyes. By exploring the lived experiences of these children this research endeavoured to gain an understanding of their notions of self and lived or constructed realities (DePoy and Gilson 2010). It was hoped that a better understanding of twice exceptional students' lives would have implications for improving policy, practice and 'management' related to these children within and outside education systems. Both parental and child consent was sought for the children and parents to take part in the research project (Hill 2005). The children were considered as the primary participants with the parent interview being used primarily to clarify or respond to specific experiences elicited during the children's interviews, if necessary.

The narrative-informed case studies involved three to four separate interviews with each child, an interview with at least one parent, and field notes. The interviews were audio-recorded and transcribed, and from these, narrative stories were developed which were member checked for veracity and accuracy. The interviews were conducted in the participants' homes using a memory box where children collected items of interest to themselves prior to each interview, for sharing with the interviewer in order to elicit further details about their lived experiences (Martin and Merrotsy 2006).

Children were given the option of having a parent present during the interviews. This generated both affordances and limitations, as the presence of a parent assisted children with responding in the interview at times, but also impeded their responses on occasions when parents interrupted or corrected their children (Harrington et al. 2013). In addressing parental influence during the interviews, the interviewer re-directed questions back to the child in order to gain their perspective and to check agreement or not with parental response (Preece and Jordan 2010).

The semi-structured interview questions were spread out over the three to four interviews, allowing 30–60 minutes for each interview. The initial interview involved an informal discussion surrounding the participant's memory box (from the pre-interview meeting where the collection box is given to the child), expectations of the interviewer and participants and focusing on building rapport and establishing trust. Questions such as *Can you tell me a little about yourself?* provided a gentle opening to the interview process, providing sufficient scope for the children to expand upon.

The first author entered the research context of the child's home as a participating adult who had the ability to assume the role of a compassionate, empathetic and sensitive adult (Birbeck and Drummond 2007). The relationship was founded and developed based on trust and mutual respect which enabled us "to uphold the ethical imperatives when working with children…this approach is entirely consistent with the social, intellectual and communication requirements of children if they are to participate in research" (Birbeck and Drummond 2007, p. 27).

Child Participants With a Disability

Prior to and during the interviews there was a need to develop "approaches and resources to address individual...needs" (Harrington et al. 2013, p. 2) of the participants. This was critical to ensure that the perspectives of the twice exceptional children were captured whilst maintaining trust and comfort for the participants. This involved an inclusive approach where the child's needs were addressed to ensure they were able to participate in the project, regardless of their disability and any communication needs. This was undertaken on an 'as-needs', individual basis (Harrington et al. 2013) and negotiated with the child and parent, to ensure appropriate and adequate approaches were used. As Harrington et al. (2013) suggest, we spent time getting to know the children to build rapport and increase comfort during the interviews, and this was primarily by engaging in activities that the children enjoyed. For some children, this meant the inclusion of pets during the interviews, along with talking about their love and enjoyment of their hobbies. For the most part during the interviews we sat on the floor and the children were able to sit how they felt comfortable, spreading their memory box items out. To allow the interviewer to support the participants' social and emotional needs during the interviews, parents were invited to share health professionals' reports and school records for their child prior to the interviews.

An integral part of the semi-structured, interviews, was the use of the memory box where children were given a box to keep items which they wished to share with the interviewer. The use of the memory box allowed the participants to include objects that were of significance to them for discussion during the interviews. The participants were able to 'show' these personal artefacts and through talking about these, we elicited further rich data to add to the authenticity of the narratives (Kim 2016). At these times the participant guided the discussion with their chosen objects, rather than the interviewer taking the lead. The use of the memory box allowed the children the opportunity to explain aspects of their life that simply talking and questioning did not facilitate (Martin and Merrotsy 2006). This approach was flexible, allowing for the inductive nature of narrative research, providing further threads which could be woven into their narratives.

Narrative Approach

A narrative approach acknowledges that stories of lived experiences are built through dialogue and experience telling (Kim 2016) both as the phenomenon studied in our inquiry into the lived experiences of twice exceptional children, and as our methodology (Clandinin and Connelly 1996). The language of the story is built up from dialogue with the participant who has constructed their narrative of self around their understanding of "the episodic and temporal qualities of lived experience … human beings live out their lives in ways that can be understood and communicated narratively" (Cresswell 2008, p. 157). In a narrative approach, the inquiry is related to the portrayal, reproduction, analysis and understanding of storied explanations of 'real' lived experiences. Narrative provides an interpretive framework as "a way of thinking about experiences… as a methodology [it] entails a view of the phenomenon. To use narrative inquiry methodology is to adopt a particular narrative view of experience as phenomena under study" (Connelly and Clandinin 2006, p. 477).

Understanding through a narrative informed case study approach is derived from "a willingness to comprehend meaning in context and to accept more than one 'truth'" (Munhall 2001, p. 380). Ambiguity is a feature of narrative research and the investigator requires flexibility and tolerance in dealing with the unexpected and viewing these variations as opportunities rather than menaces (Munhall 2001). Different threads need to be stitched together to form narrative constellations.

Clandinin and Connelly (2000) suggest that a narrative approach enables "a way of understanding experience… a collaboration between researcher and participants, over time… [where] an inquirer enters this matrix … in the midst of living and telling, re-living and retelling, the stories of the experiences that make up people's lives, both individual and social… narrative inquiry is stories lived and told" (p. 20).

This type of narrative research means that a close bond was established between the researcher and participants, which assisted in establishing the direct applicability of the research (Kim 2016). Through personal experience stories, and with the support of the memory boxes, the participant's personal narratives of twice exceptionality were explored. The personal experiences stories are both individual and personal, and shared, social experiences where individuals interact with others (Clandinin and Connelly 2000) which further emphasised the research focus of learning from children who are twice exceptional.

The field texts were made accessible and presented as narrative story constellations (following Clandinin and Connelly 1996; Craig 2007). This approach, following from Craig's work and Clandinin and Connelly's work, has been adapted to include the paired narratives of Children's Stories/Stories of Children. This approach is further expanded and explained under the story constellations section later in this chapter. This approach revealed heuristic narratives about the lived experiences of twice exceptional children, at times co-constructed with their parents, leading to a deeper understanding of what the educational and daily lives are like for children identifying as twice exceptional. The story constellations approach enabled us to analyse and re-story the children's and parents' interviews. This produced rich, in-depth stories with inimitable permutations about narratives of lived experiences, recounted at specific points of time in the children's lives, stories lived and told (Clandinin and Connelly 2000).

Polkinghorne (2007) distinguishes between 'stories' as fictional portrayals and narrative 'stories' as being the "fundamental scheme for linking individual human actions and events into interrelated aspects of an understandable composite" (p. 13). Hence, narrative refers "to both the process and the results" (p. 13) of narrative research. The narrative method enables the formulation of reasonable analysis and interpretation of findings and the building of a worthy line of reasoning (Bassey 1999).

Therefore, the resulting case study narratives are "descriptive, inductive and ultimately heuristic—[seeking] to 'illuminate' the readers' understanding of [the] issue[s]" (Cresswell 2008, p. 33). In essence narrative research is an exploration and investigation of current real-world phenomena through the in-depth analysis of a narrow series of events, interactions and/or circumstances, and how these interconnect (Yin 2009) in the lives of twice exceptional children.

The Interview Protocol

The interview protocol involved specific information relating to each child, and it was flexible, incorporating any disability adjustments necessary (e.g., breaks, moving around, playing with objects/toys during the interviews). The interview program included a pre-interview which took place at the initial meeting with each child and their parents. The aims of the pre-interviews were to familiarise the children with data collection expectations and to answer any queries that they had relating to the research. During this meeting each child was provided with their memory box which they kept for storing their items to share with the researcher during the interview process. Most of the participants already had items ready to show the author at the first pre-interview, despite not already having the box.

The parent interviews were characterised by a sense of urgency and this appeared to come from the need and desire to have other people know about their stories (Chase 2003). The stories represented a catharsis of sorts for both the children and their parents, presenting "the cathartic advantageousness of exchanging memories or lived experience" (Duffy 2011, p. 89). This process is examined further after the presentation of Ashley's story constellation.

The Interview Schedule

The interviews were guided by Seidman's (2006) three-phase interview process. In this approach, Seidman suggests that a person's behaviour becomes more comprehensible and meaningful when positioned in their life-context and in the lives of those around that individual. This contextual positioning assisted in developing our understanding though the interview process, of the daily lived experiences of twice exceptional children and the meaning these children made of their experiences.

Seidman (2006) suggests that the first phase interview (focused life history) (Figure 9.1) should place the individuals' experiences in context. In the first interview, the participants were asked about their experiences relating to their lived experiences up to the present point in time—their "focused life history" (p. 21). The second phase (the details of experience), further focused on concrete details and examined twice exceptional children's lived experiences within a context (Seidman, 2006). The third phase (reflection on the meaning) was where the participants were asked to reflect on the meaning of their experiences, and to make intellectual and emotional connections with their experiences. This increasingly focused third phase was where previous data were amalgamated with other contextual information, to reach crucial meanings that the participants had of their lived experiences (Seidman 2006). The three-phase process was spread over three to four interviews with the child participants, ensuring, as much as possible, that each stage was adequately addressed prior to moving on to the essential final stage. This process aided in initial analysis of these data from each interview stage, to inform subsequent interviews. A final interview with parents helped in clarifying and expanding on information and ideas garnered from the children. The child's verbal permission was sought for this after their final interview and prior to the parent interview, which immediately followed the child's last interview session.

Seidman (2006) recommends asking participants to "reconstruct rather than to remember" (p. 88) experiences, and that researchers should focus on concrete details that constitute particular experiences. In essence, this required asking questions such as "what happened?", rather than "do you remember …?" (p. 88). With recalling experiences being based partly on memory and partly on what participants see as being important about their past experiences, "in a sense all recall is reconstruction…in interviewing it is better to go for that reconstruction as directly as possible" (p. 88).

The interviewer did not take field notes during the interview as this could be off-putting as the children may be wondering what was being writing down. Once the interviewer left the interview location some time was spent writing field notes and observations from the interviews. Fig. 9.1.

Narrative Analysis

During the interview phase of the study there was ongoing preliminary analysis of each interview to inform subsequent interviews and to guide the three-phase process. Immediately after each interview the first author wrote field note précis, summarising the interview content and noting any features for further attention. The interviews were transcribed verbatim, including utterances, pauses, silences, false starts and other vocalisations, including laughter, and the transcript was then reviewed against the audio recordings for accuracy, and verified where applicable. This preliminary exploratory analysis gave a general sense of the data, where initial ideas were noted, and subsequent interview questions were organised (Kim 2016). The transcription of the spoken discourse became "like photographing reality, … an interpretive practice… by displaying text in particular ways, [providing] grounds for [my] arguments, just like a photographer guides the viewer's eye with lenses and by cropping images" (Riessman 2008). The field notes and memos gave guidance to our ideas, thoughts and feelings, used as an aide-mémoire technique.

Interview	Interview Focus	Task
Pre-interview meeting	Getting to know each other; establishing rapport; building trust	Introduce myself,give child memory box, interview structure, establish rapport/trust; setting -child's home -where they feel comfortable sitting).
First Interview	Questions 1-4-How Q's: Tell about self; Experiences in context;	Establish rapport/trust, memory box–setting (floor etc. child is comfortable).
Second Interview	Questions 5-11-Do Q's: Experiences in context& concrete details about lived experiences; relationships;	Continue to build rapport/trust; memory box, –interview setting (floor etc. where child is comfortable).
Third Interview	Questions 12-19 – Concrete details about lived experiences & Reflect on meaning of experiences (making intellectual/ emotional connections);	Continue to build rapport/trust memory box, –interview setting (floor etc. where child is comfortable).
Fourth Interview	Questions 20-26 – Reflect on experiences (making intellectual/emotional connections); Future;	Continue to build rapport/trust–interview setting (floor etc. child is comfortable).
Parents' Interview	Reflect on experiences–co-construction of narrative).	Questions that have arisen during the interview phase and from any documentation.

Fig. 9.1 Interview guiding schedule linked to interview questions following Seidman (2006)

After the initial review of the verbatim transcripts, these were again reviewed alongside the audio-recordings. During this re-reading and re-listening, superfluous talk was removed (or snipped) from the transcript (e.g., about the weather and talk deemed repetitive or irrelevant). This process was extensive and led to a first draft of each child's narrative. The first-draft narratives emerged from the transcripts after we began to snip away "at the flow of talk". This involved "decisions about form, ordering, style of presentation, and how the fragments of lives that have been given in the interviews [would] be housed" (Riessman 2008, p. 13). These draft narratives were sent to participants' parents for member checking in conjunction with their child.

Bruner (cited in Polkinghorne, 1995) remarks that "people do not deal with the world event by event or with text sentence by sentence [rather] they frame events and sentences in larger structures" (p. 15). It is through Polkinghorne's (1995) narrative structure of plot that people comprehend and define the relationship between events and life choices throughout their lived experiences, and it makes sense to use this method to grasp these together as one cohesive story through narrative configuration. With this in mind, we were interested in telling stories of lived experience, rather than reporting a series of sequenced, themed events from passages of transcribed text (Patterson 2013). We sought to evaluate passages of text—chunks of data—which disclosed how the participants felt about their experience "and mediated the point of [their] story" (Patterson 2013, p. 36). This was undertaken so we remained close to the nuanced features of these transcribed narratives. The goal was personalised narratives of lived experience rather than "an event-centric understanding of personal narration" (Patterson, 2013, p. 36). Therefore, a hands-on approach for the analysis ensued where we reviewed narrative drafts, which were re-read, further edited and amended, taking into account the participants' feedback. This editing re-shaped the narratives, "turning [them] into a hybrid document" (Riessman 2008, p. 13) where the participants' voices were central (Gubrium 2002). This re-reading of the hybridised-narratives took place several times, where the first author immersed herself in the details, endeavouring "to get a sense of the interview as a whole before [further] breaking" (Agar 1980, p. 103) them into segments and threads of experiences.

After initial reduction of each of the narratives, Polkinghorne's (1995, 2007) narrative analysis was used as an emplotment process in analysing the field texts. The process involved "happenings [being] drawn together and integrated into a temporally organised whole" (Polkinghorne 1995, p. 5), the outcome of which were story constellations of lived experiences. This was undertaken by using what Polkinghorne described as using "a thematic thread to lay out happenings as parts of an unfolding movement that culminates in an outcome" (p. 5), the outcome of which was the stories of lived experience—the story constellations. This narrative analysis involved the development and discovery a plot that demonstrated links among data elements as segments of "an unfolding temporal development culminating in a denouement" (Polkinghorne 1995, p. 15). This denouement (conclusion) formed the basis for each of the story constellations, drawing together the narrative threads across the children's experiences. During the latter stages of data analysis, we used the configuration process of emplotment, where plotlines began to take on narrative meaning and started to develop an understanding of the plotlines' influence on particular outcomes and experiences (Polkinghorne 1995). Emplotment was used on the hand-coded transcripts, and then further developed on the initial re-storied narratives to draw out the essence of these. We organised and constructed the elements of the textual data by emplotment, into the individual story constellations. This assisted in unifying and providing meaning to the textual data as contributing to our objective and purpose (Polkinghorne 1995) of exploring the lived experience of these twice exceptional children. This narrative analysis involved our developing and discovering a plot that demonstrated links among data elements as segments of "an unfolding temporal development culminating in a denouement" (p. 15). This 'denouement' formed the basis for the story constellations, drawing together the narrative threads.

Story Constellations Approach to Analysis

Clandinin and Connelly (1996) discuss 'working landscapes' of teachers' knowledge and relationships with this landscape to policies, theories and other educators. They talk about landscapes outside classrooms where "knowledge is funnelled into the school system for the purpose of altering teachers' and children's' classroom lives" (p. 25). This landscape of knowledge can be said to include the lives and experiences of children, both within and outside classrooms and educational institutions. This filtering occurs in not just policies and theories, but in the lived experiences of children (students), particularly those with differing experiences and backgrounds of diversity; in our case children identified as twice exceptional. Also included are the storied experiences of their parents' in the children's multi-vocal narratives (Czarniawska 2002). In this multi-vocality of children and parents, many narratives are presented. Our role as researcher is not to say one is more 'truth' than any other, but to enable readers to comprehend the similarities and differences in and between the stories.

By using Clandinin and Connelly's metaphor of landscape, the children's stories would seem to come down from the hills, filtering through the landscape like streams through the rocks and vegetation, heading to the fresh water springs of the school landscape, and distributing their experiences for educators and policy makers to learn from. Producing interpretive accounts as narratives (Clandinin 2013), which tell and re-tell of lives lived, of lives being lived and of re-living (Clandinin and Connelly 1996; Riessman 2008); the narratives operate as a process of interpretation and re-interpretation of experiences.

Clandinin and Connelly present their story sets of teachers' stories as unfolding in a landscape of paired narratives. These narrative pairs are teacher stories—stories of teachers; school stories—stories of schools. This relates to Dewey's (1997) concept of education, experience and life being indivisibly interwoven with Dewey suggesting that the study of life is the study of experience.

In Craig's (2007) story constellations approach, teacher experiences are brought to the fore, endeavouring to situate teachers' knowledge in the many environments where it is formed. Craig suggests two further companion sets of stories to Clandinin and Connelly's matrix: "stories of community—community stories, and stories of reform—reform stories" (p. 177). Craig suggests that these additional pairs allow for further "perspectives and offer a more panoramic view of the complex forces influencing school milieus and shaping the horizons of what becomes available for teachers to know" (p. 177).

Through this approach Craig seeks to uncover "experiential stories about school-based educators working in relationship" (p. 175). Our aims in this study are similar, in that we sought to uncover "experiential stories," and examine the "complex forces influencing school milieus" and societal milieus. However, the stories we wished to unearth were those of the students, the children in the teachers' landscapes and beyond. Ultimately, the lived experiences of twice exceptional children, both inside and outside traditional educational landscapes, including their home lives beyond the schools' horizons.

The story constellations approach was therefore adopted to support the relationships in and between the children's narratives, and as a way of presenting the multi-vocal narratives. We have added to Clandinin and Connelly's narrative pairs, and augmented Craig's two other companion story sets with children's stories—stories of children. The augmented story constellations approach provided the opportunity to draw together narrative thread and plotlines in the denouement process described earlier.

Re-Storying of the Research Texts

Through story constellations, the narratives we composed and re-storied were able to remain close to the data, and enabled the voices of the children to be heard (Gubrium & Holstein 2002). Through the parental narratives, which enhanced and amplified those of the children, a multi-vocal story was created. Through re-storying the plotlines and segments of narratives, taken directly from the transcribed interviews, they were first decontextualized somewhat, "but in return [this] also recontextualised them as engrossing narratives" (Czarniawska 2002, p. 744). By recontextualising the narratives they were returned to the context, through which they were told, as recollections, as parts of stories, as lives being lived and as 'messy' stories. Clandinin and Connelly (2000) speak of the ever present context in narratives which is inclusive of "temporal context, spatial context, and the context of other people" (p. 32). We endeavoured to present each child's contexts through their narrative accounts as a way of demonstrating the holistic child, contextualised by their experiences and the places where they lived, re-lived and re-told those experiences. However, all these analytical processes were dependent on thorough and thoughtful interview data. In the following section we present a section of one of the case narratives. We then return to a discussion of the interview features and practices that facilitated the data generation required for development of the narratives of these twice exceptional students.

Story Constellations

Here we set out part of one of the participant's story constellations. Although we would like to present a fuller and more comprehensive story, for the purposes of this chapter we have only included a limited version. Nevertheless, through this approach the children's lived experiences can be situated in the contexts of where those experiences are formed.

Ashley's Story Constellation

Children's Story/Story of Children

(Note: The following is re-storied and written in first person by the first author).

Through Ashley's narrative extract, we weave the interview process and our analysis of the field texts to produce our initial story constellation based round the emerging themes.

Ashley is 16 years and 2 months old. She lives with her family in a middle-class suburb in Queensland, Australia. Their home is low-set in a quiet, leafy cul-de-sac. At the time of my visits, spread over eight weeks in late summer and early autumn, I was privileged to share Ashley's unique experiences and her family's experiences; those of having a sibling with profound intellectual disability. The following narrative is a snapshot of those lived experiences.

The Interviews

Ashley and I had spoken on the telephone prior to my first visit. I'd also spent some time in email correspondence with Susanna, Ashley's mum, and we'd talked on the telephone too. We'd devoted some time to discussing Ashley's disabilities, particularly anxiety, and abilities, namely in the area of Visual Arts and music. The primary reason for our communication had been both Ashley's and Susanna's interest in taking part in my research study.

Ashley's disabilities included a diagnosis of Pervasive Developmental Disorder Not Otherwise Specified, (on the autism spectrum), Semantic Pragmatic Language Disorder and anxiety. Prior to our interview, Susanna, Ashley's mum had told me via email that;

> *Ashley was quite insistent that she did not want to be identified as disabled anymore. So two months ago we went back to [care centre] to be 'undiagnosed' [for Pervasive Developmental Disorder Not Otherwise Specified, Semantic Pragmatic Language Disorder].*

In one of her first emails, Susanna wrote;

> *Ashley is quite gifted though she is not a savant. She plays the piano quite well and can 'jam' and make up compositions on the spot. She is very good at art and loves it. Both of these subjects she is going to be studying in her final two years of high school. English, she loves and even got an A+ for her Romeo and Juliet essay, which she had deliberately set out to do. She is also doing physics, chemistry and maths. She has trouble with the algebra side of maths.*

In the same email, Susanna told me of her eldest daughter, Sarah, 18 years old, who has a profound disability, affecting her cognitively and physically. Susanna and her husband, Lesley, were placed in the principal position of having two children, both with disabilities, but profoundly different needs, particularly related to care. Sarah needed round the clock support and regularly went to respite care. On the other hand, Ashley needed interventions, particularly when she was younger, and specialist care, but with the added need of creative stimulation to cater for her giftedness.

On my first visit to their home, I heard voices from within as I approached and Susanna greeted me at the front door with a happy smile, ushering me into the coolness of their home. Ashley appeared from the darkness of the kitchen beyond the family room where Susanna and I stood. A young woman slept on the patterned sofa in one corner of the room. I presumed this was Sarah. Two cats were fast asleep at the other end of the sofa. All three looked cosy and relaxed, not stirring as I entered their home.

As we settled back in our chairs to begin our chat, one of the cats awakened, and seeing a visitor came over to check me out. I reached down to allow the cat to sniff my hand, "Oh hello gorgeous." I exclaimed as the long-haired grey cat brushed against my hand. Ashley introduced her pets "*This is Tiny Lass [pseudonym]. We have two cats, this is Tiny Lass and the other one over there, next to Sarah, is Tex [pseudonym]*". By acknowledging and talking with Ashley's pet as I do with my own, I had unintentionally begun to build rapport with Ashley. Even though we were talking in a place where Ashley felt comfortable, in the family room of her own home, she was still meeting me as a stranger; despite our brief telephone chat we did not know each other. I was aware of Ashley's autism diagnosis and anxiety from the information Susanna supplied. The presence of the cats gave me the opportunity to ease both Ashley's and my own social anxiety and act as a buffer to any difficult interview beginnings. It is acknowledged in the literature (O'Haire et al. 2015) that children with autism experience significant social anxiety, and as Ashley talked I learnt more of this.

As Ashley scooped the cats up onto her lap she caressed its belly, the cat began to purr, Ashley opened up to tell me about her disabilities and how they may have affected her; *I can tell how much of an annoying child I was. I would sort of call out when it was inappropriate in class, like yell stuff out, and it would just be like that's just rude, you don't need to speak right now. I wasn't the best with my social skills during Primary School; like I could not cope with females, too complex. My friends were all guys, because it was easy, you just had to punch them on the shoulder and they got the message.*

Sometimes it's a bit difficult getting sentences out, I've always found, to have a one on one conversation with a person, where I have to look at them for a very long time, gets stressful and I will cut off. As Ashley talks she appears comfortable, looking at me as we talk; it is more of a conversation between two people than an interview situation. Her body language shows she feels at ease, sitting back in the chair with the grey cat curled in her lap, her body turned slightly towards me as she talked.

> *Sometimes I would just shift sentences back to front, or words. Let me think of one, say 'treen grutle', I would say something like that, when I would mean to say, 'green turtle'. I would swap the front...letters and stuff around. But sometimes I do it in front of people and they just look at me, I'm like, 'Did I just say something funny?' I don't realise it at all. Not until someone goes, 'You just said this', and I go, 'Oh! What?' It's like I've swapped a whole sentence around, I will replay stuff myself... I'll probably be thinking about something else at the time or doing something and it will come out.*

Having the cat on her lap seemed to enable Ashley to be at ease with me as we talked my interest in the cats also helped build rapport. Ashley invited me to stroke the cat as it slept peacefully on her lap, a significant sign that she was open to sharing her pets with me and leading further to sharing her experiences. The cat is a living part of her 'memory box' as we talked, emphasising the ties Ashley has with her pets.

Special Education

As we stroked the cat, we talk about how Ashley felt being in the special education program at school as a result of her disability diagnosis; *Well I was like 'You don't need to treat me like this'. It just makes me very angry to have people decide who I am... because I'm not that. You don't get the right to choose. I'm sorry but having a personality and being a little bit different to everyone else, I don't think is acceptable to classify me as having a disorder, saying that I'm different and weird because of it, I don't think that's right. I think we're getting to the stage where everyone's just going to be diagnosed and no one's going to be normal. That's so the end of it, because you're going to get diagnosed for having a personality. You've got it or not! My counsellor has this on the wall, 'Everyone's normal until you get to know them.'... It's just more like you start off as a genius, we're seen as amazing but as you get older you become normal. And it's quite correct actually, because as you get older you just become normal. Oh here's the other one.* Ashley says as her other cat came to see what we are doing.

The cat came over to my bag and sniffed, curiosity getting the better of him: he stuck his head in. We paused to pay attention to the cat, chatting about his antics and laughing as he tried to climb into my bag. Susanna came in, drawn most likely by our laughter at the cat's antics.

Susanna told me; *One of the reasons why I didn't want Ashley undiagnosed, was because I was very concerned that the fact that we're now going in to year 11 and 12, when it really mattered, maybe this was the time we might have a meltdown, and anxiety.* Ashley and Susanna discussed the reasons why they both felt the opposite, as I listened intently, both sides sounded reasonable to me, Ashley doesn't feel the label helps her and Susanna would like the educational and emotional support the label brings for Ashley, especially in the final school exams and assignments coming up in the next year. They seem to have to agree to disagree.

Anxiety and Agoraphobia

Susanna told me that; *Ashley actually suffers very badly from agoraphobia and it was about a year ago that I called her aside and had a talk with her. She wouldn't go out with any friends or anything like that; she would only go out with church ladies who were in their fifties because she trusted them. It all really started I think from that big storm that we got caught in, you know the big one that happened, it's called the [name of storm]. How I remember the supercell that it was equivalent to a hurricane 2 or cyclone 2. We got caught right in the middle when we were driving. It was terrifying I have to say, it was real terrifying. Ashley was terrified of storms after that.*

"*She just wanted to be home and so I said to her, 'This is not right, we need to go and see counsellor.' Ashley's really improved from it. So a lot of that going out came from anxiety, so I think Ashley is quite an anxious child. We've just been [to the specialist centre] again and she's been totally undiagnosed with autism but with the agoraphobia the counselling has really helped. I just got to let you know, sorry to be barging in. I thought you needed to know.*" Ashley's sitting quietly, occasionally glanced at her mum and nodded in agreement as she spoke. I get the feeling Ashley wanted to tell me about the agoraphobia but perhaps didn't know how to broach the subject.

I ask Ashley how she went with getting through those feelings of not wanting to go out and being anxious;

> *The counselling was really good. Talking about it, it was the thing of coming up with plans of I'm able to get out of situations if I want to, I can have plans in place for what I can do. They originally actually put me on drugs to help along with the therapy. I tell you one thing, I did not like those! They turned me ADHD. I could not sit still, it was the most vile feeling ever, I felt sorry for those who have ADHD, because it was just terrible. I felt always on edge, and I hated it, I couldn't stand it. I was on it for a couple of weeks, I was like, 'I can't do this anymore!' I don't see the need to have drugs. It's annoying side effects getting that really, jittery stuff from it, obviously I was just possibly unlucky. It was like I didn't want to go out. Even now, sometimes I'll get quite defensive...*

I would feel really nervous, sort of sick in the stomach, stuff like that, and I'd always be on edge and I would always be watching the sky. I don't have issues now with storms, I still wouldn't want to go out in car, that's just common sense! But I don't get that whole jittery feeling when ones around, like I would get that thing sort of sick feeling I would get when going out, when I was in the house when there was a storm, and I would normally go grab the cat, try and occupy myself with something else... but I don't really have those issues anymore... thankfully. Ashley shed some light on the importance of her pet cats as part of her extended family as she cuddled up with them both when she feels anxious and stressed. The cats appear to prompt positive emotions for Ashley as O'Hare et al. (2015) found in their study with children who had autism, meaning Ashley's pets may function as effective social buffers and confidants for her (Melson 2001).

I think I'm a sort of person that needs to be told, 'It's okay to be [anxious] like this and that there's ways that you can get around it and it's not wrong to feel this.'

I just need to be able to have an action plan, because you can't let it stop you from going and doing stuff. Yeah, because I'm a sort of person who's like, 'God won't help you if you won't help yourself.' I find it irritating when people sit in the corner and go, 'There's something wrong with me,' and stuff like that. You can go do something about it, just don't sit there and complain, go do something! If you've got problems, try and solve it yourself. Like obviously I've had issues since I was young with my social behaviour and stuff, and I was still bad in grade 7 and 8. In grade 9 I felt that was a very big year of change for me socially, like I stopped associating with people who associated with others that just upset me. I thought I became much more responsible that year and much more mature and I was making more friends on my own with much more creative artsy friends. I had to do so much to change myself, I've tried really hard to get to where I am and mum's helped a lot in therapy. Ashley trailed off as one of the cats rolled over to have her stomach rubbed, and cat hair swirrled up into the air as Ashley craddled the cat lovingly on her lap.

Analysis of Ashley's Story Constellation

Through Ashley's story constellation of self-identity, the importance of her wanting to be 'undiagnosed' emerged quite strongly, she unintentionally challenged the labelling of her as a person identified as twice exceptional—she did not want to be seen as someone with a disability anymore. We had inadvertently called, or 'hailed' (to use Althusser 2001, favoured verb) Ashley, to be or become, what being twice exceptional involved—identifying as a person with giftedness and with disability. She no longer wanted to take up this identity—the disability aspect at least, which had been allocated to her by a system which had no alternative if it was to intervene and support her education and development. Ashley at 16 years old, had come to see herself differently. As far as she was concerned her circumstances had changed, she now found having a disability label to be contentious, as a source of discomfort and dislike.

She was in the process of change, not just into a young woman, but in recognising and deciding to have a say in how she wanted to be perceived by others. This is what Clandinin (2013) refers to as 'relational' in narrative inquiry; the relational between Ashley and her world, Ashley and her lived experience which had shaped and brought her to this point in time.

Ashley's evolving knowledge about her young adult self, her past experiences around disability and her disability status, had led her to her current vantage point. Thus, her knowledge about herself was "entwined with [her] identity" (Clandinin 2013, p. 53). Clandinin suggests that through thinking narratively about who we are and where we fit in "speaks to the nexus of a person's personal practical knowledge, and the landscapes, past and present, on which a person lives… a concept of *stories to live by* allows us to speak of the stories that each of us lives out and tells of who we are, and are becoming… this highlights the multiplicity of each of our lives –

lives lived out and told around multiple plotlines" (p. 53). Her present vantage point is clearly influenced by a multiplicity of different factors.

Ashley uncovered that perceptions of her by significant others; parents, friends, peers and teachers, were of importance: they mattered to her. Because of this she did not want those people to see her as incapable in any sense, as she perceived a label of disability showed her to be. She felt those narratives of disability were fixed to her by significant others (Clandinin 2013). By having others story her in these ways was immensely disturbing to her.

Ashley was seeking to construct "preferred narratives" (Riessman 2008) about herself. Riessman suggests that our propensity with identity is "no longer viewed and given as 'natural', individuals must now construct who they are and how they want to be known…in postmodern times, identities can be assembled and disassembled, accepted and contested." (p. 7).

The Interview Process

Developing the interview protocol began before the first meeting with the gathering of background information from Ashley's mother, including specialist reports and assessments, and school records (Table 9.1). This information and the email and telephone conversations with Susanna assisted in providing me with a clearer indication of any special consideration needs that Ashley might have during the interviews, which we needed to allow for. This was vital for the interview protocol, enabling us to adapt the interview process appropriately (Wilson and Powell 2001). From the background information we established that Ashley had a form of ASD which may have affected her communication, her receptive language. This meant we could approach the pre and first interviews with this in mind, to be flexible in the way we spoke and posed questions, aware of the possibility that Ashley may have had some difficulty in comprehending and processing verbal language. During the telephone conversation the first author had with Ashley prior to our first meeting, we

Table 9.1 Information checklist prior to the interview

Type of information sought
Name of child and pseudonym choice
Parents' names
Address
Date of birth/age
Disability assessment/diagnosis – any impact these might have on the interview process
Gifted assessment – any impact this might have on the interview process
Type of schooling
School reports
Out of school interests/hobbies and achievements

became aware that her receptive language was very acute; this was confirmed during our first face-to-face meeting. With this in mind we were able to proceed with the interviews, knowing that at times there might be the need to repeat or change questions as needed. Ashley also had a diagnosis of anxiety and agoraphobia which may have affected her during the interviews, even though she was in her own home, a place where she felt comfortable, she was still being exposed to myself as a stranger. This further emphasised the need to carefully build rapport and put Ashley at ease. Susanna shared some insights into Ashley's interests, which included music and art. The first author is an artist and an art teacher, this was a clear door into Ashley's world.

Preparing for the First Interview

Working from the background information and being aware that Ashley had a diagnosis of ASD and anxiety, meant we were able to consider elements of the interview protocol well before our first face-to-face meeting for the pre-interview. We considered what the interviewer would wear to the interviews; where in the home the interviews were to be conducted; the initial greeting and how the interviewer would need to place Ashley at ease straight away; the use of appropriate language—the use of voice—tone, inflection, clarity and so forth; the use of the memory box; and ending the interviews.

Dressing for the Occasion

Being a teacher the first author has a professional way of dressing for teaching situations, whereas for the interviews she wanted to present herself casually, in a less formal way so that Ashley was not intimidated by formal attire. Therefore, consideration was given to attire prior to each interview, dressing smartly, yet casually. Being aware of Ashley's ASD also made us conscious of not wearing clothing which was overly patterned or colourful, which might be distracting during the interviews. The first author did wear a small charm necklace to the pre and first interview session, which after self-reflection from the first interview, had provided Ashley with a focal point, rather than having to keep constant eye contact during our chat. This appeared to allow Ashley to focus on what she wanted to say rather than being distracted by remembering to keep eye contact.

The Environmental Context

Previous interview methods for children with disability included structured diagnostic and screening interviews usually undertaken in clinical settings. By going to Ashley's home, a place where she felt comfortable, surrounded by the familiarity of her home and her extended family of two cats, Ashley was able to be herself. Our 'free-talk' interviews provided a clear focus through flexibility and responsiveness, to Ashley and her environment. The time of day was also taken into consideration when arranging the interviews with Ashley and Susanna to ensure that they were in the mid-morning but not too early, so that Ashley was well-rested and cognitively prepared for the sessions; alternatively early afternoon, following lunch. The interviews took place mid-week of the two week Easter school break; subsequent interviews were arranged on Saturdays during the day, so as not to interfere with Ashley's school week, homework and social life. This arrangement aimed to ensure that Ashley was not too tired from a day's work at school, and the process was not perceived as a nuisance or interfering too much with Ashley's other commitments.

Initial Greetings

The initial greeting was important at each of the four interviews, but none more so than for our first face-to-face meeting. First impressions *do* count and we needed to present a positive influence (Zwiers 1999) on Ashley and her parents, whom we had not met previously. Needed to smile, looking at Ashley as Susanna introduced us, presenting our open, honest and friendly demeanour from the beginning.

The Pre-Interview

The purpose of the pre-interview with Ashley was to begin to build rapport and trust, an ice-breaking conversation. Barker (1990) underlined the importance of building rapport, not just initially but ongoing during the interview and subsequent interviews. He defined rapport as a condition of consideration, empathy, accord, and consistency, an understanding and considerate relationship personified by warmth towards each other (Barker 1990).

Initially we talked in general, making chitchat about the first author's trip up to her home, which presented an opportunity to gauge how Ashley felt in chatting. We termed the interviews 'chats' rather than 'interviews', when we needed to use the phrase, to make the conversations sound less formal. This pre-interview phase allowed us to use open-ended questions to build rapport and enable Ashley to become familiar with our child-centred approach to the interviews, where she was free to talk as much as she wanted (Wilson and Powell 2001), so that she was able to see our genuine interest in her experiences as a twice exceptional person. During this time the interviewer also told Ashley more about our study, why we were doing it and some personal information about us, such as children, pets, being an artist and art teacher, and where we lived. As the nature of communication is a reciprocal process, we encouraged Ashley to ask questions about the study. After all, we were asking her to disclose information to us, so we reciprocated by sharing some information through self-disclosure (Zwiers). One of the main subjects we began to talk about in this initial rapport building phase, was Ashley's two cats, who were asleep on the couch.

The first author has two pets, this also helped to build rapport with Ashley during the pre-interview and subsequent interviews, as she could relate to her cat stories and they became a 'bridge' to fill-in when the conversation subsided. This supports findings in the literature, particular for children with ASD, that having a pet present increases social interaction when compared to having no animal present (O'Haire et al. 2015). Ashley would often ask if my cat had similar behaviour as we exchanged stories about our cat's antics. The interviewer knew how to interact with her pet cats, and having that understanding gave her the ability to talk from a position of knowledge with her about her cats.

During the pre-interview we prepared Ashley for what was involved in the interviews; letting her know it was okay to choose not to answer any questions or not to talk about anything that she did not want to, and that she did not have to give a reason. Additionally, we let her know that she could stop at any time also without having to provide a reason to me. We informed Ashley that we was not there to be judgemental and that she was free to choose what she wished to share about her experiences and what she did not wish to share.

Language and Tone of Voice

The dynamic, child-centred interview protocol that we developed and implemented allowed for the reciprocal process of interviewing Ashley, Ashley liked to talk, and we were good at listening, but when it came time for Ashley to have feedback from us, the interviewer was able to provide supportive gestures, in the form of nodding, and vocal sounds to show active listening and taking in her sharing of experiences. This reciprocal process meant we influenced one another, by creating a discourse whereby we were inviting Ashley to share and explore her thoughts and experiences (Zwiers), then as appropriate, we could clarify and explore her responses once the free-flow had subsided. During this time, Ashley would ask questions, or ask for our experiences of certain events. It was important to share this information in a limited capacity only after Ashley had shared her experiences, so as not to directly influence what she was recounting. This developmental protocol with flexible, open-ended questions, was able to respond to new information from Ashley with further questions, and comments to gain a more thorough understanding of Ashley's lived experiences (Zwiers and Morrissette 1999).

Memory Box

The memory box served to bring into the conversation and to prompt memories from Ashley's lived experiences. The artefacts from her memory box, did not in themselves form part of the field texts, however, during the first and subsequent interviews, they provided "triggers" (Clandinin 2013) for telling her stories. The importance of Ashley's extended 'family' and support network she felt her pets provided her was reinforced with the cat collar which she included in her memory box items for the first interview. The collar was the first collar her cat had as a pet, on showing me this, Ashley expanded on the importance of her cats in teaching her responsibility: *I included that because that was just more representing how, when I first got her, the responsibility I started to learn from having a cat. That it's something to look after and the relationship because, oh a cat they're such a stress relief, because you just pat and they purr and they make you feel happy. She's like best thing in your life, I felt so happy.*

Ending the Interviews

Our chats had been extended beyond the set time on many occasions. We scheduled 30–45 min for each interview, despite protestations that we were taking up their time; both Ashley and her parents welcomed the interviewer to stay well beyond the allocated time frames. On one occasion we chatted for over two hours, Ashley occasionally stepping out of the room to collect another artefact to share, Susanna joining us to share her thoughts; me sipping my water and Ashley her coffee, as we listened intently, intermittently briefly sharing an anecdote from our experiences. They treated us like a special, important visitor, but also as a kind of collaborator, ally and cherished friend. At the end of each of our interview chats, Ashley and Susanna would accompany me to the door, chatting further as we moved from the living room to the front door, then they would stand on the driveway, we would still be talking, eventually I would make my final goodbye in their quiet cul-de-sac as they waved their last farewell.

Having spent many hours with Ashley and her family over the course of the interviews, (which took two months), to eventually have to close off the interview chats was quite difficult. We had become quite attached and almost formed a friendship of sorts based on our mutual interests. Ashley had shared her confidences with me, as had her parents during their interview; it was difficult for me at least, to accept the reality that we were not going to be visiting them anymore. The relational nature of narrative research (Clandinin 2013) meant we had both undergone a transformative process through the character of our dynamic relationship. However, as Mahoney (2007) states "Blurring the lines between our friendship (private intimate relationship) and our research collaboration (public fieldwork relationship) was a balancing act" (p. 589) throughout the interview process.

The process of exiting the field was always going to be difficult following our relational rapport, according to Michailova et al. (2014) "is a contested terrain serving as the loci of multiple and multivalent emotions, and it is because of this that it can be powerful for learning and unlearning" (p. 149). This was the start of a new part of our journey to continue to analyse and co-construct Ashley's narrative. After transcribing and re-storying Ashley's story constellation, the story was sent to her and Susanna for member checking and feedback. This to-ing and fro-ing process meant that although we had left the field, we were still in email contact. Susanna would from time to time, share Ashley's recent experiences and achievements with us. We knew this would slowly fade over time, and it provided a slow and comfortable exit for us from their lives and the stories Ashley and her parents had shared with us, stories lived and told, re-lived and retold (Connelly and Clandinin 1996).

Conclusion

The flexible and dynamic interview approach facilitated Ashley's sharing of her lived experiences of twice exceptionality. Experiences centring on self-identity, seeing herself as apart from the 'norm', yet wanting to be seen as 'normal'. Ashley's key narrative of disassociation from her disability diagnosis resulted from her multiplicity of experiences; having a sister with profound intellectual disability, perceptions of her by others, perceptions of herself and her own disability experiences. The importance of these key events in her lived experiences, shape her narrative (Boenisch-Brednich 2002). Ashley is in Turner's (1975) 'liminal space', a space of transition and transformation, where she stands on the threshold of a new landscape of experiences, moving across the limits of what she once was, into what she is going to be, but not yet knowing what that is.

Discussion Questions

1. Are there any specific needs of your participants (or a participant group with which you are familiar) that may need to be considered? How might you design an interview protocol that ensures the participants' needs are met?
2. How might a memory box be used to enhance an interview in your field of research? What types of items might prompt conversations about the things in which you are interested?
3. How might a story constellations approach be adapted for your research context? What stories might make up the constellation?

References

Agar, M. H. (1980). *The professional stranger: An informal introduction to ethnography*. San Diego: Academic.

Althusser, L. (2001). *Lenin and philosophy and other essays* (Trans.: B. Brewster). Retrieved from http://www.english.ufl.edu/mrg/readings/Lenin%20and%20Philosophy.pdf

Barker, P. (1990). *Clinical interviews with children and adolescents*. New York: Norton.

Bassey, M. (1999). *Case study research in education settings*. Ballmoor: Open University Press.

Baum, S. M., & Olenchak, F. R. (2002). The Alphabet children: GT, ADHD, and more. *Exceptionality: A Special Education Journal, 10*(2), 77–91.

Birbeck, D. J., & Drummond, M. J. N. (2007). Research with young children: Contemplating methods and ethics. *Journal of Educational Enquiry, 7*(2), 21–31.

Boenisch-Brednich, B. (2002). Migration and narration. *Folklore, 20*, 64–77.
Chase, S. E. (2003). Listening to people's stories: The use of narrative in qualitative interviews. In J. Elliott (Ed.), *Using narrative in social research: Qualitative and quantitative approaches* (pp. 17–35). Thousand Oaks: Sage.
Clandinin, D. J. (2013). *Engaging in narrative inquiry*. Walnut Creek: Left Coast Press.
Clandinin, D. J., & Connelly, F. M. (1996). Teachers' professional knowledge landscapes: Teacher stories - stories of teachers - school stories - stories of schools. Educational Researcher, 25(3), 24–30.
Clandinin, D. J., & Connelly, F. M. (2000). *Narrative inquiry*. San Francisco: Jossey-Bass.
Connelly, F. M., & Clandinin, D. J. (2006). Narrative inquiry. In J. L. Green, G. Camilli, & P. Elmore (Eds.), *Handbook of complementary methods in education research* (3rd ed., pp. 477–487). Mahwah: Lawrence Erlbaum.
Craig, C. J. (2007). Story consellations: A narrative approach to contextualising teachers' knowledge of school reform. *Teaching and Teacher Education, 23*, 173–188. doi:10.1016/j.tate.2006.04.014.
Cresswell, J. W. (2008). *Educational research* (3rd ed.). Upper Saddle River: Pearson Education.
Czarniawska, B. (2002). Narrative, interviews and organizations. In J. F. Gubrium & J. A. Holstein (Eds.), *Handbook of interview research: Context and method* (pp. 733–776). Thousand Oaks: Sage.
DePoy, E., & Gilson, S. (2010). *Disability design and branding: Rethinking disability within the 21st century*. Maine and Astos: Office of Special Education and Rehabilitative Services. Retrieved from http://www2.ed.gov/rschstat/research/…/nidrr-lrp-05-09-exec-summ.pdf
Dewey, J. (1997). *Experience and education*. New York: Touchstone.
Duffy, M. (2011). *Paul Ricoeur's pedagogy of pardon: A narrative theory of memory and forgetting*. Retrieved from https://books.google.com.au/books?hl=en&lr=&id=4VLNM_dqrVUC&oi=fnd&pg=PP2&dq=narrative+as+cathartic&ots=G4vr3oZZi5&sig=ckFvyTa_U3HlJiqEYUYNzU0Oy-c#v=onepage&q=%20cathartic&f=false
Foley-Nicpon, M., Allmon, A., Sieck, B., & Stinson, R. D. (2011). Empirical investigation of twice-exceptionality: Where have we been and where are we going? *Gifted Child Quarterly, 55*(1), 1–15.
Foley-Nicpon, M., Assouline, S. G., & Colangelo, N. (2013). Twice-exceptional learners: Who needs to know what? *Gifted Child Quarterly, 57*(3), 169–180. doi:10.1177/0016986213490021.
Gagné, F. (2009). Building gifts into talents: Detailed overview of the DMGT 2.0. In B. MacFarlane & T. Stambaugh (Eds.), *Leading change in gifted education: The festschrift of Dr. Joyce VanTassel-Baska*. Waco: Prufrock Press.
Gubrium, J. F., & Holstein, J. A. (2002). From the interview to the interview society. In J. F. Gubrium & J. A. Holstein (Eds.), *Handbook of interview research: Context and method* (pp. 3–32). Thousand Oaks: Sage.
Harrington, C., Foster, M., Rodger, S., & Ashburner, J. (2013). Engaging young people with autism spectrum disorder in research interviews. *British Journal of Learning Disabilites, 41*(3), 1–9.
Hill, M. (2005). Ethical considerations in researching children's experiences. In P. Christensen & A. James (Eds.), *Researching children's experiences: Approaches and methods* (pp. 61–86). London: Sage.
Kim, J. H. (2016). *Understanding narrative inquiry: The crafting and analysis of stories as research*. Thousand Oaks: Sage.
Mahoney, D. (2007). Constructing reflexive fieldwork relationships: Narrating my collaborative storytelling methodology. *Qualitative Inquiry, 13*(4), 573–594.
Martin, J., & Merrotsy, P. (2006). Portfolio of artefacts: Promising data for qualitative research. *Australasian Journal of Gifted Education, 15*(1), 39–43.
Melson, G. F. (2001). *Why the wild things are: Animals in the lives of children*. Cambridge: Harvard University Press.

Michailova, S., Piekkari, R., Plakoyiannaki, E., Ritvala, T., Mihailova, I., & Salmi, A. (2014). Breaking the silence about exiting fieldwork: A relational approach and its implications for theorizing. *Academy of Management Review, 39*(2), 138–161. doi:10.5465/amr.2011.0403.

Munhall, P. L. (2001). *Nursing research: A Qualitative perspective* (3rd ed.). Sudbury: National League for Nursing.

O'Haire, M. E., McKenzie, S. J., Beck, A. M., & Slaughter, V. (2015). Animals may act as social buffers: Skin conductance arousal in children with autism spectrum disorder in a social context. *Developmental Psychobiology, 57*(5), 584–595. doi:10.1002/dev.21310.

Patterson, W. (2013). Narratives of events: Labovian analysis and its limitations. In M. Andrews, C. Squire, & M. Tamboukou (Eds.), *Doing narrative research* (pp. 27–46). London: Sage.

Polkinghorne, D. E. (1988). *Narrative knowing and the human sciences*. Albany: State University of New York Press.

Polkinghorne, D. E. (1995). Narrative configuration in qualitative analysis. *Qualitative Studies in Education, 8*(1), 5–23.

Preece, D., & Jordan, R. (2010). Obtaining the views of children and young people with autism spectrum disorders about their experiences of daily life and social care support. *British Journal of Learning Disabilities, 38*(1), 10–20.

Reis, S. M., Baum, S. M., & Burke, E. (2014). An Operational definition of twice-exceptional learners: Implications and applications. *Gifted Child Quarterly, 58*(3), 217–230. doi:10.1177/0016986214534976.

Riessman, C. (2008). *Narrative methods for the human sciences*. Thousand Oaks: Sage.

Seidman, I. (2006). *Interviewing as qualitative research: A Guide for researchers in education and the social sciences* (3rd ed.). New York: Teachers College Press.

Turner, V. (1975). *Dramas, fields and metaphores: Symbolic action in human societies*. Ithaca: Cornell University Press.

Wilson, C. J., & Powell, M. B. (2001). *A guide to interviewing children: Essential skills for counsellors, police, lawyers and social workers*. Crows Nest: Allen & Unwin.

World Health Organisation. (2011). *World report on disability*. Geneva: The World Health Organisation, United Nations.

Yin, R. K. (2009). *Case study research: Design and methods* (5th ed.). Thousand Oaks: Sage.

Zwiers, M. L., & Morrissette, P. J. (1999). *Effective interviewing of children: A Comprehensive guide for counselors and human service workers*. Philadelphia: Taylor & Francis.

Chapter 10
The IELTS Roller Coaster: Stories of Hope, Stress, Success, and Despair

Megan Yucel and Noriko Iwashita

Abstract This chapter discusses how a narrative approach can be used to investigate the key constructs of language, culture, identity, and learner beliefs about English language testing. With the globalisation of English and its spread in use, there is a need for a reliable means of assessing English language proficiency. Governments, employers, professional bodies, and educational institutions rely on large-scale international tests to provide them with English language proficiency information. The chapter features participants preparing to take the International English Language Testing System (IELTS), a high-stakes test of English language proficiency largely taken for the purposes of immigration and entry into tertiary academic institutions.

The specific methodological issue that this chapter explores is how to frame the stories of language learners. We draw on Clandinin and Connelly's (2000) model of the three dimensions (temporality, sociality and place) which provide the context for a story. To capture these dimensions, details of the candidates' life history, interaction with IELTS testing and their story 'after' IELTS are specifically written in to their stories, as are the relational and social contexts and the places. We also use Barkhuizen's (2008) model of interconnected stories (from individual to broader contexts) to frame analysis of the data. Our framework choices allowed us as researchers to gain a deeper understanding of the varied reasons that language learners may have for wanting to acquire and use a new language, from personal or family reasons to social, economic or political reasons, and provided a way to capture the participants' experience of the phenomenon of IELTS test candidacy. They also facilitated the analysis of micro stories of individuals in the context of their wider resonance on a macro or societal level.

Keywords IELTS • English language proficiency • English language assessment • High-stakes tests • Narrative inquiry

M. Yucel (✉) • N. Iwashita
The University of Queensland, St Lucia, QLD, Australia
e-mail: m.yucel@icte.uq.edu.au

© Springer Science+Business Media Singapore 2017

R. Dwyer et al. (eds.), *Narrative Research in Practice*,
DOI 10.1007/978-981-10-1579-3_10

Introduction

> It's very stressful this situation, because I have to pass the IELTS test, so when I'm thinking about IELTS I feel stressed, nervous… I think this was my main problem in the last test. I couldn't pass it because of my stress, maybe, I don't know. (Pamela)

This chapter reports on a qualitative study involving a narrative inquiry of candidates taking the IELTS test. IELTS, which stands for International English Language Testing System, is a high-stakes English language test that is conducted globally on a large scale. The growth of testing as an industry and the move in society towards what Brown and Abeywickrama call a "test-oriented culture" (2010, p. 100), mean that testing has become an increasingly important component of English language education. At the same time, an increase in the number of non-English speaking students wishing to undertake all or part of their university education abroad, and in English, has led to steady growth in the higher education sector in English speaking countries such as Australia. The rising number of international students seeking to gain a place at university has created a need for large scale, consistent, centralised and trustworthy gatekeeping examinations to help determine these students' suitability for tertiary study in English. Large-scale English language tests such as IELTS are commonly used to decide who is able to gain access and who is not. The rising demand for IELTS has also been fuelled by government immigration policy, with the granting of Australian work and residency rights being tied to IELTS scores. As a gateway to study or work in Australia, success on the IELTS is thus a focal point for many individuals for whom English is not their first language.

Conceptualizing the effects of a gatekeeper exam such as IELTS necessitates understanding the multifaceted and longitudinal nature of the setting in which the phenomenon occurs. The study participants' perceptions of IELTS developed across time and in various settings, including the home countries where English language study and IELTS preparation was undertaken, and the Australian setting where they ultimately planned to work or study. A variety of research tools were used to gather data including questionnaires to gain background information about the participant and semi-structured interviews. Interviews with participants were conducted periodically over a six-month period, at various stages of their journeys, from the early stages of preparing for the IELTS test to reflecting on the test in hindsight. After interpretation of the interview data, learner narratives were generated, which were then verified by the participants. This chapter features the narratives of three of the five participants in the study.

The underlying premise of many Narrative Inquiry research methodologies is that we as human beings understand or make sense of our lives through narrative (Bruner 1990). The stories at the centre of this particular inquiry are those told by test-takers; candidates taking the IELTS test. It is worth noting that it is not enough simply to collect the stories and tell them, however interesting they may be. As Murray points out, the story only becomes research "when it is interpreted in view of the literature of the field" (2009, p. 46) and can be put to practical use, lead to further research, or contribute to theory. In this case, the test-taker narratives that were produced in the study make a contribution to scholarship on test impact, including candidates' attitudes and perceptions of IELTS, and the uses of large-scale English language tests in international education and employment.

Background to the Study

The Socio-cultural Context of Taking the IELTS Test in Australia

The candidates' lived experiences and the authors' analysis of their content are inextricably linked to the context in which these experiences took place. The IELTS test was taken by approximately 2.5 million candidates in over 140 countries around the world in 2014 (IELTS 2015). Stakeholders (students, teachers, institutions, professional associations and government departments) are assured that the test offers a reliable and rigorous measure of a candidate's proficiency in English, through tests of reading, listening, writing, and speaking. To that end, significant amounts are invested in test development and validation, as evidenced by the IELTS Joint-funded Research Program, which offers funding for IELTS-related projects (IELTS 2015).

In the Australian context, the IELTS test is one of only a few tests that are used to make decisions about immigration, professional registration and university entrance. In terms of immigration, for example, under the Immigration Points Test, applicants seeking a Skilled Visa can attain valuable points by demonstrating English language proficiency with an IELTS band score of 7 or above (Department of Immigration and Border Protection, 2015). Professional associations set their own language requirements; the Nursing and Midwifery Board of Australia, for example, requires a minimum standard of IELTS band 7 for registered nurses (2015), while the Australian Institute for Teaching and School Leadership (2015) requires teachers to attain an average band score of 7.5, with no less than 8 in listening and speaking. In the tertiary sector, university administrators must consider academic qualifications and language proficiency when making decisions about the admission of international students. In a case study of one Australian university, O'Loughlin (2008) found that administrators relied solely on IELTS scores to assess language proficiency. There was no flexibility from one individual applicant to the next. This system was seen to be fair by one set of stakeholders, the university administrators, as the decision to admit was not a subjective one, but rather an objective one based on an IELTS score. This is by no means an isolated example. It is standard practice for Australian universities to set a minimum IELTS score for prospective international students. At the University of Queensland, for instance, where this study took place, the minimum IELTS requirement ranges from 6.5 to 7, according to the degree program being applied for (2015). As such, a single test score can be the catalyst for momentous, life-changing events, such as studying abroad, being accepted by a professional body, or gaining immigration clearance.

Lived Experiences and Narratives

This study focused on both the content and the context of the narratives; that is, the experiences of the candidates and how they understood them was explored and analysed by coding and categorising themes that emerged from the data. At the same time, the context of the stories was considered. We drew on Clandinin and Connelly's (2000) model of the three dimensions; temporality, sociality and place. To capture these dimensions, details of the students' life and language learning histories, interaction with IELTS testing and their story 'after' IELTS were specifically written into their stories, as were the relational and social contexts and the places. We also used Barkhuizen's (2008) model of three interconnected stories to frame this context analysis:

1. story – a particular individual's story.
2. Story – the wider context, beyond the personal level such as the school or workplace.
3. STORY – the broader socio-political context in which teaching and learning takes place.

This involved viewing each individual's story in reflexive relation with the wider context of Story and then again with the broader socio-political context (their STORY). Choosing this framework enabled us as researchers to gain a deeper understanding of the varied reasons that language learners have for wanting to acquire and use a new language, from personal or family reasons to social, economic or political ones, while also providing a way to capture the participants' experience of the phenomenon of IELTS test candidacy. This framework also relates in an interesting way to test impact, which can also be seen as the effect of a test on the individual at the micro level, and on society at the macro level. In other words, the micro stories of individuals can have a wider resonance on a macro or societal level. In terms of test validity, it is also the stories of individuals that can help us to understand this multi-faceted concept from the perspective of the test-taker.

Using narrative inquiry as our overall research framework, we aimed to explore candidates' beliefs about the IELTS test, and themselves as test-takers. In other words, we wished to explore each candidate's subjective system of knowledge and beliefs about the IELTS test. We are interested here in what meaning test-takers attach to the IELTS test and what this tells us about the experience of taking a high-stakes test like IELTS.

This research is situated within the broader contexts of language assessment research, and narrative inquiry in educational research. Traditionally, language-testing research has favoured a predominantly quantitative approach to test validation, while narrative research in TESOL has tended to focus more on the lived experiences of teachers rather than learners. To date, narrative research has not been applied to the context of the IELTS and its effect on English language learners. This project makes a significant contribution to TESOL assessment research through a focus on test takers' narratives. By allowing the candidate's voice to be heard, it contributes to a deeper understanding of the IELTS test-taker, and also provides useful insights for other stakeholders, such as teachers, administrators, and policy makers.

Theoretical Context

This research project is situated within the broader contexts of test washback (Alderson and Wall 1993; Green 2007), or the effect of a test on teaching and learning. It also relates to test validity (Messick 1996), and use (Fulcher 2010). It provides a unique and illuminating view of an arguably somewhat neglected group of test users, the candidates. Preparation for the IELTS test influences the emotional and learning experiences of candidates seeking to meet the language requirements for work, study, and/or immigration.

This study investigates test-takers' views of the validity of the English language test they are taking. A traditional view of test validity confines its developers' role to ensuring that the test "measures what it purports to measure" (Ruch 1924, p. 13). From this perspective, validity is defined in terms of test items being reasonable samples of the knowledge and skills that candidates are expected to possess. More recently, Messick argued for consideration of the consequential aspect of validity and called for evidence of "…unfairness in test use" (1996, p. 251). This suggests that the responsibilities of the test developer may also extend to how the test is used to make decisions about test candidates (Fulcher 2010). Test developers can make recommendations, but in the case of IELTS in Australia, test use is ultimately determined by government departments, educational institutions and professional bodies. Some argue that the focus on "social consequences" (Brualdi 1999, p. 1) leads to a "cluttering" of the notion of validity, resulting in "confusion, not clarity" (Popham 1997, p. 9). It is perhaps for this reason that the issue of personal, professional and academic consequences stemming from IELTS has received scant attention from researchers.

Data Collection and Analysis

Participants were recruited from a range of programs, from one week intensive IELTS preparation courses to long-term English for Academic Purposes programs. When selecting participants to interview, we were seeking a range of different types of IELTS candidates in terms of aspects such as gender, nationality, and reason for taking the test. Each participant was interviewed at least twice for about an hour at a time. In the interviews, the interviewer simply asked each participant to tell the story of their IELTS journey, from first contemplating taking it, to studying for the test, to receiving their results. The participants were asked to describe how these things made them feel. The researchers and participants also had other contact apart from the interviews, such as emails.

The interview data was then coded and categorised and themes and patterns were identified, for each individual and across the whole group. There were, for example, some concerns that were mentioned by every participant, such as the perception of IELTS as an impediment to their progress, or the lack of time allowed to complete the test, which added to the pressures experienced by the candidates on test day. The expense of the test and the repeated attempts to take it were also frequently mentioned. There were some unique concerns too, such as the candidate who experienced crippling test anxiety, or the participant who decried the lack of feedback given to candidates. Surprising perceptions emerged, such as concepts of passing or failing the test, even though there is no pass mark as such on IELTS, just a band score from 1 (non-user) to 9 (expert user). Nevertheless, each participant had a target score that they needed to attain, which evidently loomed large in their minds.

Next, the interviewer developed a short narrative account for each participant recounting their IELTS story, loosely using Clandinin and Connelly's (2000) model of the three dimensions; temporality, sociality and place, and Barkhuizen's (2008) concept of three interconnected stories as aides-mémoire in incorporating the different strands of each individual's story. These accounts are a form of what Clandinin and Connolly (2000) call an interim text. The narratives were then verified with the participants. Three of these narratives are featured in the next section. At the same time, the IELTS test partners gave the researchers permission to access these participants' writing test scripts and speaking test recordings so that a comparison could be made between the candidates' perceptions and their performance on these parts of the test, although this information is not included in this chapter.

The Stories

Pamela's Story: No Exceptions

Meeting Pamela for the first time, I was struck by her air of strength and confidence. Our interviews would take place in an empty classroom, after her English classes had finished. Even after a long day of study, her energy and dynamism filled the room.

Pamela had left her home country of Colombia to do a Master's Degree in Geometallurgy at an Australian university. Unlike some students who may not have formulated clear ambitions before commencing their university studies, it was immediately apparent that Pamela had a strong sense of her professional identity and her research goals. In other words, she had a definite purpose for being in Australia and a clear scholastic goal that she wished to achieve. Having received a conditional offer to do a Master's, she had already found a supervisor and had even begun to collect data for her research project in her home country. Pamela, a geological engineer, was being sponsored by her employer, a large multi-national firm, and the research that she was to

(continued)

complete at the university would feed into a multi-million dollar project in her home country. Pamela was able to readily explain to me, a layperson, how her research fit into this project:

> This project at this moment is in the exploration stage so we are working on the prefeasibility stage, and writing, we are writing the prefeasibility document in order to send this document to [the parent company] and they need to check that everything is OK. They will send money in order to make a mine, to start to develop the mine, and infrastructure and things like that. Geometallurgy helps us to understand the hardness of the rock type so we need this model now in order to continue with the prefeasibility stage, but because of my IELTS score I cannot start to work on this model.

She had also presented at an international mining conference in Australia and co-authored a paper in English on the project in a peer-reviewed journal. Attaining the required IELTS score to commence her studies was the final hurdle. Unfortunately, this hurdle became a seemingly insurmountable one. As she took one test after another, the pressures on Pamela – both from within and without—began to mount.

> My supervisor says, "Pamela, you don't need IELTS because you can communicate with everybody. I know you can make mistakes when you speak or something but you can start a Master's. It's not a problem." I say, "Yes. But what can I do? I tried to talk to [University] Admissions."

Understandably, Pamela felt a sense of obligation to her employers to succeed in her IELTS. She was conscious of the costs involved in her Australian sojourn and she was also cognisant of the potential scale of the mining project that her research was contributing to, and the effect that this project could have on the local economy if it proceeded. A sense of bewilderment became apparent, as Pamela tried to reconcile her lower-than-expected IELTS scores with her confidence in her knowledge of her chosen field and her ability to carry out research successfully. She frequently referred to the stress that she experienced when taking the test and wondered if this response was quite normal. She noted that tasks that she completed quickly and easily in her English class, such as reading comprehension questions, became much more difficult under exam conditions. She concluded, humorously, "maybe I don't need more English courses…maybe (I need) yoga to manage my stress!"

When, at the end of her English course, it was time for her to return home, Pamela had fallen just short of attaining the overall IELTS band score that she needed. After taking the test on five separate occasions, she remained in limbo. She spent her final days in Australia dealing with university officialdom, unsuccessfully trying to find a way around the IELTS hurdle, only to be told to come back when she had an IELTS score. She articulated her feelings thus: "So frustrating. I know I can do this. That's the frustration. I know I can do this. But they [University Admissions] won't even look at it, [her current IELTS score] they won't look at me. It's the idea that, is there any exception? But of course they don't make exceptions."

Pamela's Story: Commentary

Pamela's story exemplifies the plight of those international students who somehow fall through the cracks by failing to reach the language requirements of their chosen university, despite their aptitude and desire to study there. Her story also illustrates the disconnect between university admissions departments wishing to have a clear and unambiguous set of requirements for entrance, and prospective international students who feel that they have the ability and the credentials to undertake their chosen course of study but are being kept out by a reliance on just one, narrow definition of language proficiency.

Basing entry to universities solely on meeting language proficiency test requirements has the potential for unfavourable personal and academic consequences. It favours students who are more familiar with and skilled at this style of assessment, while potentially shutting out others. University administrators must certainly consider academic qualifications and language proficiency when making decisions about the enrolment of international students, but how this should be done is a matter of some conjecture. By relying solely on proficiency test scores to assess language ability, there is no flexibility from one individual applicant to the next. So, while this system is seen to be fair by one set of stakeholders, as the decision to admit is apparently objective, based on an IELTS score, students like Pamela slip through the cracks. It is little wonder that these students begin to question the validity of the IELTS test.

If the practice of making judgments about people based on a single, high-stakes test is perceived by one group of stakeholders—the test-takers—as lacking fairness, this leads to the question of what form of assessment might be a more suitable replacement for the traditional psychometric language test. The answer seems to lie in a more diverse range of assessment options, such as portfolios, observations, and projects, which cater to different learning styles and preferences and require different modes of performance. However, these forms of assessment can be impractical, unreliable and even biased if they are introduced without adequate training and support and this may lead to ethical concerns for those administering them. Any alternative measure to IELTS would need to have comparable levels of convenience, validity and reliability for those users.

Toshi's Story: Never Say Die

It was always a delight to meet with Toshi. This polite and cheerful young man was eager to meet me after class, and displayed an unfailingly positive attitude when describing his IELTS-related travails. Toshi was an exchange student from Japan who was doing an undergraduate degree in Education at a Japanese university. He was determined to immerse himself in campus life and Australian culture, had made many friends in his multilingual class, and spoke fondly of his Australian host family.

(continued)

Toshi had originally planned to study at the University of Queensland for two semesters, but a lower-than-expected IELTS score meant that he spent one of those semesters studying English intensively and taking IELTS preparation classes at the language institute attached to the university. Toshi saw the positive side of this, explaining that as he hoped to become an English teacher one day, the experience would be beneficial in giving him an insight into the latest English language teaching methods used in Australia. Nevertheless, during our interviews, Toshi expressed his eagerness to begin his university studies as soon as possible. Like Pamela, Toshi had taken the test on multiple occasions and had come very close to the required band score to enter UQ, but still needed an overall average of 6.5 on one test. Despite this predicament of being so near and yet so far, Toshi displayed unfailing optimism in our interviews. He was fully aware of his strengths and weaknesses and was convinced that with enough hard work in the right areas, he would achieve his goal. He frequently referred to this hard work, e.g. "I'm trying very hard for almost 10 weeks, yeah. I've been trying very hard and studying every day and talking. Sometimes my friends say like, you're very studious, you're doing a lot, so you don't need any more, but I feel like I need more, I have many weaknesses, so I have to tackle this."

Toshi spent a lot of time in our interviews talking about each skill tested in the IELTS test, and the strategies that he was employing to improve his results. He gave an amusing example of one such test strategy that he had used in his most recent speaking test. When asked about a particular type of hobby, he found himself with nothing to say because he had no interest in it. "But I had to say something," he went on, "so I told a lie. It's a kind of strategy. One of my friends likes that hobby so I just talked about that. But in my heart I was like, I'm so sorry for telling lies." Toshi had grasped the fact that the examiner was not overly concerned about the nature of the hobby itself, but rather the English language proficiency that was displayed in describing it.

In our penultimate interview, Toshi had good news—he had achieved the 6.5 he needed to begin his university studies. However, this was not without some difficulty. When he first received his scores, Toshi had received a lower score than expected. After some deliberation, he exercised his right to a remark and was awarded a higher mark in one of the skills, which was enough to give him the overall score that he needed. We met again some months later, just before he was about to return to Japan. He had had a wonderful semester and had achieved good marks in the assessment for his university subjects.

Toshi's Story: Commentary

Toshi's story is somewhat typical of the many international students who strive to meet the language requirements of the university that they have chosen. Unlike Pamela, although these students take the IELTS test again and again, they refuse to be disheartened by their inability to reach the language requirements, studying diligently until they are successful. Toshi's story, therefore, illustrates how success may be achieved through diligence, motivation, and a positive attitude towards tests. Rather than seeing the IELTS test as an unnecessary hindrance, as Pamela had, Toshi accepted its existence and worked steadily and optimistically towards reaching his goal of 6.5. He spoke of the connection between preparing for the test and seeing an improvement in his language skills, thereby exhibiting confidence in the validity of the exam. Toshi, therefore, is typical of those international students who accept the need for universities to ascertain English language abilities through language proficiency tests and are prepared to work within those parameters to gain a place.

Sandra's Story: Under Pressure

Meeting Sandra in the leafy surrounds of the Brisbane backpackers' hostel where she and her partner were staying, I would never have known that this was a woman under immense pressure. She just looked like a typical European backpacker, laughing and joking without a care in the world.

Sandra and I agreed to meet in the garden of her backpackers' accommodation. As we sat at a picnic table, looking out over the pool, Sandra explained her story to me. Sandra had visited Australia some ten years before, as a tourist, and had "fallen in love" with the country. She made a decision then to try to come back to live and work here. Sandra was a highly-qualified and experienced ICU nurse in her home country, the Netherlands. As she spoke, she was able to fluently and humorously recount her IELTS experiences to me. From our casual conversation, her communication skills seemed more than adequate, but of course to be registered as a nurse in Australia, there are strict rules. As well as meeting the qualification and experience requirements, international nurses are also required to prove their language proficiency. One way of doing this is by achieving 7s in all four skills in the IELTS test. When Sandra had first looked into working in Australia, the language requirement for nurses was lower. She had even accepted a job here, until her plans changed and she didn't take the offer. Some years later, she would come to regret this decision as she now found that 7 so hard to attain.

Like the other candidates I interviewed, Sandra spoke of taking her first IELTS test without knowing very much about it. Like Toshi, for example, she was pleasantly surprised at her score on her first attempt, and thought that it would be a relatively straightforward matter to get the required 7. How wrong she was. Sandra found herself in Australia, two years later, still trying to get the 7, with the added pressure of time ticking away on her visa and mounting expenses. She also had a partner, who had decided to embark on the adventure with her, depending on her getting the work visa so that he could also stay and

(continued)

study or work. She was undergoing a sort of crisis of confidence. She said, "I can't believe I still haven't achieved that band score 7. And then it sort of gets to you, you know? IELTS recommends you as well, take a year, go and do reading, you know? So I done all that, I have never read a Dutch book again, so I'm only reading English books, I've been preparing myself knowing that I had to score this band 7, and, the test gets to me now, I get so nervous that I, you know. Recently I done the test and during my speaking test, I'm just stuttering, and then I think, I know I can speak English, and why am I so nervous? It's because this test is so important for me to achieve 7." It seemed apparent that Sandra's state of mind was affecting her proficiency in a skill, speaking, where she had previously felt confident.

Her main hurdle, like so many of the participants that I contacted in this study, was writing. Sandra had consistently received a lower score in this skill than the others and was 'stuck' on 6.5. She had sought help from a tutor in her country but had largely studied by herself until taking the IELTS strategies course offered at ICTE. She realized that she needed more feedback on her writing if she was going to improve. "I've been practicing, that's how desperate you get you know, you just ask people you don't even know, can you please mark it? Because I need to know if I'm doing well. And apparently if I do it here I can do it, but once I'm in the test room I can't do it anymore." The feedback that she had received from her teacher on the course had been helpful and had helped to increase her confidence. Her teacher had given her advice on paragraphing, for example. "My teacher showed me some things I'd done wrong, and that's my writing style, she says, you paragraph too much. I just jump to the next line because for me it's reading clear. She said, you're just making new paragraphs." Sandra felt that this revelation might make a real difference to her writing grade. Although Sandra had found the strategies course helpful, she was adamant that the test itself should offer better feedback to the candidates, and that a problem such as this should have been made known to her when she received her results. "Maybe I should have done the strategy course in Holland and then I would have achieved IELTS quicker, but then again I think they should give feedback. Feedback is what people deserve if they take an exam."

Sandra was ultimately able to achieve her IELTS overall band score of 7 in the first test that she took after the strategies course. She describes the moment when she learned her scores thus: "Then you have to pick up this envelope, and I thought, you know, it's close. So I thought, I'll just go outside, I won't apply for another test today. So I just walked outside and then I opened the envelope, because I can't wait, and it's like, 8, 7.5, 7—and I was disappointed because I had only a 7 for writing—and I was like, Oh my God, but that's not a 6! So yeah, I was very, very happy."

Sandra's Story: Commentary

Sandra's story illustrates the difficulties faced by professionals—often highly qualified and experienced in their respective fields—seeking to prove their language proficiency and attain permission to ply their trade in a new country. Her lack of success, despite her professional expertise and apparent linguistic fluency, highlighted the importance of effective feedback, preferably from a teacher. Until her teacher pointed out an obvious deficiency in her writing, Sandra was unaware that she was making the error. It is not uncommon for professionals taking the IELTS test to underestimate its linguistic demands and a preparation course can allow them to familiarise themselves with the test format and gain beneficial skills and strategies.

The standards required for health-care professionals such as Sandra are of necessity stringent; they could, after all, mean the difference between life and death. There is a place for well-designed, valid and reliable standardized tests that professional bodies can use as part of the process of ascertaining whether a prospective entrant meets the minimum required standards that they need to carry out their professional duties. Large-scale, high profile English language tests such as IELTS and TOEFL will continue to be used for gatekeeping purposes because of logistical considerations, but a positive development in recent years is the emergence of tests such as the Occupational English Test (OET), which is designed specifically to assess the language skills of health-care professionals like Sandra.

Reflections

The use of the IELTS test to make decisions about the future of individuals raises ethical questions. Tests seem to offer clear, objective results, but they are not infallible and there are limitations in how much they can tell us about the test-taker. Spolsky (1997, p. 246) cautions that while efforts to make gatekeeping tests as reliable as possible through psychometric means are commendable, "we still need to be troubled by how much confidence to place in using results like these in making fateful decisions about people". In making decisions today about university entrance, for example, Spolsky recommends making use of other sources of data apart from gate-keeping tests. McNamara (2000) concurs, arguing that a socially responsible view of language testing requires consideration to be given to a test's consequences, both intended and unintended. It is clear then, that ongoing research and continual improvement processes must be undertaken to ensure that English language proficiency tests are used ethically and appropriately in the interests of all stakeholders. This study aimed to contribute to those efforts by examining the test from the perspective of the candidate.

The intense focus on succeeding on the IELTS exam resulted in consequences for learning and teaching, or washback. Individuals noted the improvement in their language skills and this was reflected in the gains that some made in their IELTS scores. Thus, some positive washback from studying for the IELTS exam was reported. However, the impact of taking the IELTS test went beyond the academic aspects of language proficiency. A recurring theme in the interviews was the pivotal role that IELTS had assumed in these individuals' lives. Of those interviewees who were preparing to take the test, it seemed to dominate their thoughts and actions, so that their lives revolved around it. This preoccupation with IELTS did not end after they had sat for the test, with all of the participants taking the test multiple times. Planning the timing and budgeting the expense of the next test had to be carefully considered along with actual test preparation and study. Waiting for their results, they tried to plan for the future, hoping for a positive outcome while also envisaging worst-case scenarios and making contingency plans. These considerations all took place while they juggled other aspects of their lives, such as their English classes, part-time jobs, and relationships. As a consequence, stress and anxiety were frequently mentioned, with participants feeling the pressure as time began to run out for them to achieve IELTS success. These insights indicate the emotional impact that taking a high-stakes gatekeeper test may have on the test-taker.

The decision to use narrative research methods in this research study brought both challenges and benefits. We were aware of the need to do more than just tell stories. The stories needed to be told in the socio-cultural context in which they occurred, in order to understand them. We were also conscious of the fact that, due to time constraints and the amount of data generated, we could only have a small number of participants compared to other forms of research. Nevertheless, we hoped that our interviews with them would yield rich and in-depth data. When it was time to present the data that had been collected and analysed, we grappled with the question of how best to bring the participants' stories to a wider audience. We considered whether it was better to select individual anecdotes that were told by the participants within the interviews or to try to construct a coherent story about the participant. We decided that the interviewer should write a narrative for each participant, what Barkhuizen (2011) calls a bigger story of the individual, which was based on the entire interview. The process of transcribing and analysing the interview data helped to facilitate the production of the narratives, as the researcher was already familiar with the experiences that had been shared by the participants. Ethically speaking, because the participants' own words were being transformed into narratives by the researchers, it became even more important for checks to be carried out so the participants could verify that our interpretations matched what they had intended to say. To this end, even when the participants were no longer on campus, we kept in touch via email, and sent the narratives to them for feedback.

Choosing to use narrative inquiry allowed the researchers to gain a deeper understanding of the varied reasons that language learners may have for wanting to acquire and use a new language, from personal or family reasons to social, economic or political ones, while also providing a way to capture the participants' experience of the phenomenon of IELTS test candidacy. Using the Clandinin and Connelly (2000) and Barkhuizen (2008) models enabled the researchers to write up the individual test-taker narratives with an awareness of their social, political, and cultural context. The findings provide new insights into the effects of a high-stakes language test on the individual at the micro level, and the implications for society at the macro level.

In terms of the three individuals' narratives, they provide valuable insights into the impact that preparing for and taking a gatekeeper test can have on a person's life. They show the washback effects on these language learners, both academic and personal. The narratives also contribute to the debate on how concerned test developers should be about the consequential validity of an exam; that is, how it is used by stakeholders and the consequences of those uses. These individual cases help to illustrate these ethical concerns. Each individual invested a considerable amount of time, money and effort pursuing their dream of studying or working in Australia. Their success or failure in the test also had significant repercussions. Pamela's desire to undertake further study (her story) was necessary for her to fulfil her role in her workplace team and was encouraged and sponsored by her managers (her Story) in order to contribute to the commencement of a multi-million-dollar mining project in her country with global economic implications (her STORY). Similarly, Toshi's wish to complete a university exchange (his story) was expected by his university and supported financially by his family (his Story) and would equip him with the spoken English fluency to teach English in a Japanese high school, as part of the Japanese government's endeavour to raise English language proficiency levels in the population (his STORY). Sandra's dream of living and working in Australia as an Intensive Care nurse (her story) had led her across the world with her partner in tow to a Brisbane backpackers' hostel to start again (her Story). Her skills and expertise were in demand in the Australian healthcare system (her STORY). These narratives have allowed the uncovering of test-takers' experiences, including their beliefs about the IELTS test, its significance in their lives, and the experience and process of taking it.

Discussion Questions

1. What are the features of Barkhuizen's 3 interconnected levels of story in your research? What are the features of individual participants' stories on a personal level, in a broader context of work or family, and at the socio-political level?
2. What can be learned by reading the stories of the three participants that is not evident from studying and analyzing their performance on the test?

References

Alderson, J., & Wall, D. (1993). Does washback exist? *Applied Linguistics, 14*, 115–129.

Australian Institute for Teaching and Learning and School Leadership. (2015). *AITSL induction and registration*. Retrieved from Australian Institute for Teaching and Learning and School Leadership: www.aitsl.edu.au

Barkhuizen, G. (2008). A narrative approach to exploring context in language teaching. *ELTJ, 62*(3), 231–239.
Barkhuizen, G. (2011). Narrative knowledging in TESOL. *TESOL Quarterly, 45*(3), 391–414.
Brown, H. D., & Abeywickrama, P. (2010). *Language assessment: Principles and classroom practices* (2nd ed.). White Plains: Pearson Education.
Brualdi, A. (1999). Traditional and modern concepts of validity. *ERIC/AE Digest*, 1–3.
Bruner, J. (1990). *Acts of meaning*. Cambridge: Harvard University Press.
Clandinin, D., & Connelly, F. (2000). *Narrative inquiry: Experience & story in qualitative research*. San Francisco: Jossey-Bass.
Fulcher, G. (2010). *Practical language testing*. London: Hodder Education.
Green, A. (2007). *IELTS Washback in context: Preparation for academic writing in higher education*. Cambridge: Cambridge University Press.
IELTS. (2015). *IELTS*. Retrieved from IELTS Web site: http://www.ielts.org
McNamara, T. (2000). *Language testing*. Oxford: Oxford University Press.
Messick, S. (1996). Validity and washback in language testing. *Language Testing, 13*, 241–256.
Murray, G. (2009). Narrative inquiry. In J. Heigham & R. Croker (Eds.), *Qualitative research in applied linguistics* (pp. 45–65). Basingstoke: Palgrave Macmillan.
Nursing and Midwifery Board of Australia. (2015). Retrieved from http://www.nursingmidwiferyboard.gov.au/
O'Loughlin, K. (2008). The Use of IELTS for university selection in Australia: A case study. (J. Osborne, Ed.) *IELTS Research Reports, 8*, 3–98.
Popham, W. J. (1997). Consequential validity: Right concern – Wrong concept. *Educational Measurement, 16*(2), 9–13.
Ruch, G. (1924). *The improvement of the written examination*. Chicago: Scott, Foreman & Company.
Spolsky, B. (1997). The ethics of gatekeeping tests: What have we learned in a hundred years? *Language Testing, 14*(3), 242–247.
The University of Queensland. (2015). *International students: English language requirements*. Retrieved from The University of Queensland Web site: http://www.uq.edu.au/international-students/english-language-requirements

Chapter 11
The Power and Possibility of Narrative Research: Challenges and Opportunities

Ian Davis and Rachael Dwyer

Abstract From the very conception of this book project, we have been concerned about the confusion that can arise for novice researchers due to the lack of transparency in the various ways narrative methods are theorised and applied. As we have seen in the previous chapters, research that is informed by narrative can take a variety of forms, and may be called any number of things (narrative inquiry, narrative studies, narrative research, narrative focus). As Rachael and elke pointed out in Chap. 1 (this volume), this can be viewed as either a strength or a weakness; as diverse applications of a flexible approach, and/or as inconsistent interpretations of theory. There are certainly examples of both, and the difference is not always clear. Our intention in this chapter is to explore the current and future perspectives on working with narrative methods, by drawing on the perspectives of leading scholars in the field.

Keywords Narrative methods • Narrative research • Narrative inquiry • History of narrative • Narratology • Future of narrative

Introduction

From the very conception of this book project, we have been concerned about the confusion that can arise for novice researchers regarding the lack of transparency in the various ways narrative methods are theorised and applied. As we have seen in the previous chapters, research that is informed by narrative can take a variety of forms, and may be called any number of things (narrative inquiry, narrative studies, narrative research, narrative focus). As Rachael and elke pointed out in Chap. 1 (this volume), this can be viewed as either a strength or a weakness; as diverse

I. Davis
Griffith Institute for Educational Research, Griffith University, Brisbane, Australia

R. Dwyer (✉)
Queensland Conservatorium Research Centre, Griffith University, Brisbane, Australia
e-mail: rachael@rachaeldwyer.com

© Springer Science+Business Media Singapore 2017

R. Dwyer et al. (eds.), *Narrative Research in Practice*,
DOI 10.1007/978-981-10-1579-3_11

applications of a flexible approach, and/or as inconsistent interpretations of theory. There are certainly examples of both, and the difference is not always clear. Our intention in this chapter is to explore the current and future perspectives on working with narrative methods,[1] by drawing on the perspectives of leading scholars in the field.

With this in mind, we approached three established scholars of narrative research—Michael Bamberg, who is currently Professor of Psychology at Clark University (United States) and editor of the journal *Narrative Inquiry*; Maria Tamboukou, who works from the University of East London (UK) and heads up the Narrative Research Centre there; and Debbie Pushor, who is based at the University of Saskatchewan (Canada) and previously worked with Jean Clandinin. The interviewees were chosen to, we hoped, represent a diverse range of perspectives regarding the history, practice and future direction of narrative methods.

Questions for the interviews were developed to elicit stories from our participants about their own experiences, histories, views and use of narrative methods. We also included questions about the various strengths and challenges of using narrative methods, and what each interviewee saw as possible directions for the future of narrative research.

The interviews were transcribed and form the basis for this chapter.

Interviewees articulated their specific concerns relating to three main areas. Firstly, the tensions that arise when considering definition and delineation of the terms, and approaches concerning the use of narrative methods as a research tool. Secondly, the differences, both ethical and practical, in how narrative data is collected and used. And finally, the differences in the historical trajectory of how narrative methods have been utilised in research.

The following chapter is divided into three key sections broadly following the pattern of how each of the interviewees were questioned. In the first section we investigate the *stories and histories* of our participants and how their own histories have influenced their own incorporation of narrative methods into their work. The second section discusses what each interviewee considers to be the *strengths and challenges* current in working with narrative methods. The third and final section reveals what our interviewees consider to be new and *emerging developments* in the field of narrative research and briefly discusses both the potential and the difficulties present in these initiatives.

Stories of Histories, Divisions and Boundaries

When asked to speak on what they felt was the history of narrative inquiry, all of our interviewees expressed caution: they each stated that there is not just one history, and that different histories are allied to different disciplines; as Maria reminded us

[1] A term we use in this chapter to inclusively to encompass any research that draws upon narrative as data, means of interpretation or re/presentation.

"stories have many and multiple beginnings". A need to distinguish a narratological view from how, for example, narrative is used in the Social Sciences was key in establishing boundaries, our reading of the interviews also suggests that there are significant divisions within the disciplines of linguistics and the social sciences in terms of how narrative methods are used.

Maria talked to us about her introduction to using narrative methods. She discusses how a focus on the narrative method was often occluded by the subject or indeed the research position. In her description, as she admits, there appears to be little understanding that narrative methods were perhaps an expression of an ontology in itself.

> MT: I looked at women teachers' autobiographical writings, and these included the autobiographies, memoires, diaries, letters, and tried to understand through these writings how they were creating themselves in the way that Foucault has talked about in his late work in the technologies of the self. So I guess it was this effort of mind to see whether what Foucault was talking about could be applied to women teachers and my only source then was the personal narrative. At the time I had not really understood the importance of narratives themselves.

Narratology is a field dedicated to the study of textual narrative, which is often defined in highly technical ways. As Michael suggests, narratology concerns itself with "trying to figure out what is a narrative … what kind of formal aspects and structural components make a narrative, and possibly even a good narrative…". He proposes that the tension arises because of a lack of understanding of the differences between narratology and what is commonly referred to as "the turn to narrative in the social sciences." He goes on to suggest that, "within the social sciences we are forced, occasionally at least, to define narrative and that is where we borrow structural and formal principles and components".

Maria agrees with this difficulty arising from a lack of knowledge about the different disciplines in which narrative is used:

> MT: people who do narrative studies in the humanities or literary studies most probably will know very little about what is going on in the social sciences, for example, or people who do mostly digital narratives or other kinds of new media narrative. We know very little sometimes about some of the histories of narratology. So I think we should try to be more serious when doing interdisciplinary narrative. We need to have more connections across disciplines

The "turn to narrative in the social sciences", a phrase that was originally coined by Norman Denzin (2000), is considered to be a defining feature of the history narrative, taking the focus away from purely textual investigations and into the process we now refer to as narrative inquiry. Maria proposes that within a sociological frame, this trend has a much longer history.

> MT: Denzin thought these turns happened around in the 1980s but actually as a sociologist I think it goes back to the beginning of the twentieth century. I think that if we think sociologically about the history of narrative studies I would locate it in the publication of the Polish peasants in between 1918 and 1920: this is where these letters of Polish immigrants to the US were published, and Thomas and Znaniecki (1996/1918) considered these letters as important in understanding issues around migration and the lives of these people. I think there is a rich history in the US that goes through symbolic interactionism, the words of Cooley (1902) and Mead (1913) … and of course a very important influence for me is C. Wright Mills and the *Sociological Imagination* in 1959, and

this idea of how we can think together through biography, history and structure. And I think these are the important moments in the history of narrative studies that eventually brings us in the 1980s and, you know, a very significant turn. That was a moment when the social sciences in general turned to language.

In the broader social sciences however, Michael suggests that narrative research is far more focused on identity, and

MB: questions around identity, but very broadly defined... we are much more turned toward the functions that these narratives serve when it comes to reflection, looking at who we are and what holds us together in terms of our identity, and also what drifts us into different groups, into different organisations, you know, what keeps us apart.

Michael believes that a concern with identity "has unified, to a degree, this narrative approach". However, in some branches or strands of narrative inquiry, it would be more common to read of a focus on Dewey's notions of experience than identity. When Debbie spoke about the history of narrative, a vastly different story emerged:

DP: I guess for me, given that I'm a Canadian, I see story really arriving from our First People. I see it as an oral tradition of telling stories, of teaching through story, that was in place well before our country was settled by Europeans ... And I think with industrialisation ... the scientific push, that wanting to be first, wanting to make a mark, that we really lost some of what we knew. We moved to a place of ... reductionism, of objectivism, and felt that we could capture things more effectively with a quantification. And so I think a lot changed and I really do think when we look back to the roots of Dewey, and we look at the work of Schwab, and we look at the work of Michael Connelly and Jean Clandinin, it was really a push against that way of thinking, against that lack of humanism in what we did. And so I think it was a hard fight for a long time to establish narrative knowing as a legitimate way of knowing and as one that had value and was valid.

The Ontological Significance of Boundaries

Rachael and elke put forward in the opening chapter of this volume that a single definition of narrative methods is not necessarily possible or even desirable. Rather, an open acknowledgement of the differences, particularly how the same terms are used in different ways, is a necessary development in how we can more fully understand narrative methods. While the different strands and sub-strands of narrative methods were not a specific question in our interviews, different views did emerge.

Michael raised the question of narrative inquiry losing its meaning due to an *anything goes* attitude. Michael discusses the idea of working towards a "core around which the narrative work can oscillate". Alternatively, he suggests that perhaps it is more productive as it is, a methodology that has no centre but is instead with a "free floating innovative interdisciplinary orientation". Michael further explains that if we remain where we are, although currently a dynamic space, it could result in the purity of narrative "ultimately, potentially at least, disintegrate[ing]". From what appears to be quite a protective position Michael is concerned that unless we find, or at least seek to find, a central set of beliefs and actions in relation to narrative methods we will ultimately continue to "talk past each other not making any sense to the outside world when we use the term *narrative*".

MB: So that, I think, should be a challenge right now, but at the same time there's the counter position that these narrative approaches are sitting in the social sciences nicely between all these different fields and do their innovative work there, but in a way they are not going anywhere. So there has to be something like an interesting important integration and differentiation of narrative moving into the discipline, but not too much so that they are not absorbed, but not staying totally in this free field of non-disciplinary alignment.

For Debbie, the diverse, innovative and creative use of narrative inquiry is its strength:

DP: What I love about it [narrative inquiry] is all of the ways that people are using it creatively, artistically, for varied kinds of purposes. I think it's really an exciting time … we're in a place where we can be imaginative and creative and we can play with that work so much more.

However, Debbie also cautions that creativity should not mean a disregard for methodological rigour; in whatever way that may be defined. Like Michael, she is concerned about the anything goes approach and what it might mean for those using narrative methods.

DP: My interest in narrative is particular to narrative inquiry, the kind of Clandinin and Connelly school of narrative inquiry, and one of the things that I think sometimes people struggle with is the idea that narrative inquiry is more than telling stories, that narrative inquiry is both the telling of the story and then the enquiring into the story … And so I think it's that sense of, it's more than telling a story, becomes really important that we preserve that notion and we preserve that understanding that it's about telling the story but then it's about unpacking that story, asking ourselves, "Why did I tell that story? Out of all of the stories I could have told, why do I want to tell this one? What work do I want that story to do from a research perspective? And as I unpack that story, what am I going to do to make those connections, to pull the threads forward to link it to concepts, to link it to other literature, to begin to take that thread and weave it into something more."

As we reflect on this, it would appear that there is some value in clarifying the different perspectives on narrative inquiry, which draw on vastly different theoretical underpinnings. However, we also recognise that this clarification should not reify, or place limits on innovation and creativity.

Maria suggests that perhaps the manner in which we are introduced to narrative methods then influences how we view the use of narrative within our work or discipline.

MT: I don't think there is just one history in narrative studies. I think that there are many histories and these many histories depend on the disciplinary field you are working with. If you are a literary scholar, for example, you will have a different history in mind.

What appears to be the case in each of the three interviews is that our interviewees' relationship to the idea of narrative methods is not only about differences in approach and utility, but is also driven by the expression of quite different ontological viewpoints. As described earlier, Michael talks about narrative as a, "free floating innovative interdisciplinary orientation", raising the notion that this needs to be anchored in some way to maintain rigor in the approach. However, this is a complex question, one to which we will return in later sections of this chapter.

It would appear anyway, despite the different disciplinary backgrounds, narrative work, in the broadest sense, is underpinned by *the ways stories are structured, designed, communicated and/or utilised to make sense of the world and the individual's place within it.* While there appear to be significant differences in the ways in which those ends are pursued, there is perhaps more common ground than seems initially apparent. What is emerging, however, is how each of our interviewees have very different and individual pathways in how they began using narrative methods; pathways that have influenced their ontological position in relation to narrative methods. In each case the use of a narrative method appears to be secondary, with the primary focus being the participant or anticipated outcomes of the individual study. In this sense, narrative appears to be often employed as a methodological means to an end.

Strengths & Challenges of Narrative Methods

Among other issues deliberated by our interviewees, we also discussed what they saw as the key strengths and challenges facing research that employs narrative methods today. Three areas of consideration emerged. *Interdisciplinarity* was identified as an issue that could both contribute as well as divide those working in the field, including some of the tensions already referred to earlier in this chapter. Maria mentions the language focus identifying the *hegemony of the English language* in narrative methods, and finally Maria also refers to the ways in which we may seek to *hear the silences* that become part of our work.

Interdisciplinarity

Addressing the notion of challenges within the field, Maria discusses key areas of facing our use of narrative methods regarding the concept of *interdisciplinarity*. One of the major difficulties she cites is communication. How do we communicate across the multifarious differences that are present in approach, in design and, often in intention?

MT: One great challenge that I have identified is that when we are in narrative studies very easily we talk about interdisciplinarity and how important interdisciplinary narratives and narrative studies and how narratives are in a way lending themselves to interdisciplinarity but actually we are not very good at doing interdisciplinarity and if you go into narrative scholars you will see that people are trends within their disciplines. So people who do narrative studies in the humanities or literary studies most probably will know very little about what is going on in the social sciences, for example, or people who do mostly digital narratives or other kinds of new media narrative. We know very little sometimes about some of the histories of narratology.

To counter this, Maria suggests we should intentionally increase our connections and communications across and also with the various disciplines that use narrative methods. She reminds us that:

MB: We should try to be more serious when doing interdisciplinary narrative. We need to have more connections across disciplines, faculties, universities, colleagues. That's one of the challenges that we have to face.

As alluded to in the previous section, Michael expresses an anxiety with reference to the issue of *interdisciplinarity*. He describes a tension that asks if we should be striving for the development of a core or central understanding regarding narrative methods that cuts across disciplinary boundaries and provide a greater degree of coherence. Or, he suggests, would developing such a central system of language and or process undo the richness and diversification that can be found in how narrative methods are theorised and applied?

MB: Does narrative and do narrative inquiry and narrative studies need a core or a centre around which the narrative work can oscillate or fly … it should remain where it's at and that is that there is no centre, they are not even different centres, but narrative is this free floating innovative interdisciplinary orientation, let me put it this way. The problem with that, that I have is, if we remain there, then narrative as a study, as an inquiry, we ultimately potentially at least, disintegrate.

Michael is unable to resolve this tension for himself or us. Instead he presents us with that problem and cites the potential threat that might result from a lack of action in this area.

Debbie, however, points to what narrative can offer in terms of providing connections across disciplinary lines, providing a means of accessing and learning from work in related and unrelated disciplines.

DP: I think it enables us to work with colleagues in ways that we wouldn't otherwise, that the medical work would stay in this place and our educational work would stay in this place, and we wouldn't speak to each other. But when we start to share those narratives, we see opportunities to learn from one another… narratives about children with traumatic brain injury become something that can speak to my work as an educator or my work with parents or my work with children.

Although all interviewees approach the difficulty of *interdisciplinarity* from different perspectives, all present a clear message, a 'call to arms' for some clear action in this area. The imperative referred to by all parties here is to be more intentional, more strategic and remain cautious as to what might be lost in any process of hemoginisation.

Language Hegemony

Maria draws our attention to the hegemony of the English language in relation to narrative methods.

MT: Another important challenge for narrative studies right now and it's starting to come up more and more is the hegemony of the English language and how do we deal with questions around translation. What does it mean to have transnational narratives? What

> are the boundaries of the language? They are so important things that have been in French, for example, or in Italian or in Spanish speaking areas and we cannot communicate with them because of this hegemony of the English language.

Within a globalised environment where barriers around communication are being collapsed further and further, how can we as researchers begin to encompass work that is being done in nations and cultures that are not English speaking? This raises interesting questions regarding the cultural specificity not only of language structures, but also narrative structure and how these are read, in which contexts and cultures, and for which audiences. Maria suggests that:

> MT: we need to do more about what we call now transnational narrative, so narratives in translation, and we need to face the fact that if we are talking about narratives and it's a question of language we need to engage the subtleties and the intricacies of different languages. So I think this is very important.

Hearing Silences

Finally, Maria points to the challenges involved in hearing and interpreting the *silences*. She discusses how we not only are required to hear the story that is spoken or covertly demonstrated but she suggests we need to develop analytical frameworks which would enable us to notice the absences and silences that are created within stories.

> MT: [Another] challenge I think is how we can create the sort of framework to consider silences. Sometimes we talk about silences but what is the narrative method to discern silences, to understand how silences are part and parcel of stories and to be more analytical, more hermeneutic about this.

This might demonstrate a point of potentially productive hybridisation of narrative methods, fusing the narratological view where recently silences within the literary text have been viewed in a poststructuralist, deconstructionist framework proposed by Derrida (1998) and his unravelling of the concept of presence as both trace and absence. Alongside either exists psychodynamic views of silence characterised by discussions of the tension between "self-reflection and unformulated experience" (Stern 2002, p. 228), or more socio-political notions of silence and silencing.

Absences, silences are now commonly considered in postmodern socio-political terms, asking whose voices are heard and whose are not. In this perspective absences are viewed as specific conscious or unconscious gaps in a text or story where people, groups, ideas or issues have been omitted or silenced—sometimes to maintain the structure of a story or the structure of a societal norm.

Whatever combination of perspectives are utilised, literary or narratological, psychodynamic or socio-political, Maria's call for a more hermeneutic approach to understanding silences can potentially bring disparate approaches together, producing new ways to view narrative forms.

Debbie speaks of her own experience of feeling silenced as the impetus for the beginning of her personal journey with narrative research.

> DP: … what I found in those early experiences of being a parent on the school landscape was it was a really different experience … I didn't feel welcomed; I didn't feel I had a place or a voice, and all of a sudden my whole understanding of schools was shaken, and I realised that there was a really marginalised group in our schools. And those experiences, after having been an educator probably 15 years by that point, those experiences for me were significant and in some way life-changing and I wanted to tell my stories to everyone who would listen.

Could it be that using narrative methods assists in giving a voice to marginalised populations? The sheer commonality of stories and storying can unite groups who are silenced—or in some cases erased from texts and stories—and help them articulate their experience so it can be heard and further understood.

New and Emerging Developments

Turns and the Post Humanist Turn

The concept of *turns* has been used a way of describing junctions and trends within disciplines, or of developments in critical theory. The idea of *turns* is often used as a way of periodising or classifying trends within research and academia. Maria challenges the idea of the big *turn*, which she alludes to as oversimplifications and which potentially inaccurately represent how ideas become developed and entrenched within our work. She suggests that instead what we retrospectively view as *turns* are often the result of a number of smaller innovations developed over time.

> MT: I don't believe in "big things". I don't think that something big is coming up or we can foresee or discern it. Usually we have small things happening and then when they … when we look back at these things small things that have already happened, then we give it the form of the big.

Maria refers to our current theoretical climate, which attempts to move beyond post structuralism and the anthropocentric, humanistic philosophical tradition, and instead supports what is being heralded as the *post humanist turn*.

> MT: Maybe in 10 or 20 years' time when we look back the big thing would have been how narratives started in general. We have a date with what we now call the post humanist turn. For me, there is a lot of discussion around post humanism

What interests Maria is a consideration of what a theory such as posthumanism—that specifically aims to decentralise the conception of the human—does with a method such as narrative that is so essentially and centrally human.

> MT: Narrative studies have always been centred around language and the human. What is going to happen with the post humanism turn? I think that would be a big thing maybe in 20 years' time and I'm very curious to see how narratives will feature in there.

Maria points out that like postmodernism, which challenged the nature of truth, and poststructuralism the hegemony of language, posthumanism is yet another "grand ideology": a further binary position created to challenge, in this case, the Humanistic, Enlightenment project of the late Renaissance.

MT: I have not been persuaded by the post humanist discourse in the same way that I have been also very sceptical about the post modernism or the post structuralism. I am against these grand ideologies, these isms, whatever they are or whatever they represent.

However much we may agree or disagree with the influence of such "grand ideologies", we must concede that they do have an effect on how we operate within the field of narrative methods. As Maria says:

MT: The fact is whether I agree with the grand post humanism or not, the fact is that we are all in a phase where we are thinking that humans should not or need not be at the centre of our epistemologies or knowledges or, you know, in general of our concerns.

For a collection of methods that considers storying and the story as central to its analysis and almost glories in the humanness of its approach, we must seek to understand how this big *turn* will impact on our work.

Attending to the Visual and Sensory

The development of narrative emerged from a turn towards using words as data (Pinnegar and Daynes, 2007), and it is thus natural that language—written and oral—has narrative researchers' focus. However, the late twentieth century expansion of the definition of what counts as a "text" has opened up a new range of possibilities for exploring the ways in which texts that are not language-based have the potential to convey narratives. As lisahunter (Chap. 5, this volume) describes, visual images provide means of communicating something richer than text alone, and may provide opportunities for narrative research at the field text/data, interim text/analysis and/or research text/(re)presentation stages.

Visual narrative is something that Maria identified as a new direction for narrative inquiry, but one that needs further exploration.

MT: the visual turn in narrative studies where people thought a lot about the image and how can we think about narrative through images and I think this is still going on because particularly who we are, sociologists or historians, we don't have what we call a visual vocabulary or a visual grammar to think about the image in relation to narratives. Although we are working hard on it and I think that's a very exciting area because up until now when we think about narratives and images two things can happen: we use narratives as captions of images, or on the other hand we use images as illustrations of our narratives. But I think that a more serious engagement with storylines and images can show us that the relation is much more dynamic and organic and it's not just additive or complementary. So I think there is a lot of work to be done in this area and, as I said, we need to educate ourselves in the grammars and vocabularies of the image.

Michael also considered the importance of visual narratives, suggesting a rigid focus on a linguistic or narratological method may result in some of the meaning being lost.

MB: when stories are told with visual means and not just like movies where we have actors who speak and actresses and they interact and carry out the action so to speak, but if we have now these commercials, in particular, where you have [actors] interacting but without words, it's all with gestures, with gaze, so the body language rituals that hold for humans are transferred. But this is where traditional narratologists expand the notion of texts to capture film and to capture also these visual narratives without words.

However, as well as recognising the importance of using the richness apparent in visual narratives, Michael also warns against developing a "catch all", which may distort what we consider to be a text that expresses a narrative.

MB: This is exactly where the notion of texts that we have been working with … is breaking down. Narrative is, the notion of texts and the interpretation of texts as the core of narrative, has held us back from realising that within the narrative performance there's a lot more going on …

This attention to other aspects of story-telling, such as gesture, is not always overlooked in narrative research. Narrative researchers in the phenomenological tradition, in their attention to temporality, and particularly, sociality and place, illustrate their stories with rich detail. The following example gives us a sense of the characters'/participants' histories, relationships, physical environment and facial expressions, demonstrating how these contextual details are as much a part of the social interaction as the words they exchange:

"Ms. K, Ms. K, looked what I got here." Two bright shining eyes look up to me from the floor. There sits George, a little boy who usually does not talk much. In fact, he has been seeing the Speech and Language Pathologist to help with both language acquisition and articulation. George is so excited he can hardly contain himself. Standing beside him is his step-mother, Patty, who also has a huge smile on her face. George produces a big Ziploc bag with a very large snake skin inside it. I ask him what it is, and he proceeds to tell me about the four and a half foot long corn snake they have at home and how the snake had shed its skin that morning. He wants to share with everyone in the classroom. (Kowaluk 2013, p. 131)

Narrative research presented in this style tends to merge with arts-based research, particularly in the use of evocative language, literary genres and devices.

DP: narrative isn't just the words on the page or the story told, but it becomes the whole way the story is told as well. We're seeing … plays and poetry and we're seeing work with hypertext, and we're seeing works like Vera Caine's where there's just a few words on a page or where her spacing is completely different.

Emotional Resonance

Michael discusses the influence of gestures and visual cues on the story, or as he puts it: the "micro stuff that is doing the bonding". Here he refers to two new, largely literary, innovations within the field: specifically *narrative transportation*, and *narrative empathy*. These are new areas of development within narrative methods. Both concepts acknowledge and explore our other senses, our tacit identification with the emotional world of stories and narratives, by examining how we empathise with texts and stories, and also how we move into and away from the world on the text or story.

MB: There's the issue of narrative transportation or narrative empathy that is now being circulated … I think the core of this question is, what do we really do when we hear a story, how do we understand and make sense and then also feel for what is going on, not just rationally but in terms of our emotional moving into the story, and then at the end moving out again. That's where the discussion has circled a little bit around, is it, and I'm over simplifying here, is it the plot, or is it the characters that we identify and identify with?

Michael explains how marketing and branding has seized upon the idea of *narrative transportation* (Brechman and Purvis 2015) and has sought to use all of our senses. Our empathic responses, along with our inherited understanding of narrative structures and how stories work are used to deliver evermore effective and persuasive messages; suggesting that advertising is using storytelling in an affective as well as an intellectual way.

MB: Our bodies resonate with other bodies—that's where the resonating activity, so to speak, happens micro genetically over the micro cues that are visual most of the times, rather than in words or textual in that sense. And these lead to an identification that we then can argue our identifications with characters or identifications with plot expectations. But there's a micro stuff [cues] that are doing the bonding, that is doing the alignment, that has been left out very much out unless people have pushed the performative aspects of storytelling.

Also, in the field of medicine (Carmel-Gilfilen and Portillo 2016), Michael alludes to how understandings of *narrative transportation* and *narrative empathy* have been used to enhance how employees within these professions work with the stories of the people they encounter.

MB: it's fascinating to see how narratives now are becoming a big part in medical humanities … a sub field of medical training …where narrative …become the means, the prerequisites for doctors to become people who also have empathy, who share empathy with their patients, in order to bring empathy, being a part, a big chunk of the diagnostic procedure.

Debbie also discusses our empathic responses to a narrative both in our own storytelling and in listening to the stories of others.

DP: I think one of the things about narrative work always is that notion of resonance that, "I read your story but it resonates – it could be my story too", or, "It evokes my own story [that is] like yours." And so I think it's one of those things that truly crosses boundaries, crosses borders, attends to some of the things that sometimes keep people separate, and I think, you know, that's so exciting.

It seems surprising that the idea of acknowledging the empathic emotional content of the narratives we encounter when using narrative methods should be such a new area and one that is approached with such care and a little trepidation. Exploration of the emotional element of our work that, with some notable exceptions (Goldie 2012), is otherwise overlooked in much of the literature that surrounds the field of narrative methods. Perhaps in our quest for rigour and alignment with more mainstream qualitative methods we may have overlooked how to bring the feeling back in to our work as researchers, or as Michael puts it: "what we really do when we hear a story".

Conclusion

The exercise of bringing three key narrative practitioners together in this chapter to discuss the history, practice and future of the narrative methods appears to have been a successful one or intriguing at the very least. As is evident, there are clear divisions within the field relating to general differences in ontological viewpoints, as well as specific pathways into using narrative as a research method. There is also a tension shared by all interviewees that exists not only in the multiple uses of narrative as a method, but also in disciplinary origins of the those methods, how they were classified and how they will be further developed.

Throughout the interviews there was expressed an often-mentioned hope, at times even a need, to develop a greater commonality in our understanding about what narrative methods are and what they do. It occurs to us, however, that we could alternatively conceptualise this lack of clarity and the tensions alluded to in this chapter, as a productive working space. This space would act as an arena where there is no resolution; or even the desire for clarity or commonality.Instead this space would contain the existing push and pull between the processes employed by these competing narrative methods and the ideas exemplified by their use. By viewing the tensions that exist in our work not as a deficit but instead as a methodological *atelier*, we could actively employ the notion of narrative or story as the common focus enabling an active and effective dialogue. Such a dialogue can assist a discussion regarding our differing views of the world and our often-polemic approaches to understanding our diverse methodological and theoretical environments. We propose that embracing this space promises a productive outcome to our work, and is perhaps more desirable than a homogenous common ground without diverse edges and unexpected pitfalls and the richness that navigating these obstacles can often bring.

Acknowledgements We would like to take this opportunity to thank our interviewees Michael Bamberg, Maria Tamboukou, and Debbie Pushor for their time and participation in this project. Due to the time differences between us in Australia and the northern hemisphere, interviews often took place at inconvenient times in the working day for our interviewees. We would also like to thank the IT communications team at Griffith for their support and GIER staff for assistance in the administration of this project. Finally, a big thank you to Greer Johnson who interviewed each of our participants and who has supported this project from its inception.

References

Brechman, J. M., & Purvis, S. C. (2015). Narrative, transportation and advertising. *International Journal of Advertising, 34*(2), 366–381. doi:10.1080/02650487.2014.994803.

Carmel-Gilfilen, C., & Portillo, M. (2016). Designing with empathy. *HERD: Health Environments Research & Design Journal, 9*(2), 130–146. doi: http://dx.doi.org/10.1177/1937586715592633

Cooley, C. (1902). *Human nature and the social order*. New York: Charles Scribner's Sons.

Denzin, N. (2000). Preface. In M. Andrews, S. D. Sclater, C. Squire, & A. Treacher (Eds.), *Lines of narrative*. London: Routledge.

Derrida, J. (1998). *Of grammatology*. New York: JHU Press.

Goldie, P. (2012). *The mess inside: Narrative, emotion and the mind*. Oxford: Oxford Scholarship Online.

Kowaluk, C. (2013). A boy, his snake and their story: Building authentic relationships on and off the school landscape. In D. Pushor (Ed.), *Portals of promise: Transforming beliefs and practices through a curriculum of parents*. Rotterdam: Sense.

Mead, G. H. (1913). The social self. *Journal of Philosophy, Psychology and Scientific Methods, 10*, 374–380.

Stern, D. B. (2002). Words and wordlessness in the psychoanalytic situation. *Journal of the American Psychoanalytic Association, 50*(1), 221–247. doi:10.1177/00030651020500011201.

Thomas, W. I. & Znaniecki, F. (1996/1918). *The polish peasant in Europe and America: A classic work in immigration history* (E. Zaretsky, Ed.). Urbana/Chicago: University of Illinois Press.

Teaching Resources

It is hoped that excerpts and extracts from this book will be used in the teaching of narrative methods at a tertiary level. To this end we have developed two key resources for teachers who may wish to use this book as part of a research methodology course or perhaps with the specific disciplines. Firstly, below you will find a series of questions that have been designed by the editors based on the content and ideas elucidated in each chapter. These have been designed to promote discussion and aid the reading process. You will also find below a reading list. These are works considered seminal by the authors, some of which have been used as sources within this volume. These works either characterise narrative methods in a useful and productive way or in some cases describe the process of using narrative methods in a research setting. We hope you find these resources helpful and they enhance your experience of this volume.

Chapter 1. Narrative Research in Practice: Navigating the Terrain

1. Map your own research (or a project you have read about in a journal article, book or dissertation) on the 'position of narrative' diagram (Fig. 1.1). Consider what this means in terms of what the data/evidence, analysis and (re)presentation of the research.
2. Choose the author/s cited who you think aligns best with your own ideas about narrative and research. Write a paragraph explaining your choice.

© Springer Science+Business Media Singapore 2017

R. Dwyer et al. (eds.), *Narrative Research in Practice*,
DOI 10.1007/978-981-10-1579-3

Chapter 2. Autoethography: Is My Own Story Narrative Research?

1. We often enter a research topic because of something in our own experience – what is your story? How might your story of your interest contribute to your research?
2. What are the ethical concerns in your project for either including your autoethnography or asking your participants to produce autoethnographies as field or research texts.

Chapter 3. Saying Goodbye to Mr Chips: Masculinity, Narrative and Identity Construction

1. In what way do you think the fictional characters from books, film and television you have encountered are significant in how you have developed your identity either as a professional or in your personal life.
2. When collecting narratives from research participants what do you think are the key considerations in terms of how you might read the story in light of an understanding of how fiction narrative structures might influence how stories are constructed?

Chapter 4. Critical Junctures in Narrative Research: Collaborative Reflections on Methodological Issues

1. Consider the three critical junctures that the authors identify in this chapter. How might those same junctures be encountered in your own research? Are there others that you can predict?
2. Are there particular ethical considerations that are unique to your research context? How do you plan to address them? Are there steps you could take in your design that would help to avoid or alleviate problems later?

Chapter 5. If You See What I Mean? Visual Narratives – Stories Told Through, with and by Visual Images

1. Consider your research question or topic. Map how visual elements could complement your field texts (or data). Consider analysis of those texts.

2. How might you use visual texts to disseminate your research both to a scholarly audience and beyond the scholarly audience. Be sure to consider the ethical concerns and how you might navigate them.

Chapter 6. Where Words Fail: Storying Audio-Visual Data

1. What are the ethical requirements at your institution regarding the use of video data, including its storage, the rights of participants to anonymity and privacy, and the dissemination of video footage to the wider academic community? Consider how your research project traverses these ethical issues.
2. Who is your intended audience, and how will you disseminate your findings? Have you considered multi-platform dissemination, such as podcasts, academic journals, audio-visual documentary, art-centred research?

Chapter 7. Sensual, Sensory and Sensational Narratives

1. Consider your research question or topic. Map how sensory or sensual elements could complement your field texts (or data). Consider analysis of those texts.
2. How might you use sensory devices within your research texts? How might this enhance the reader's experience?

Chapter 8. Who Is Asking the Questions? Using Co-constructed Interviews in the Study of Perceived Discrimination from a Discourse Analytical Perspective

1. How might use of an 'in-group' interviewer affect interviews in your field? Speculate on how an insider might respond differently to an outsider interviewer?
2. Compare the benefits and challenges of each of the types of interviews mentioned on page 162. Make a decision about which might be best suited to your own research project and explain your choice.

Chapter 9. Insights into Disability and Giftedness: Narrative Methodologies in Interviewing Young People Identified as Twice Exceptional

1. Are there any specific needs of your participants (or a participant group with which you are familiar) that may need to be considered? How might you design an interview protocol that ensures the participants' needs are met?
2. How might a memory box be used to enhance an interview in your field of research? What types of items might prompt conversations about the things in which you are interested?
3. How might a story constellations approach be adapted for your research context? What stories might make up the constellation?

Chapter 10. The IELTS Roller Coaster: Stories of Hope, Stress, Success, and Despair

1. What are the features of Barkhuisen's 3 interconnected levels of story in your research? (What are the features of individual's stories, stories in context, and at the socio-political level?)
2. What can be learned by reading the stories of the three participants that is not evident in studying and analyzing their performance on the test?

Reading List for Orientation in Narrative Research

Andrews, M., Squire, C., & Tamboukou, M. (Eds.). (2013). *Doing narrative research*. London: Sage.

Bamberg, M. (Ed.). (2007). *Narrative: State of the art* (pp. 165–174). Amsterdam: John Benjamins Publishing.

Bamberg, M., & Andrews, M. (Eds.). (2004). *Considering counter-narratives: Narrating, resisting, making sense*. Amsterdam: John Benjamins Publishing.

Clandinin, D. J. (Ed.). (2007). *Handbook of narrative inquiry: Mapping a methodology*. Thousand Oaks: Sage.

Connelly, F. M., & Clandinin, D. J. (2006). Narrative inquiry. In J. L. Green, G. Camilli, & P. B. Elmore (Eds.), *Handbook of complementary methods in educational research* (pp. 477–488). Washington, DC: American Educational Research Association.

Polkinghorne, D. E. (1995). Narrative configuration in qualitative analysis. *International Journal of Qualitative Studies in Education, 8*(1), 5–23.

Riessman, C. K. (2008). *Narrative methods for the human sciences*. Thousand Oaks: Sage.

Index

© Springer Science+Business Media Singapore 2017
R. Dwyer et al. (eds.), *Narrative Research in Practice*,
DOI 10.1007/978-981-10-1579-3

Made in the USA
Las Vegas, NV
09 May 2026

46666799R00149